Peaceful Neighbor

Also by Michael G. Long

Gay Is Good: The Life and Letters of Franklin Kameny

Beyond Home Plate: Jackie Robinson on Life after Baseball

Martin Luther King Jr., Homosexuality, and the Early Gay Rights Movement: Keeping the Dream Straight?

I Must Resist: Bayard Rustin's Life in Letters

Marshalling Justice: The Early Civil Rights Letters of Thurgood Marshall

Christian Peace and Nonviolence: A Documentary History

First Class Citizenship: The Civil Rights Letters of Jackie Robinson

The Legacy of Billy Graham: Critical Reflections on America's Greatest Evangelist

God and Country: Diverse Perspectives on Christianity and Patriotism

Billy Graham and the Beloved Community: America's Evangelist and the Dream of Martin Luther King Jr.

Against Us, but for Us: Martin Luther King Jr. and the State

Peaceful Neighbor

Discovering the Countercultural Mister Rogers

Michael G. Long

WESTMINSTER
JOHN KNOX PRESS
LOUISVILLE · KENTUCKY

© 2015 Michael G. Long

First edition
Published by Westminster John Knox Press
Louisville, Kentucky

15 16 17 18 19 20 21 22 23 24—10 9 8 7 6 5 4 3 2 1

Book design by Drew Stevens
Cover design by designpointinc.com
Cover art: Fred Rogers during a May 27, 1993, taping of his show Mister Rogers Neighborhood *in Pittsburgh;* © *Gene J. Puskar/AP Photo*

Scripture quotations from the New Revised Standard Version of the Bible are copyright © 1989 by the Division of Christian Education of the National Council of the Churches of Christ in the U.S.A. and are used by permission.

Excerpts from the writings of Fred M. Rogers provided courtesy of The Fred Rogers Company and are used by permission. Art used in chapters 1, 3, 5, 6, 7, 8, 9, 11, and 12 provided courtesy of The Fred Rogers Company and is used by permission. Art used in chapter 4 is used by permission of Boston University. The art used in chapter 10 is used by permission of Vincent Jones.

Library of Congress Cataloging-in-Publication Data
Long, Michael G.
  Peaceful neighbor : discovering the countercultural Mister Rogers / Michael G. Long. — First edition.
    p. cm.
  Includes index.
  ISBN 978-0-664-26047-7 (pbk.)
  1. Rogers, Fred—Religion. I. Title.
  PN1992.4.R56L66 2015
  791.4502'8092—dc23

2014031602

Most Westminster John Knox Press books are available at special quantity discounts when purchased in bulk by corporations, organizations, and special-interest groups. For more information, please e-mail SpecialSales@wjkbooks.com.

To Kathleen, my favorite neighbor

War isn't nice.

—Fred Rogers

Contents

Acknowledgments   ix

Introduction: Just the Way He Was: Meeting the Real Mister Rogers   xi

Part One: War and Peace in the Neighborhood

1. "Isn't Peace Wonderful?": Against the Vietnam War, for Gandhi   3
2. "War Isn't Nice": Against the Arms Race,
   for Peaceful Imagination   9
3. "I Like You": Against the Cold War, for Puppet Détente   21
4. "Just the Way You Are": A Theology of Peace   27
5. "It's Okay to Be Angry": A Psychology of Peace   45
6. "A Gross Form of Abuse": From the Persian Gulf War
   to the War on Terror   63

Part Two: Peace as More Than the Absence of War

7. "A Black Brother": Race and Diversity   81
8. "Food for the World": Tears for Hungry Children   99
9. "I'm Tired of Being a Lady": Tough Girls, Sensitive Boys   119
10. "He Understood": Homosexuality and Gay Friends   143
11. "I Love Tofu Burgers and Beets": Animals and Mothers   157
12. "Take Care of This Wonderful World": Peace on Earth   169

Conclusion: The Compassion of Fred Rogers   177
Notes   183
Index   197

Acknowledgments

I am deeply grateful to the following individuals and institutions: The Fred Rogers Company for permission to use material from the Fred Rogers Archive at the Fred Rogers Center for Early Learning and Children's Media at St. Vincent College; Kevin Morrison, chief operating officer of the Fred Rogers Company; Emily Uhrin, archivist at the Fred Rogers Archive; editor Jessica Miller Kelley and production director Julie Tonini of Westminster John Knox Press; Dean Fletcher McClellan of Elizabethtown College; student assistant Kelsey Walck; Tim Lybarger of neighborhoodarchive.com; François Clemmons of Middlebury College; Betty Aberlin; Kathleen Murphy; Tony Chilrodes; the Reverend John McCall; Michael John Dabrishus, assistant university librarian at the University of Pittsburgh; Georgia Locke of Boston University Marketing & Communications; Darla Moore, archival specialist at Rollins College; Jessica Barr and Diana Da Rocha of the Henri J. M. Nouwen Archives and Research Collection, John M. Kelly Library, University of St. Michaels; Bob Frymoyer; copyeditor Don Parker-Burgard; David Beckmann of Bread for the World; Vincent Jones, formerly of Middlebury College; Andrew Armstrong, formerly of Greater Latrobe Senior High School; and two kids I love just as they are, Jack and Nate Long. Special thanks to friends Elaine Tinari Benedetti and Sharon Herr for proofreading and editing.

Introduction

Just the Way He Was: Meeting the Real Mister Rogers

*F*red Rogers was concerned. Ellen Goodman, a syndicated columnist for the *Boston Globe,* had just criticized one of his public service announcements for preschool children during the Persian Gulf War. "Mr. Rogers decided to make a special public service announcement to anxious children that 'you'll always have someone to love you, no matter what,'" she'd written. "But the dateline of his report is the Kingdom of Make Believe."[1]

The words stung, but rather than simply stewing, Rogers took to the pen, as he often did, writing Goodman a heartfelt response. "Having been an appreciative reader of your excellent work for years, I was concerned when I read the column in which you 'clicked' our public service announcement for preschool children in this horrendous world crisis," he wrote.

Rogers did not launch at Goodman, but he did feel the need to explain his actions, gently but firmly, so she might better understand. "When PBS asked if I would speak about conflict to families of preschoolers, my first reaction was not to do anything about the war in this medium which seemed to broadcast nonstop the 'Scud v. Patriot Show,'" he offered. "But then I started to hear more and more about young children's fears, and I prayed for the inspiration to do something helpful."

Rogers added that the result of his prayers, the PSAs Goodman criticized, echoed his earlier work in another time of crisis. After the assassinations of President Kennedy, Martin Luther King Jr., and Robert Kennedy, he had written and taped a program in which he asked families to include their children in the grieving process. "Our country was in mass mourning," he explained. "It was then that I realized more fully how speaking the truth about feelings—even on television—could be exceedingly curative."

So in spite of his initial reticence, Rogers accepted the invitation from PBS by doing what he did best—speaking directly to children and their families about their hopes and fears. He summed it up for Goodman:

Even though I don't make policy in this country, I do feel an obligation to give the best I know how to families with young children when policies (of government and television) are affecting those families so directly. That's why I agreed to do anything at all. I lament for the world (not the Neighborhood of Make-Believe!) because the abuses of war breed abusers who grow up to sow the seeds of future wars. Anything I can do to bring a modicum of comfort to a little one, I will do. (How I would love for my 2½-year-old grandson to be able to grow up in a world which refuses to abuse its children!) Even though I felt helpless in some ways (because of the onset of the war), I was grateful (as I imagine you must be at times) to have an avenue in which to express the truth as I felt it for the children I've always tried to serve.

But it wasn't just gratitude that Rogers was feeling as he finished his letter. "You can imagine my grief," he wrote in a postscript, "when I think of the many 20+-year-old men and women on 'active duty' in this war who grew during their earliest years with our 'Neighborhood' program. How I long for them to be able to come back here and live the rest of their lives in peace."[2]

Fred Rogers was a pacifist. He was not a Navy Seal sniper with thirty confirmed kills during the Vietnam War. Nor was he an accomplished Marine who sought to hide his death-dealing skills by presenting himself as a kind and gentle soul. Although it's easy to find these crazed claims on the Internet, the real truth is that Rogers's spiritual beliefs led him to oppose all wars as well as all barriers to individual and social peace.

Rogers was an ordained Presbyterian minister, and although he rarely shared his religious convictions on his program, he fervently believed in a God who accepts us as we are and loves us without condition, who is present in each person and all of creation, and who desires a world marked by peace and wholeness. With this progressive spirituality as his inspiration, Rogers fashioned his children's program as a platform for sharing countercultural beliefs about caring nonviolently for one another, animals, and the earth.

We don't typically think of Rogers as a radical, no doubt partly because he didn't appear that way: His voice was gentle, his body was vulnerable, his hair was in place. He wore colorful, comfortable, soft sweaters made by his mother. Nor do we usually imagine him as a pacifist; that adjective seems way too political to ascribe to the host of a children's program known for its focus on feelings.

In a very real sense, we've domesticated Fred Rogers and his radical pacifism. We've restricted him to the realm of entertainment, children, and feelings, and we've ripped him out of his political and religious context.

The most popular YouTube video of Rogers—with over 10 million views—is a remix created for PBS Digital Studios by the mash-up artist John D. Boswell.[3] The fun and engaging piece shows Rogers singing a lovely song about growing ideas in our minds. But there's no hint anywhere in the video that, for Rogers, our ideas would do well to include really radical thoughts—such as imagining the Persian Gulf War as a form of child abuse.

Another YouTube video—this one with over 2 million views—shows Rogers appearing at a 1969 U.S. Senate hearing on cutting the proposed budget for the newly formed Corporation for Public Broadcasting.[4] The video is powerful and compelling because Rogers uses slow and gentle language to persuade a fast-talking, slick, and rough-and-tumble senator, John Pastore of Rhode Island, to reinstate funds President Nixon wanted to cut. What the 2 million viewers don't learn from the video is that in the late 1960s, Rogers used his program to offer a counter voice to Nixon's conduct of the Vietnam War and his concerted effort to depict poor people as lazy and subversive of the American work ethic.

Still another wildly popular video of Rogers attracts hundreds of thousands of views every time there is a violent crisis in the United States, especially those involving school shootings. In the emotionally gripping clip, Rogers tells us that looking for "the helpers" in violent situations can comfort us and provide us with a sense of hope.[5] But the backstory to the video is that Rogers made it during the War on Terror, and that he was deeply opposed to President George W. Bush's violent response to terrorism—points left unknown to the viewers watching the decontextualized clip.

The popular image of Fred Rogers, as depicted in these videos and many other places, separates him from his faith-fueled pacifism and progressive politics as well as from the historical context in which he shared his treasured convictions. The result is that Rogers often appears benign, anemic, even "namby-pamby," as the late folk singer Pete Seeger once described him.[6]

Rogers disliked that image of himself—especially when he sensed it in parodies served up by Johnny Carson on *The Tonight Show* and Eddie Murphy on *Saturday Night Live*. "I've told Johnny that I like humor as much as anybody," Rogers stated in 1983. "But what concerns me is the takeoffs that make me seem so wimpy! I hope it doesn't communicate that Mr. Rogers is just somebody to be made fun of. Only people who take the time to see our work can begin to understand the depth of it."[7]

The purpose of this book is to take Fred Rogers and his Neighborhood seriously. And why not? For more than three decades, *Mister Rogers' Neighborhood* was a "national powerhouse" that reached more than 3.5 million viewers weekly.[8] Nielsen ratings indicate that at certain points, the number of viewers even ran as high as 9 million people a week. While the program's target audience was children ages two to five, its viewers also included countless siblings, parents, and grandparents, to the point that Rogers became a national icon by the time of his death in 2003. Ongoing sales of his program and books, coupled with online views of him and his work, suggest he remains a beloved figure more than a decade after his untimely death from stomach cancer.

Discovering the real—and radical—Fred Rogers requires setting aside the video clips and the parodies. For me, it demanded suspending my own initial point of entrance into the life and legacy of Fred Rogers. Because I was at the back end of his target audience by the time his program went national in 1968, I did not spend my childhood years watching *Mister Rogers' Neighborhood.* But I did eventually grow to be a huge fan of *Saturday Night Live,* and if truth be told, my first significant encounter with Mister Rogers was through Eddie Murphy's hilarious character "Mister Robinson."

It was thus quite an eye-opening experience, as if I was meeting him for the first time, when I began to dig through his papers at the Fred Rogers Archive at St. Vincent College in Latrobe, Pennsylvania; to read his speeches at the Mister Rogers' Neighborhood Archive at the University of Pittsburgh; to study numerous episodes of the national run of *Mister Rogers' Neighborhood* (1968–2001); to listen to the many interviews he gave; and to talk with people who knew him well. Here, at last, was the Fred Rogers far beyond the comedy sketches of *Saturday Night Live.*

What I found, much to my delight, was a quiet but strong American prophet who, with roots in progressive spirituality, invited us to make the world into a countercultural neighborhood of love—a place where there would be no wars, no racial discrimination, no hunger, no gender-based discrimination, no killing of animals for food, and no pillaging of the earth's precious resources. This is the Fred Rogers I have come to know: not a namby-pamby, mealy-mouthed, meek and mild pushover, but rather an ambitious, hard-driving, and principled (though imperfect) creator of a progressive children's program designed to subvert huge parts of the wider society and culture.

That's right. Rogers was politically subversive—and stubbornly so. Of course, this is not the figure many of us typically remember celebrating as a national icon. We normally recall an angelic figure hovering above the dirtiness of politics and culture, smiling tenderly at our spellbound children, and speaking to them ever so peacefully. But, as he told Goodman, Rogers sometimes felt obliged to address public policy issues when they negatively affected the children and families who comprised his viewing audience.

Although he was deeply engaged in politics and culture, Rogers was well aware of his personal and professional limitations in addressing public policy. As he conceded to Goodman, he well understood that he was not a policymaker who could craft legislation or sign executive decrees to eliminate war and its abuse of children. But he also realized he could use his own particular bully pulpit to shape the moral character of his viewers and extol certain virtues and practices subversive of public policies that enshrined violence, discrimination, and injustice.

That's exactly what he did, and not just with public service announcements. Rogers hinted at this in his letter to Goodman when he noted that he did not lament for the Neighborhood of Make-Believe. Rogers did not have to lament for Make-Believe, with its colorful mix of puppets and adults, or for the "real" neighborhood in which his television house was situated, because he created both as provinces within the peaceable kingdom he desired for humanity and all of creation.

While it's true that many of his shows "tackled the fears and the sadnesses of childhood," they also focused on the politics of violence and injustice—a fact that becomes all the clearer when we study them in their historical context.[9] Indeed, his television neighborhood and the Neighborhood of Make-Believe are virtual oases of peace and justice in a violent and unjust world. But they're more than that, too; they're plain and simple invitations for his viewers to adopt the virtues and practices of peace and justice as they negotiate a world that conquers and kills so much.[10] *Mister Rogers' Neighborhood*, it turns out, is far from sappy, sentimental, and shallow. It's a sharp political response to a civil and political society poised to kill, a fact that will surprise all those elites who dismiss him as a lightweight not worthy of critical engagement.

Rogers also extended his peaceable invitation through numerous sermons, prayers, speeches, letters, books, and interviews, understanding all this countercultural work as part and parcel of his vocation as a Presbyterian minister—a minister called to embody and enact the unconditional and expansive love of God revealed in Jesus of Nazareth. In fact, Rogers sought to ensure that his work of creating peacemakers was a faithful continuation of the ministry of Jesus—an ongoing effort to create the peaceful and just reign of God on earth.

As a Christian peacemaker, Rogers understood Jesus to be the nonviolent love of God incarnate, and he turned to the life of Jesus for concrete guidance about ways to create the peaceable kingdom right here and now. As he put this in a 1979 letter to a friend, "What a tough job to try to communicate the gift of Jesus Christ to anybody. It can't be simply talked about, can it?

Jesus himself used parables—so I guess that's our directive: try to show the kingdom of God through stories as much as possible."[11]

Hence, Rogers's bully pulpit wasn't really about bullying at all. He fashioned his program and outside engagements as opportunities to tell compelling and inviting stories about peace and justice. Fred Rogers was a storytelling peacemaker, and a powerful one at that.[12] His activism, at once militant and gentle, came to expression not through making policy, marching in the streets, or rallying in the squares, but in the stories he shared on his program and in other public venues. By turns affectionate and comical, poignant and provocative, these stories—a major subject in this book—came straight from a heart concerned for the underprivileged, oppressed, and wounded.

Rogers was also a Zen-like peacemaker. His personal and professional style, especially as revealed on his program, demonstrated a deep appreciation not only for quiet storytelling but also for slow pacing and the sounds of silence—those moments when "inner turbulence can settle."[13] The slow way he talked, the careful transitions he made from his "real" television neighborhood to Make-Believe, the silence he insisted on—all this gave us a model for *being* peace.[14] As a model of being peace, Rogers showed us how to practice deep listening, deep thinking, and deep understanding—each of them antidotes to violence in any form.

He also showed us how to take tough action when others undermine our efforts to be peacemakers. In December 1998, for instance, he instructed his lawyer to file a lawsuit against a Texas novelty chain store that was selling T-shirts depicting him, clad in his red sweater, as sporting a handgun and saying, "Welcome to my hood."[15] He was so angry that he insisted that the store not only stop selling the shirts but also destroy them. Fred Rogers was no passive pacifist.

Modeling peacefulness was one of his preferred methods for creating peacemakers because he believed the old Quaker saying "Attitudes are caught not taught."[16] It's perhaps this belief, coupled with his quiet style, that is the underlying reason for our failure to recognize Fred Rogers as one of the most radical pacifists of contemporary history. Because he did not grab headlines by pouring blood on files at the Pentagon, climbing atop the cones of nuclear weapons, leading rallies against the Persian Gulf War, or publicly lobbying against the War on Terror, Rogers has long remained deep in the shadows of the history of progressive dreamers—a history populated in the United States by the likes of William Garrison and Lucretia Mott, Jane Addams and Bayard Rustin, Martin Luther King Jr. and Dorothy Day, Robert Kennedy and Marian Wright Edelman.

But as you will see in the pages ahead, although he is one of the most underappreciated peacemakers in U.S. history, Fred Rogers richly deserves a place in the pantheon of pacifists who tried to shake the foundations of society and culture. To the day of his death, he was a radical Christian pacifist—fervently committed to the end of violence and the presence of social justice in its full glory. The time has come for us to pull him out of the shadows so we can celebrate him just as he was—a fierce peacemaker.

PART 1

War and Peace
in the Neighborhood

Mister Rogers' Neighborhood had its national debut in 1968, during the height of the Vietnam War, and Rogers used his first week of programming to share his antiwar beliefs.

Chapter 1

"Isn't Peace Wonderful?"

Against the Vietnam War, for Gandhi

*J*ust three weeks before the national launch of *Mister Rogers' Neighborhood* in February 1968, Ho Chi Minh and his advisers in North Vietnam marked Tet, the Vietnamese lunar New Year, by carrying out a surprise assault on cities and villages across South Vietnam. The Tet Offensive was massive, with 84,000 pro-Communist troops staging attacks throughout the South, and although U.S. and South Vietnamese forces took just several days to repel the attackers, the sheer power of the assault suggested that President Johnson and General Westmoreland had been less than forthcoming in their earlier assurances that the Vietnam conflict was near its end.

Frustration at home was palpable. "What the hell is going on?" CBS news anchor Walter Cronkite angrily asked. "I thought we were winning the war!"[1] Cronkite's network and other major media outlets had been bringing home the horrors of war by offering daily doses of violent images and death counts. Coupled with this ongoing barrage of negative images, the shock of Tet contributed to the public's growing disapproval of the war and President Johnson's handling of it.

Although only a small minority of citizens were antiwar activists, protests were on the rise, and just two weeks before *Mister Rogers' Neighborhood* debuted nationally, Martin Luther King Jr. had led 2,500 members of a major antiwar group, Clergy and Laity Concerned about Vietnam, in a silent vigil at Arlington National Cemetery. Far from monolithic, the growing antiwar movement ranged from mainstream protests like King's to violent confrontations at military sites to Yippie activist Abbie Hoffman's mystical efforts to levitate the Pentagon.

Fred Rogers was no Abbie Hoffman—levitating the Pentagon was not his thing—but viewers tuning in to his new national program would have had no doubt he opposed the war. Rogers communicated his antiwar views

3

that first week primarily through a timely storyline in the Neighborhood of Make-Believe.[2]

War in Make-Believe?

Rogers typically crafted *Mister Rogers' Neighborhood* with weekly themes (for example, pets, food, or recycling) that he addressed in his television neighborhood and in the Neighborhood of Make-Believe. He devoted the theme of his first week of national programs to war and peace. Rogers's approach to this topic, like his approach to less controversial themes, was not "in your face"; his style was far from dogmatic or confrontational, and he often surrounded the week's theme with lessons that did not seem directly related to the theme. For example, in the series on war and peace, he used "peace balloons" to teach not only about peace but also about the physics of flying balloons. His gentle approach to the theme sometimes belied its hard-hitting message.

In our very first visit to the Neighborhood of Make-Believe, we discover that the ever mischievous Lady Elaine Fairchilde, a rather unattractive puppet with a long and crooked nose, has used her magical boomerang to rearrange the landscape, even moving the Eiffel Tower to the other side of the castle. The mischief so angers King Friday XIII—the titular, egotistic, and often bumbling head of Make-Believe—that he establishes border guards so other changes "cannot come in."

When Mister Rogers shares this news with neighbor Betty Aberlin back at his television house, she exclaims, "That sounds like a war!" Distressed and concerned, she dons a burlap cape and leaves to find out what's going on in the normally peaceful Make-Believe. Once there (she's now Lady Aberlin, the niece of King Friday), she discovers King Friday and Edgar Cooke, the singing castle cook, dressed in full military regalia and prepared to use force to turn back anyone seeking to make further changes, although, truth be told, Cooke seems more worrier than warrior.

Sporting a helmet with thirteen stars, King Friday then instructs Lady Aberlin to check the north gate while Edgar checks the castle gardens. When Lady Aberlin protests, saying she was not planning to stay, the king will have none of it. "You have come during a state of emergency," he says, "and I have *drafted* you!" Unbelievably, the military draft has come to Make-Believe—and so too has resistance. Although Lady Aberlin hesitantly agrees to be drafted, the Neighborhood has had at least one draft-resister along the way, because the oversized uniform she puts on was actually intended for a draftee who dared not to show up.

Unaffected by such dissent, King Friday continues to militarize the castle, even adding barbed wire around the walls. But guards Edgar and Lady Aberlin are not comfortable with either the militarized Neighborhood or their jobs, and it does not take long for Aberlin to ask for a day off. She uses her time away to follow up on a creative idea first suggested by the once-wild-but-now-tame Daniel Striped Tiger: to send peace balloons onto the castle grounds so King Friday will know that "the whole Neighborhood wants peace."

Safe and sound back in Mister Rogers's house, Betty Aberlin talks with Mister Rogers about the plan, showing him a bunch of balloons with little signs tied to them. The signs include words of peace: *love, peaceful coexistence, tenderness,* and *peace* itself. Mister Rogers is not entirely sure the idea will work, because the king is in "such a fighting mood." But after he and Betty do a successful test run together, he smiles and says, "I think this can work!"

Back in the Neighborhood of Make-Believe, Lady Aberlin joins Daniel and others for the balloon launching at the factory owned and operated by Cornflake S. Pecially. Everyone waits. As the peace balloons float onto the castle grounds, King Friday mistakes them for paratroopers and begins to shout, "Fire the cannon! Fire the cannon! Fire the cannon! Man your stations! Paratroopers! Paratroopers!" Because he's in such a "fighting mood," the king has imagined that paratroopers have invaded his land with dangerous designs to change Make-Believe.

But Lady Aberlin quickly intervenes, pleading with Friday and his soldiers to read the messages "before you start shooting." Guard Negri, one of the king's faithful soldiers, reads the messages aloud and, lo and behold, the surprised king immediately says, "Stop all fighting! Stop all fighting!" Of course, no fighting had ever broken out, but the neighbors of Make-Believe translate the king's directive as an order to stop guarding the Neighborhood and return to their everyday lives. At last, King Friday is very pleased with these peaceful developments, and so are Lady Aberlin and Daniel Striped Tiger. "It *worked*, Daniel," Lady Aberlin says, with a lovely smile. "Oh," Daniel replies, "It *did* work. . . . I'm so glad, because we wanted everybody to have peace, didn't we?"

Back in his house, reflecting on the exciting events, Mister Rogers admits he was not entirely certain the idea of floating peace balloons around the castle would actually succeed. "Floating things!" he says. "How did we know that that was going to be the way the Neighborhood of Make-Believe told the castle they wanted peace?" But Mister Rogers is just as pleased as everyone else with the way things turned out. "Isn't peace wonderful?" he says.

Peacemaking Works

Fred Rogers has taught us in this inaugural week that peace is indeed wonderful. King Friday no longer needs to draft soldiers, post guards, and shout orders to fire the cannon. Neighbors no longer have to give their name, rank, and serial number when traveling throughout Make-Believe. Henrietta Pussycat can stop worrying about being shot and come out from hiding deep in the roots of X the Owl's tree. X no longer has to promise to protect Henrietta from flying bullets. And no one has to shoot invading paratroopers, or even balloons with peace messages. Everyone can go back to the peace and quiet that marked their lives before the crisis.

Rogers thus deliberately used his storyline to build a rational case against war. Like the rationalist Progressives of the 1920s, he sought to school us in the overwhelmingly negative effects of war: disturbing fear, disrupted lives, and distorted thoughts and actions. By the end of the week of programs, war seemed absolutely crazy—the height of irrationality.

Nevertheless, while he emphasized that peace is wonderful, Rogers was not altogether starry-eyed in this first week. In fact, he seemed quite the political realist in teaching us that peacemaking will be hard work. It will certainly require the most creative thoughts our moral imagination can muster. Like Daniel Striped Tiger, we will have to move beyond typical options and come up with creative strategies that surprise and shock the warmongers we seek to influence. Peacemaking will also no doubt be time-consuming. It will require us, as it did Lady Aberlin, to take time off from our regular work to create and carry out unique plans we would not normally even consider. And peacemaking will lead us into moments of doubt and uncertainty. Like Lady Aberlin and Mister Rogers, we will find ourselves wondering whether our ideas will really work.

But the stronger message from the first week is that peacemaking can indeed work. In emphasizing this hopeful and pragmatic point (Mister Rogers, Lady Aberlin, and Daniel use the word *work* at least half a dozen times in reference to the peace balloons), Rogers echoed an individual he often identified as one of his personal heroes: Mohandas Gandhi. Unfortunately, Rogers never spelled out the exact ways in which Gandhi influenced him, but it's not too difficult to see his ideas in this first week overlapping with Gandhi's.

Like Gandhi, Rogers depicted political power as derivative. He did not develop this thought, of course, but the first week in Make-Believe certainly showed Rogers's belief that a ruler's power, like King Friday's, is ultimately dependent upon complicity or cooperation from those he or she rules, and that when the governed begin to withdraw their cooperation, as

Lady Aberlin and Daniel Striped Tiger did, the power of the ruling authority begins to crumble.

Like Gandhi, Rogers also embraced the practice of civil disobedience and its underlying notion that people *should* withdraw their cooperation with unwise leaders. Again, he did not expound on this, but the first week clearly revealed his belief that it's good and important when individuals, like Lady Aberlin and Daniel Striped Tiger, peacefully dissent from a ruler intent on using force to impose his unjust or irrational will throughout the land.[3]

Finally, Rogers firmly believed, as Gandhi did, that nonviolent dissent can indeed work. A pragmatic pacifist, Rogers showed us that if the people withdraw their cooperation from a ruler intent on taking them to war, they will ultimately succeed, one way or another, because political power ultimately resides with the people. Particular peacemaking strategies may fail along the way—we won't know whether peace balloons will work until we try them— and rulers may resist dissent in a variety of ways. But if the people remain resolute in their peacemaking, they will win the day, and rightly so, because power belongs to the people.

Echoing Gandhi, Rogers gave voice to the 1968 peace movement in the United States. Context matters, and when placed in its historical context, Rogers's message from the Neighborhood of Make-Believe packs a punch: The power of President Lyndon Johnson, like King Friday's, depends upon the people he rules. If peacemakers withdraw their cooperation from the president's commitment to Vietnam, they will succeed. They may not succeed in the short term, but if they remain resolute and identify the right strategies, they will ultimately win. And their hard efforts will be worthwhile because peace, as the people know, is always far more desirable than war.

Fred Rogers was no wild-eyed Abbie Hoffman during the Vietnam War. Mystical levitation wasn't his forte. Nor, for that matter, was he a Martin Luther King Jr. Marching for peace in noisy streets wasn't his chosen method, either. But in the quiet of a television studio, behind the staring eye of a camera, Rogers was a leading peace activist in his own right, intent on showing the beauty and power of peacemaking to children and adults mired in a war with no end in sight.

"And they shall beat their swords
into plowshares,
And their spears into pruning forks;
Nation shall not lift up sword
against nation,
Neither shall they learn war
any more."

Rogers showed the biblical roots of his pacifism
when he broadcast this image of Isaiah 2:4 in his
1983 series on war and peace.

Chapter 2

"War Isn't Nice"

Against the Arms Race, for Peaceful Imagination

Many opponents of the Vietnam War were not pacifists. John Kerry, for example, was a leading activist in the peace movement of the 1960s, but in the 1980s he was not a prominent voice in popular campaigns opposing nuclear weapons or various U.S. military excursions. Fred Rogers, by contrast, was opposed not just to the Vietnam War but also to all wars. He was a dyed-in-the-wool pacifist who saw war and its preparations as always wrong—yesterday, today, and tomorrow. As a committed pacifist, Rogers continued to broadcast his antiwar views long after the conclusion of the Vietnam War. When he did so in the 1980s, he intentionally offered a counterpoint to the militaristic foreign policy of President Ronald Reagan.

The Context: War and Weapons

In November 1983, Rogers aired a remarkable weeklong series of *Mister Rogers' Neighborhood* on the theme of conflict. The series resurrected themes from the 1968 programs on war and peace but also advanced them in new and creative ways. The episodes of November 7–11, 1983, remain the most concerted antiwar effort of Rogers's entire television career, and there has since been nothing like it in all of children's programming.

War and weapons, as usual, were in the air in 1983. PBS was using the new fall television season to broadcast its thirteen-part history of the Vietnam War, or, as media critic John Corry aptly characterized it, "the longest and most misunderstood war that Americans ever fought."[1] The somber documentary resurrected old images of body bags and soldiers wading through muddy waters and rice paddies, and many viewers no doubt saw the footage as a ghastly reminder of the dangers of U.S. foreign policy run amok.

They also would have seen the footage as timely. Once again, the American public was debating the wisdom of employing U.S. military might to combat communism abroad. This time the focus was on Central America—Nicaragua, Honduras, Guatemala, and El Salvador—and President Reagan's fervent commitment to using U.S. forces there to conquer communism and establish U.S.-styled democracy. John B. Oakes, a *New York Times* editor during the Vietnam War, snorted at that mission, speaking for many liberals when he warned that summer that unless Congress stopped him, "Ronald Reagan could plunge this country into the most unwanted, unconscionable, unnecessary, and unwinnable war in its history, not excepting Vietnam."[2]

But the most significant military event occurred in October, just before Rogers's weeklong series, when the virulently anticommunist Reagan authorized a U.S. military intervention in Grenada, a small Caribbean nation whose Marxist leader, Maurice Bishop, was overthrown by members of his own party. At the request of the Organization of Eastern Caribbean States, Reagan sent U.S. troops to the tiny island to restore order, safeguard American students, and prevent Cuba from establishing control over the nation's politics. It took U.S. forces only a few days to accomplish their mission, and the successful intervention received widespread support from the American public, including John Kerry.

Finally, worldwide protests of nuclear weapons also set the backdrop to Rogers's special series on conflict. On October 22, ten days before U.S. cruise missiles were set to arrive at an airbase in Great Britain (compliments of the Reagan administration's policy of selective nuclear proliferation), nearly 250,000 people converged in London to stage massive demonstrations against nuclear weapons on British soil. Just a week earlier, 10,000 protestors had held a protest rally at a nuclear weapons plant in Denver, Colorado, even attempting to form a human chain around the facility. And in early November, antinuclear groups shouted enthusiastic support for both Lynne Littman's *Testament*, an artsy film depicting the horrors of nuclear war, and ABC's *The Day After*, a widely publicized television series about the same topic.

While the media devoted sustained attention to these various types of protest, President Reagan seemed unfazed by the "antinukes" and continued to support the proliferation of U.S.-controlled nuclear weapons. Eight months before Rogers's series aired, for instance, Reagan had traveled to Orlando, Florida, to speak to the National Association of Evangelicals (NAE), and in what is now known as "the evil empire speech," he sharply criticized those who "speak in soothing tones of brotherhood and peace" while failing to recognize the ferocity of our godless, aggressive, and totalitarian adversaries. He had the Soviet Union in mind, of course, and he cautioned against "those who would place the United States in a position of military and moral inferiority." Setting the immediate background for his thoughts was the NAE's plans to devote some of its discussions to the topic of halting the production of nuclear weapons. "I urge you," Reagan added, "to beware of the temptation of pride—the temptation of blithely declaring yourselves above it all and label both sides equally at fault, to ignore the facts of history and the aggressive impulses of an evil empire, to simply call the arms race a giant misunderstanding and thereby remove yourself from the struggle between right and wrong and good and evil."[3]

An Arms Race in Make-Believe

Fred Rogers was no Ronald Reagan. With war and weapons in the air, Rogers used his own airspace to launch a creative assault on both. The 1983 special series, now titled "Conflict Week" but originally titled "War and Peace," delivered an antiwar message repeatedly, beginning with the first visit to the Neighborhood of Make-Believe.[4]

In an early scene, Prince Tuesday, the son of King Friday and Queen Sara Saturday, is at school, learning about war from his teacher, Harriet Elizabeth Cow. The stunning dialogue between Ms. Cow and her eager students, including the Prince, Daniel Striped Tiger, and Ana Platypus, reveals the week's hard-hitting theme:

Ms. Cow: Now which country do you think this is, class?

Daniel: That looks like Upaboveland to me.

Ms. Cow: You're absolutely right, Daniel. Now what about this one?

Ana: I think that's from Downunderland.

Ms. Cow: Yes, Ana, it used to be Downunderland, but not anymore.

Prince: Oh, I know.

Ms. Cow: Yes, Prince Tuesday?

Prince: That's the one that had the war with Sidestepland, so now everything from Downunderland is in with Sidestepland.

Ms. Cow: That's correct.

Ana: I'm glad I didn't live there.

Daniel: I am, too. I wouldn't like to live where they're having a war.

Prince: We've never had a war here in Make-Believe, have we?

Ms. Cow: Not that I know of. There's no mention of a war in this Neighborhood in any of the history books.

> Ana: We've had fights: when people get angry about things.
>
> Daniel: Everybody has those, but we don't have fights with guns and bombs and stuff.
>
> Ana: That kind of thing must be awful.
>
> Prince: But, what if you win? You get to take everything the losers have.
>
> Ana: That wouldn't be nice.
>
> Ms. Cow: No, it wouldn't, and war *isn't* nice, Ana. We've been very fortunate here in this Neighborhood of Make-Believe not to have any wars.

Upon returning home, Prince Tuesday asks his father whether Make-Believe has ever had a war. "No," King Friday replies. "Your grandfather and your great-grandfather and your great-great-grandfather never believed in war. They used to say, 'There are other ways to solve a problem.' They even taught us a song at the Kingly School about that." Surprisingly, the normally reticent king then breaks out in song: "There are other ways to solve a problem. There are other ways to solve a nasty problem. Other ways, other ways." But as his shaky singing drifts off, it's clear his mind is elsewhere.

King Friday has just learned that nearby Southwood has placed an order for one million "parts" with factory owner Cornflake "Corney" S. Pecially. News about the order has made Friday wonder whether the mysterious parts might pose a real and present danger to Make-Believe. Fueling this thought is Prince Tuesday's suggestion that because Southwood has already experienced war and thus knows how to "build bombs and make bullets and make all kinds of bad stuff to hurt people," perhaps the million parts are for the construction of bombs—bombs to be dropped on the Neighborhood.

King Friday agrees, and while carefully inspecting a part he has secured, gives urgent instructions to Handyman Negri: "You are to order a million of these from Cornflake S. Pecially and conscript everyone in the Neighborhood to help put the bombs together." When the baffled handyman seeks to confirm the stratospheric number, the king holds the part high and states, "Yes, a million. If Southwood has a million, we will have a million and one!"

The arms race is on.

King Friday acts with lightning speed in advancing his plans to build bombs, conscript everyone in the Neighborhood, and prepare for war. "No time for questions," he tells Handyman Negri. "This is a time for *action*." But not everyone agrees with the royal rush. Lady Aberlin, ever the sensitive dissident, sees the king's rush to war as wrong, and she tells him so.

> King: Niece Aberlin, there is no more time for discussion. I wish you to come to the AB room and help to assemble more bombs.

L.A.: I can't help you, Uncle Friday. I've told you over and over I believe this whole thing is wrong. There is something terribly wrong about it.

King: Don't you want this neighborhood to be protected? If Southwood is building bombs, we must do the same.

L.A.: Why?

King: Well, because, it's just the thing to do.

L.A.: Uncle Friday, we don't even know the people of Southwood.

King: We know that they *might* be building bombs.

L.A.: That's not enough proof for me.

[King reaches for some computer readout sheets, which make no sense to anyone.]

King: Here's proof enough, Lady Aberlin.

L.A.: What's this?

King: It's computer readout.

L.A.: So?

King: So, when you have computer readout that long, you know that something is going on.

L.A.: Honestly!

King: I have no more time for debate. I must go train my generals and their staffs. Farewell, Niece.

Lady Aberlin is exasperated, at least as much as one can be in Make-Believe, and so is the contrarian-in-residence, Lady Elaine Fairchilde. When she hears that Southwood is building a million bombs and that King Friday wants to respond by building one million bombs plus one, she scoffs. "That's the craziest thing I ever heard of," she says. Then when others seek to enlist her in making bombs, she replies, "Not on your life. I've got to know a lot more about this situation before anybody gets my help."

Smart as whips, Lady Elaine and Lady Aberlin join forces to create a team of vigorous dissent in Make-Believe that is intent on checking King Friday's unbelievable claims about the neighbors to the south. While Lady Aberlin has only a hunch that her warmongering uncle is mistaken, Lady Elaine bases her critical reaction on a known fact. "They'll never get me to believe all that bomb stuff," Lady Elaine snorts. "I knew somebody from Southwood one time. She was in my class at school. She was a great person."

The ladies quickly set out to identify this great person, and after they learn her name is Betty Okonak, they seek King Friday's permission to visit Betty and "find out what is really going on . . . the truth." In the meantime there's a possible glitch: Bob Dog has shown up at the castle with a piece of paper with bumps on it, and he believes it's a war secret or a code—something that could reveal real dangers confronting the Neighborhood. But Chef Brockett, schooled in much more than baking delicious cakes, sets everybody straight when he rightly recognizes the "code" as braille and then translates the message: "That which is essential is invisible to the eye." (The message is actually Fred Rogers's favorite sentence from *The Little Prince*.)

Perplexed, King Friday wonders aloud about the meaning of this curious quotation. "I guess it means that there's a lot more to things than what we see," Chef Brockett says. "Or hear, or touch, or imagine," adds Lady Elaine. "I think it means that there is a lot more to Southwood than our thinking up some story about their making bombs."

After consulting his generals, King Friday relents and agrees to send Lady Aberlin and Lady Elaine as a "peace delegation" to discover the truth about Southwood and its plans for the million parts supplied by Corney. Delighted with their new commission as "soldiers of peace," the ladies visit Southwood and soon come across Betty Okonak, now Betty Okonak Templeton, on their travels. Lady Elaine and Betty exchange warm greetings, and when Betty learns the ladies are soldiers of peace, she announces her appreciation. "I love peace," she states. "I mean, if there's anything that's truly wonderful, it's peace. All these people that talk of war and shooting and all. That's just the worst."

Betty adds that the rest of Southwood joins her in feeling the same. "Well, you'll never find a war down here," she says. "In fact, hardly anybody ever comes here." That's why Southwood is building a new bridge—to make it possible for other people to "come and visit." The million parts are not for bombs at all but rather for a bridge that will establish a lasting connection between Southwood and its neighbors.

Lady Elaine and Lady Aberlin are thrilled to receive Betty's assurance, to learn the real reason for the million parts, and to discover the essential truth about Southwood. And what is the essential truth? As Lady Aberlin puts it to Betty, "Well, I just see that you all here in Southwood are very much like we are in the Neighborhood of Make-Believe. You like good things to eat. . . . And you like peace. . . . And you like people to come and visit. . . . And you think that wars are terrible things."

The wise ladies of peace return to Make-Believe at last and announce their findings, sparking a dramatic response from the warriors. The very moment General Negri learns that Southwood is not building bombs, he takes off his general's insignia. "I'm so relieved," he says. And when King Friday learns of the bridge, he expresses regret about being so thoughtless in his decision to train generals and build bombs. As relieved as he can be, he then declares that everyone in Make-Believe will be "generals of peace," and he calls for a report on what can be done with the million and one pieces he has ordered.

His call for a report resurrects a nagging problem. King Friday's order of one million parts plus one has bankrupted the Neighborhood's coffers, and this means he cannot fulfill his prewar promise to purchase a record player for the children's school. When Lady Elaine first learned this awful news, she directly confronted King Friday. "What about the gift for the school?" she demanded. "After the war," he replied. "We'll talk about that after the war."

Now that the crisis has passed, Queen Sara adds to the expression of disappointment. The queen has been absent most of the week because as director of the World Peace Movement, she has been very busy working for peace behind the scenes. Now, even though peace has been maintained, the queen remains irked and disappointed. Wondering aloud what "in this peaceful world" could be done with the million parts, she states, "And to think there's no money left for the record player that we had saved for the school children. War is such a waste."

Why War Is Not Nice—and Often a Mistake

Thus concludes Rogers's unequivocal, unbending, unqualified depiction of war as "not nice." There's nothing subtle or nuanced about the message: War is nasty, period. By the end of the weeklong series, we've learned at least three reasons behind Rogers's entirely negative assessment of war.

First, war is not nice because it leads winners to steal from losers. Unlike Prince Tuesday, who suggests, with some enthusiasm, that winners in war "get to take everything losers have," Rogers sides with Ms. Cow's insistence that it's never good to steal property, land, and people from losers in the conflict. War means theft, and thievery is wrong.

Second, war is not nice because it fails to recognize the essential truth that all people, including our enemies, are just like us: inherently good and deserving of care and concern.[5] For Rogers, if we look deeply enough, as Lady Aberlin and Lady Elaine do, we will come to understand that reasonable people, wherever we find them, even in uniforms on battlefields, are largely alike. They are good and decent folks who long for peace and appreciate the goodness of life's bountiful offerings.

Third, war is not nice because it's such a waste, as Queen Sara puts it. It wastes precious resources that could otherwise be used for programs designed to help people flourish. For Rogers, tax dollars are for record players that can help children appreciate music; they're not for weapons designed to slaughter the parents of children or, worse, the children themselves.

Placed in historical context, Rogers's message that "war isn't nice" stood in direct opposition to Ronald Reagan's foreign policy. At the very least, his radical message implied that the invasion of Grenada was not nice; that the plot to use military force in Latin America was not nice; that spending money on nuclear weapons, especially while slashing social programs, was not nice; that identifying our enemies as "evil" was not nice; and that our own government was not nice for trying to get us to support war and nuclear weapons. Using the plain and simple language of Make-Believe, Rogers directly and intentionally voiced his opposition to the prowar and promilitary policies of the Reagan administration.

But the special series also told us much more than that war is not nice. By week's end, we had also encountered Rogers's belief that war can result from rather idiotic mistakes. In commenting on the series just before it was broadcast, Rogers pointed this out much more gently. "So often conflicts arise from a lack of communication, false assumptions or confusion, and that's what happens in the Neighborhood of Make-Believe," he explained.[6]

In fact, King Friday was utterly confused about Southwood, and his decision to rush to war came across as intellectually shallow, as an abject failure to ask hard questions and to subject initial and early suppositions to critical query. King Friday was not the brightest crayon in the royal box—Lady Elaine was.

When applied to its historical context, this message too packed a tremendous subversive punch. At the very least, it implied that President Reagan might have been wrong about Grenada, the contras in Nicaragua, and the leaders of the Soviet Union. President Reagan, like King Friday, might have just been confused.

This invites the question: What if King Friday had been *right* about Southwood? What if he hadn't been confused? What if the people of Southwood really had been intent on dropping bombs on the Neighborhood?

Importantly, Rogers did not want his viewers believing that if the right facts are discovered, or if certain suppositions are proven false, going to war will be the right thing to do. Getting the facts right is certainly important, partly because they may show that the stated reasons for resorting to war are flat-out wrong. But because he was an absolutist on the issue of war, believing that war can never be nice, Rogers held that there is not one fact or piece of data that will ever make war (or even preparing for war) morally permissible.

The Possibility of Peace

While the message of war's stupidity had enough kick to stand alone, our television neighbor did not want to conclude the weeklong series on a downer.

Rogers was never wont to leave us stuck in negativism, so he nicely arranged for King Friday to throw a "peace passing party" for the residents of the Neighborhood of Make-Believe as well as the "dear friends of Southwood."

The ever friendly Betty Okonak Templeton comes to the peace party—she's so pleased to be back in the Neighborhood—and so does Keith David, the very nice man who has been building the beautiful bridge in Southwood. Together with all the other neighbors of Make-Believe, the visitors dance, eat peace pancakes, hug, and celebrate "lasting peace."

King Friday takes the occasion to apologize to the people of Southwood ("I'm very, very, very sorry"), and—perhaps best of all—Keith David uses some of the leftover parts to make a record player. In a moment of remarkable generosity, Friday then orders that all of the other parts be used to make enough record players so he can give one to every school in the world "as a reminder that fine people can and do help others correct their mistakes."

The Make-Believe segments thus conclude on a hopeful note. Yes, Rogers has used them to teach us, in plain and simple language, that war is not nice, that it destroys the essential goodness of humanity and squanders precious resources that can otherwise help people flourish in their goodness. He has also shown us that war can be the result of poor thinking. But equally important, Rogers leaves us with a sense of hope—an empowering moral sense that peace is really possible. He did the same in 1968, when Daniel Striped Tiger floated his peace balloons, but this time Rogers has given us several additional reasons to adopt an optimistic peace ethic.

Peace is possible, according to Rogers, first because each of us is equipped with a powerful moral imagination—the ability to see goodness in moments of crisis and danger. As Mister Rogers puts this in his concluding monologue, "You see, people can *imagine* bad things, hurtful things, angry war-like things, but people can also *imagine* good things, helpful things, happy, peaceful things." Like King Friday, we can imagine our enemies are bad and try to destroy them so we can at last be safe. Or, like Lady Elaine and Lady Aberlin, we can imagine they are essentially good and, like us, desire peace. For Rogers, our vocation as neighbors is to imagine the goodness we cannot always easily see: "enemies" as individuals who are like us, "bomb parts" as components for record players, and unwise kings as fonts of wisdom. With the right vision—a moral imagination that insists on seeing people and places as positively good—we can begin to envision the peace that is possible.

Second, peace is possible because we are actors, not passive victims, who can always choose to create the peace we have envisioned. On the one hand, we can always act directly against war and its preparations. We do not have to build bombs, for example, even when the legal authorities conscript us to do so. Like Lady Elaine and Lady Aberlin, we can refuse to obey unjust and unfair orders; we can become dissidents, practice civil disobedience, and resist preparations for war. It's that simple. And if war does come, we do not have to fight. As X the Owl told a tearful and fearful Henrietta Pussycat as they were assembling bombs together, "You don't have to fight, Henrietta. And I'll take care of you."

Even once we start warring, we always have the capacity to self-correct, to change our actions midcourse. We can stop, apologize, and make amends. Again, it's that simple. Like King Friday, who was terribly wrong about Southwood's intentions, we can say we're "very, very, very sorry," make amends by inviting our old enemies to peaceful activities, and then demonstrate to others our commitment to a lasting peace. For Rogers, repentance in word and deed is the stuff of peace.

On the other hand, long before war looms, we can always choose constructive actions designed to help people flourish. Like Keith David, for example, we can build bridges rather than bombs. As Mister Rogers himself points out in the series, "People can make machines do helpful things, or they can make them do harmful things." Indeed, one of the most fascinating parts of the weeklong series comes at the end of the first episode, when Rogers shows footage, provided by the U.S. Air Force no less, of a food airlift. He explains that the film is "of people in airplanes dropping some cartons of food on a place where the people had been in a war and their food was all gone so the people in the airplanes were trying to help them have something to eat." His point is clear: We can use planes to drop bombs, or we can employ them to supply food to hungry people.

We can also choose peaceful actions when we really do face intimidating situations and problems, including those in which an enemy directly threatens our very existence. If King Friday had been right after all, and Southwood had indeed been building bombs, posing a real and present danger, Rogers would no doubt have fallen back on one of his major tenets: that there are always "other ways to solve a problem," as King Friday put it, no matter how serious the problem.

Unfortunately, Rogers did not develop this thought in any systematic way. He did not, for example, analyze and critique the major responses to conflict that social theorists have identified: conflict resolution, conflict management, and conflict transformation. Rogers was no conflict theorist, but he did affirm in the 1983 series that we can resolve some conflicts by finding and then correcting the false assumptions we may have about the roots of the conflict or those we have pinpointed as our enemies. For Rogers, this practice requires sitting with our enemies, listening to them, inviting them to listen to us, and using each other's expressed hopes and fears to add substance to our respective initial presumptions. Finding "other ways to solve a problem," as Lady Elaine and Lady Aberlin do, requires talking—deep, searching, and open-ended conversations.

This positive message from the series—peace is always possible—is just as subversive as the message that war isn't nice. In context, it implied at the very least that, unlike President Reagan, we should imagine our so-called enemies in the Soviet Union and elsewhere as potential friends, resist plans for war and the construction of nuclear bombs, and advocate for nonviolent solutions to conflicts in Latin America and Grenada. The message from the Neighborhood of Make-Believe, it turns out, was radically different from the one in the Reagan White House.

But a nagging question remains: What if our enemy does not concede that there are other ways to solve a problem and thus refuses to talk with us or anyone else, including Queen Sara's World Peace Movement, or other organizations with skilled experts in conflict theory? What if our enemy remains intent on attacking and killing us? What if our enemy actually attacks us?

Rogers never dealt with these questions directly, but perhaps part of the answer lies in his adamant refusal to qualify what he considered to be an essential truth: that all people are basically good, worthy of our care and love. It's a point he emphasized time and again.

"I guess you know how important I think people are," he states, unqualifiedly, during the series. "When we start thinking about everything in the world, it's the people who are the most important of all." That means *all* people, not just those who are our friends and allies. And if this is true, we have no reason to kill our enemies, even ones who attack us.

With nonviolence instilled in us, Mister Rogers encourages us at the end of the series to help make the world "a better and better place for people to live so that people won't have to be scared of other people." As he brings the series to a close, he sings "Peace and Quiet," a simple song he had written for his father long ago:

> Peace and quiet. Peace, peace, peace.
> Peace and quiet. Peace, peace, peace.
> Peace and quiet. Peace, peace, peace.
> We all want peace;
> We all want peace.

Mister Rogers smiles as he finishes the song. "I wish you peace," he says. And as he walks out the door and leaves, we know his wish is our command.

In 1987, as relations between the United States and the Soviet Union were beginning to thaw, Rogers traveled to Moscow and appeared on a Soviet children's television show called *Spokoinoi Nochi (Good Night, Little Ones)*.

Chapter 3

"I Like You"

Against the Cold War, for Puppet Détente

*B*y 1987, President Reagan was no longer calling the Soviet Union an evil empire. He was instead talking directly with Mikhail Gorbachev, the likeable new Soviet leader who, shortly after coming to power in 1985, had initiated domestic reforms and made peaceful overtures to Western leaders. Reagan even welcomed Gorbachev at the White House in December 1987 for the signing of a treaty that provided for the dismantling of all U.S. and Soviet medium- and shorter-range nuclear missiles—a move adamantly opposed by political conservatives such as Senator Jesse Helms of North Carolina.

At the signing, Gorbachev stressed the role of safeguarding children: "It is our duty to . . . move together toward a nuclear-free world, which holds out for our children and grandchildren, and for their children and grandchildren, the promise of a fulfilling and happy life, without fear and without a senseless waste of resources on weapons of destruction."[1] Fred Rogers agreed wholeheartedly. In fact, he had even carried out his own détente in the weeks and months preceding Gorbachev's visit.

A Trip to the Soviet Union

In the spring of 1987, David Newell—who worked as Rogers's public relations man and also played the character of Mr. McFeely—heard Ted Koppel, host of the ABC news program *Nightline*, comparing *Mister Rogers' Neighborhood* to a Soviet children's television show called *Spokoinoi Nochi* (*Good Night, Little Ones*). Inspired by the comparison, Newell soon approached Rogers with the idea of a possible cross-cultural exchange between the two programs.

Rogers liked the idea, and although he was initially unsure of its workability, just six months later he and his crew found themselves on a two-week trip to the Soviet Union. The purpose of the trip was for Rogers to appear in an episode of *Good Night, Little Ones*, finalize plans for the Soviet host Tatyana Vedeneyeva to visit *Mister Rogers' Neighborhood,* and secure footage of Soviet people and sites that he might show back home.

The exchange required detailed, on-site negotiations between Rogers and Soviet authorities, and when the discussions in Moscow bogged down, Rogers reached for his trusty puppet—Daniel Striped Tiger. Rogers had long used Daniel, a shy little tiger, to help children conquer fears that prevented them from trying new things. As a tame tiger—he no longer bit anything other than his food—Daniel was nonthreatening and inviting, and his very presence made children and adults feel as if they were in a safe place where they could imagine big and bold ideas.

Daniel looked sheepishly at his Soviet hosts, and in his sweet and quiet voice, said the Russian word for "hello"—*zdravstvuitye*—just before burying his little head into his handler's comfortable sweater. "They just lit up," Rogers later explained. "It was as if the child in them came out. I handed Daniel across the table, and they all started putting him on their hands." The negotiations soon came to a relatively successful end, although neither side got exactly what it wanted.

Rogers wanted to film workers making the world-famous *matryoshka* dolls, and while the Soviet authorities nixed that idea, he was able to secure footage of officially approved scenes and sites, including the high-tech studios where *Good Night, Little Ones* was filmed. The Soviets were hoping for an animated cartoon like *Tom and Jerry*, but Rogers gently told them that his work was markedly different from that bop-'em-and-sock-'em cartoon. "I'm sorry, I don't like *Tom and Jerry*," he said just before promising them to send something more in line with his style.

Rogers's visit to *Good Night, Little Ones* was historic in the sense that he was the first foreign guest in the twenty-three-year history of the program. The political significance of the moment was not lost on him. As the Soviet crew prepped the set, he stood in the studio and characterized the scene as part of the wider context of détente between the United States and the Soviet Union. "At first I thought this was a lark, I thought the exchange would never happen," he told a reporter. "I think, with a lot of other things, this shows the increasing good will."[2]

Extant footage from his visit on the set shows him wearing a bright blue sweater and marveling at the nicely appointed studio. In the segment filmed for *Good Night, Little Ones,* he greets Tatyana with a warm smile and says hello in Russian. Dressed in a black leather skirt, she invites him to tour the studio, and Rogers puts his arm around her waist as they take a short walk that ends at the piano, where she asks whether he would like to play. "Of course I would!" Rogers says, and as he begins to play "Won't You Be My Neighbor?" he does his best to sing it in Russian: *"Budyesh Ty Moi Sosyed?"*[3]

A palpable sense of warmth and neighborliness continues in a brief puppet scene when an assertive pig named Hryushka plants a kiss on Daniel Striped Tiger. Rather than shyly disappearing, as he's wont to do, Daniel stands his ground and says, "Thank you. I like you!" The two have become fast friends, just as Mister Rogers and Tatyana have. It's a remarkable scene in light of the Cold War fought through the years.

Rogers and Vedeneyeva met again two months later, near the end of November, at the Soviet embassy in Washington, DC, where Soviet diplomats hosted an event to celebrate the cultural exchange between the two programs. Soviet ambassador Yuri Dubinin was present for the occasion, and he and Rogers chatted briefly about the exchange. "They call it puppet détente," Rogers told the ambassador. Another Soviet official also stressed the importance of friendship between the two countries while speaking to a group of thirty Soviet and American children gathered for the celebration. "Your concerns are the same," he told them. "It's important for you to be friends, friends across the borders."[4]

A few days later, Vedeneyeva arrived at WQED-TV in Pittsburgh for a taping of *Mister Rogers' Neighborhood.* A message board outside the studio read, in English and Russian, "On the bridge of trust and the rainbow of love, Mr. Rogers' Neighborhood Welcomes Tatyana Vedeneyeva."[5] The warm welcome continued for all to see and hear during the filmed episode.[6]

When Tatyana arrives in Mister Rogers's house, the two hug as she beams warmly—a shocking scene for those of us familiar with dour-faced and arm-folding Soviet premiers like Leonid Brezhnev. Mister Rogers then notes with delight that she's wearing a sweater—"You like to wear sweaters, too!" he says—and he walks her to the closet and shows her his own many colorful sweaters. He also shows her his fish and even allows her to feed them—an act that depicts Tatyana as caring and trustworthy. So too does the conversation she and Mister Rogers have as they sit at his table and sip apple juice.

Mister Rogers asks about her five-year-old son Dmitri, and she shows a picture of him wearing the colors red, white, and blue. "He loves to play with small cars," she says, "but most of all he loves to draw." This prompts Mister Rogers to return to his point about similarities between Soviets and

Americans. "Oh, he likes to draw pictures?" he asks. "Very much like children here in our country!"

"Soviet children also like to play," Tatyana adds. "They like to read fairy tales, and they have small tables and beds where they sleep—just like American children." Mister Rogers wonders whether Soviet children become frightened sometimes, and Tatyana confirms as much before noting they also like music. With that cue, Rogers says he has a present to give her and walks her over to the piano. "Tatyana," he says, "it's a song I wrote for you." As she stands next to him at the piano, he begins to play and sing:

> We would like to welcome you.
> It's good to be in touch.
> We would like to welcome you.
> Our friendship means so much.

"Thank you very much," Tatyana says as she leans down, gives him a kiss on the cheek (not at all a common occurrence in the Neighborhood!), and then joins him in singing the song in English. With her brief visit over, she shares her wish that all children will be "healthy, happy, and have wonderful friends like Mister Rogers."

After she departs for the airport with Mr. McFeely, Mister Rogers explains the meaning of the cross-cultural exchange. "I remember so well the kindness people showed me when I visited Russia, so it's so special that Tatyana would come here to carry on our friendship," he says. "Everybody in the world loves to be loved. There are people all over the world who want to be loving and do loving things to each other."

Rogers's message was clear: The Soviet people are a lot like us. They are loving, not evil, and they want to love others, not hate and kill them. And they certainly don't want us to hate and kill them; like everyone, they just want to be loved. This message could not have been more at odds with the Cold War propaganda in which many of us had been steeped.

After the taping, Vedeneyeva and Rogers returned to their themes of peace and friendship as they spoke to the media. "Small children will be looking at this show, and they're going to understand that children around the world are really similar," Vedeneyeva said. "We all want to get along with one another, we all want friendships, we all want to be cared for."

Rogers took the moment to express a religious sense of wonder at the timing of the taping—just a few weeks before Gorbachev's landmark trip to the United States. Rogers fully realized the taping had made him vulnerable to political conservatives unhappy with such a positive depiction of Soviet life, but he was fully confident—spiritually confident—with his small and quiet version of political détente. "Talk about the Holy Spirit moving," he said. "I tell you, there are times when you just have to stand back in surprise." Deep in his heart of faith, Rogers believed he and Vedeneyeva were instruments of a peaceful Spirit blowing down walls and barriers between people who, in their own heart of hearts, just want to be loving and lovable.

An ordained Presbyterian minister, Rogers was an active member of Sixth Presbyterian Church in Pittsburgh, a congregation known for its progressive ministries.

Chapter 4

"Just the Way You Are"

A Theology of Peace

Fred Rogers often noted that his obligation as a public broadcaster was to avoid religious proselytizing, but at the end of the conflict series in 1983 he shared a key message he had left out of the 1968 antiwar episodes:

> They shall beat their swords into plowshares;
> And their spears into pruning hooks;
> Nation shall not lift up sword against nation;
> Neither shall they learn war anymore.

The message was taken verbatim from the book of Isaiah (2:4) in the Hebrew Bible. Rogers ran the passage as a screenshot, without spoken commentary, just before rolling the credits. He was targeting his adult viewers, of course, letting them know that underlying his antiwar week was the radical vision of peace depicted by the prophet Isaiah.[1]

Rogers was a believer, not only in God and peace, but also in a God of peace. His identity as a religious believer suggests that while he was a pragmatic pacifist who believed in the effectiveness of nonviolence, he was also a *principled* pacifist—someone who embraced pacifism, first and foremost, for reasons of principle, even in situations where it might not be effective. In fact, the substance of Rogers's principled pacifism came from his progressive spirituality, his abiding faith in a God of unconditional love.

Faithful and Nonviolent

As a child, Rogers worshipped at the First Presbyterian Church of Latrobe, Pennsylvania, where he so admired the ministers that he decided to attend seminary. It took him awhile, but Rogers became an ordained Presbyterian minister in 1962, charged with working with families through the mass media.

He was already steeped in children's television programming by this point, so he was quite pleased with the charge from his ministerial colleagues. But there was another reason he was happy with the charge. "I've never felt comfortable proclaiming from a pulpit," he said years later. "When you look at the lens of a camera, which is just one machine, you think of just one person. I like that, as opposed to facing a sea of congregated faces."[2]

Rogers was a gentle Presbyterian. He was not inclined to speak of God as full of wrath and vengeance, ever prepared to wipe out the earth and send sinful people to hell for eternity. "The BIG thing about God," Rogers wrote, "is God's faithfulness: not giving up on those with whom God has made a covenant . . . not even giving up on them as they torture and kill each other."

Rogers was reflecting on the Holocaust when he emailed those words to writer Tom Junod in 1998. That horrific event, so full of hatred and violence, had given Rogers reason not to question the existence of God, as so many others had, but to express sheer wonder at God's ability to endure suffering patiently. "Don't you think that if you were God you would have wiped out the whole world . . . the whole of humanity . . . in the wake of the Holocaust?" Rogers wrote. "But, like a parent whose child insists on a path of careless dalliance leading to an eventual downfall, God refuses to force the Way at the same time being always available."[3]

As one schooled in the Hebrew Bible, Rogers no doubt realized he was ignoring considerable biblical evidence in making that claim. After all, the story of Noah and the flood depicts God giving up on almost all humanity and using force to wipe out countless children, women, and men from the face of the earth. Similarly, the Hebrew stories of God commanding the Israelites to use overwhelming and indiscriminate violence, even against children, to secure land and resources seem to counter Rogers's claim that the God of the Bible neither gives up on people nor uses force to accomplish the divine will.

But Rogers held to a progressive view of divine revelation. "God evolves, learns, grows, knows," he explained to Junod, adding that this view was "probably heretical in some circles." It was indeed. Contrary to Christian fundamentalism and its millions of adherents, Rogers refused to believe that the God of yesterday remains the same today and tomorrow. So if there was a time when God quickly gave up on people and used violence to force obedience to the divine will, all that has changed. God has repented of those actions and now simply allows humanity to make its own choices, for good and bad, while always being present to any who call out. Changed, God is now faithful and nonviolent. Or, as Rogers once put it, "God doesn't POW anybody." God is not a superhero who zaps, zings, and pows his way to justice.[4]

To help describe his faithful and nonviolent God, Rogers turned to two parables found in the Gospel of Luke: those of the lost sheep and the lost coin. The former speaks of a sheep owner who leaves behind ninety-nine sheep in the wilderness in order to find the one that has strayed, and the latter of a woman who, having lost one of ten coins, lights a lamp, sweeps the house, and searches until she finds it. In reflecting on these parables to Junod, Rogers wrote, "I think that the woman (in the one) and the shepherd (in the other) represent God. They do all they can to look for and find the lost. Not knowing that they will, they just set out and they do." This is what God always does: "God continues to try and find us . . . by any means," except force.[5] Consistent and reliable, "God doesn't ever give up on us completely."[6]

The Great Appreciator

But Rogers's God does much more than not give up on us; his God also accepts and appreciates us, right here and now, just as we are. "I'm convinced that, for me, God is the Great Appreciator, that God would look for whatever is best in all of us," Rogers stated.[7] In making this claim, he set himself miles apart from countless other Christians of his era who were all too happy to envision God as the Great Judge—the robed righteous one whose main mission is to scour the Book of Life in search of guilty parties. Rogers's God is not the judgmental type.

When explaining the affirming character of God, Rogers often appealed to a lesson about Jesus he had learned from William Orr, his favorite professor at Western Theological Seminary in Pittsburgh. As Rogers shared in a 1997 sermon, Orr was not inclined to characterize Jesus as the violent Son of Man who sends people to eternal torment, or as the Lord of lords who wages war against the terribly ungodly. On the contrary, Orr taught Rogers that the Spirit of Jesus "will do anything to encourage us to know that God's creation is good, that we, his brothers and sisters, can look on each other as having real value. Our advocate will do anything to remind us that we are lovable and that our neighbor is lovable, too."

Rogers extolled Orr's depiction of Jesus as an advocate who never judges or condemns us as unlovable. And although he never referred to Satan or the devil as a real figure in human history, Rogers also valued Orr's characterization of "the evil one" as "the accuser." Opposed to Jesus, the accuser "will do anything to make you feel as bad as you possibly can about yourself, because if you feel the worst about who you are, you will undoubtedly look with condemning eyes on your neighbor and you will get to believe the worst about him or her."[8]

Rogers believed in God the Great Appreciator, then, because he fully embraced Orr's understanding of Jesus as advocate and accepted the basic Christian tenet that Jesus reveals the character of God. Not altogether unconventional in his theology, Rogers believed Jesus is the second person in the Holy Trinity, the one who reveals the innermost character of God the Creator. But far from conventional, Rogers also held that God, as revealed by Jesus, affirms exactly what the advocate embodies (and the accuser rejects): that *every* human is good, valuable, and lovable.

For Rogers, then, the advocate reveals not only the innermost character of God but also the innermost character of the person: God is the Great Appreciator, and we are the greatly appreciated. Although Rogers was a Protestant, he sharply differed from Protestant reformers who emphasized the depravity of humanity (Martin Luther and John Calvin) or with twentieth-century Protestant theologians obsessed with the immorality of human society (Reinhold Niebuhr). This is not to say that Rogers found any or every person to be altogether good. "There's the good guy and the bad guy in all of us," he often said. Or, as one of his songs put it, "the very same people who are good sometimes / are the very same people who are bad sometimes."[9]

But Rogers's belief in Jesus as advocate meant that "the bad" can never rightly become the defining characteristic of our identity. On the contrary, as the advocate reveals, the human character is always and everywhere essentially good, valuable, and lovable. So we can forever take heart that "the bedrock of our very being is good stuff."[10] Believing in the goodness of humanity, Rogers criticized his fellow ministers who focused on the sin and sins of humanity. "In fact," he wrote in 1975, "I'm weary of people who insist on trying to make other people feel bad about themselves. The more I look around me and within me the more I notice that those who feel best about themselves have the greatest capacity to feel good about others."[11]

Radical Acceptance

Rogers had an abiding respect for William Orr, and when his mentor became hospitalized after a stroke, Fred and his wife, Joanne, visited him in his hospital room. One Sunday, after Rogers and his home church had sung "A Mighty Fortress Is Our God," the famous hymn penned by Martin Luther, Rogers questioned Orr about this particular verse:

The prince of darkness grim
We tremble not for him.
His rage we can endure.
For lo! His doom is sure.
One little word shall fell him.

In recounting the verse for his mentor, Rogers asked, "What is the one little word that will fell the prince of darkness, the word that will strike down evil?" Orr thought for a moment and then said, "One little word: forgive. 'Father, *forgive* them for they know not what they do.'"[12] Rogers knew Orr was recounting the famous words of Jesus on the cross—words of unearned love, sheer grace, for those who never thought to seek forgiveness for their cruel and violent actions.

Rogers often recounted this story when explaining his own belief that the Spirit of Jesus will advocate even for those we might deem utterly unlovable. This doesn't mean that the advocate does not want us to grow away from attitudes and actions that reflect the accuser. Even as the advocate accepts us "exactly as we are," Rogers claimed, he also invites us to grow right along with him. Jesus' message is thus one of affirmation and encouragement at the same time: "Be who you are. We'll grow from there."[13] But even when we choose not to grow in love, the Spirit of Jesus still advocates for our forgiveness. And God, as revealed in Jesus, will listen and forgive. Far from vengeful, God never allows the evil within us to obstruct love for us.

Rogers thus had a radical notion of divine forgiveness and redemption. It certainly ran counter to those conservative ministers who, like Billy Graham, preached that, while God loves us, for God to love us *fully* we have to confess our sins, seek forgiveness, and accept Jesus as our personal Lord and Savior—otherwise, God will send us to eternal torture. Rogers balked at this violent message. Making God's love conditional in any way was not part of his theology.

Rogers's God forgives everything and everyone; there is nothing God does not forgive, and no one God does not forgive. As the Great Appreciator, God cannot help but find us good, valuable, and lovable, no matter what we have believed or done. "When we hear the word that we are not lovable, we are *not* hearing the Word of God," Rogers stated. "No matter how unlovely, how impure or weak or false we may feel ourselves to be, all through the ages God has still called us lovable."[14] Rogers meant this about everybody. Rogers's God is stunningly gracious in offering forgiveness and redemption to all who seem entirely unforgivable and unredeemable.

Rogers was universalist in his approach to heaven; he believed there is no point at which God does not forgive everyone. Even after we die, God is radically generous, granting eternal life and love to everyone, no matter what he or she had thought, said, or done in this life. There are no gates in Rogers's heaven; the place is wide open.

Rogers communicated this universalist message of radical acceptance throughout his writings and even on the streets of Pittsburgh. In May 2001, for example, he was walking on the street after his daily swim when he encountered a man arguing with his co-workers about salvation. The man recognized Rogers, grabbed him, and said, "Tell these people there's only one way to God." The man seemed quite intent on convincing his co-workers of the literal truth of Jesus' words in the Gospel of John: "I am the way, the truth, and the life. No one comes to the Father except through me." But Rogers did not take the bait of Christian exclusivism. He simply responded, "God loves you just the way you are."[15]

Rogers held this belief, just as he held his other convictions described in this chapter, for a very long time. In 1978, for example, in a letter to a woman who had asked about heaven, he wrote, "I believe we participate in eternal life through the grace of God. We are accepted as we are and loved exactly as we are. In other words, I believe heaven is sheer gift."[16] And in a 2000 interview with *Christianity Today*, a magazine favored by conservative evangelicals, Rogers added, "When I think about heaven, it is a state in which we are so greatly loved that there is no fear and doubt and disillusionment and anxiety. It is where people do look at you with those eyes of Jesus"—the eyes of an advocate who sees you as good, valuable, and lovable.[17]

God within Us

Rogers readily conceded that the context of our lives often makes it challenging for us to believe in a God who never gives up on us, who sees us as good and valuable and lovable, and who accepts us, on earth and in heaven, exactly as we are. "With all the sadness and destruction, negativity and rage expressed throughout the world," he wrote, "it's tough not to wonder where the loving presence is."[18] Knowing some of us might give up on God, Rogers encouraged us to look deeply.

His pastoral counsel for us in those moments of sadness and rage is unmistakably mystical. We need not look very far, he advised. God is not merely out there, somewhere in the mist hovering above the far horizon, or in a time beyond time. "Deep within each of us," Rogers believed, "is a spark of the divine just waiting to be used to light up a dark place."[19] God is *within* us.

Officially, Rogers was Presbyterian. Unofficially, he was Quaker. Although his counsel—that we look within ourselves to find God—was most likely straight from the writings of Henri Nouwen, one of his favorite writers in Christian spirituality, it had deeper roots in George Fox, the founder of the Religious Society of Friends, whose mystical doctrine of the "inner light" has inspired Quakers and other mystics since the seventeenth century to refrain from violence.

Like Fox, Rogers held that the divine spark is in everyone. It is a democratic, ubiquitous spark, refusing to be confined and controlled by a handful of religious professionals. The spark is not in a tabernacle, a baptismal font, or the church chancel; nor is it with only those who believe in Jesus. The spark is in all of us.

But Rogers also gave the divine-spark doctrine his own peculiar twist, suggesting that the spark manifests itself in our longing to be seen as lovable and capable of loving—as trusted and trustworthy partners in relationships of love. "Everyone longs to be loved and longs to know that he or she is capable of loving," Rogers often said.[20] All people, no matter what they believe or do, have this longing—this deep desire—to love and be loved. After all, where there is God, there is love, and God is in everyone.

But Rogers was careful to note that whether our longing comes to fruition depends upon our response to the spark within us. Although he was Presbyterian, Rogers was not the type of Calvinist who believed in predestination. He was more akin to liberal Protestants who see free agency as a hallmark of human existence. Consequently, he held that because our gracious God does not force us into following the divine will, "we have the free choice of using [the divine spark] or not. That's part of the mysterious truth of who we human beings are."[21]

Extraordinary, Ordinary People

What does it mean for us to use the divine spark? Rogers's answer was plain and simple: to love as God loves. We use the divine spark by consistently choosing attitudes and actions that reflect the love of God revealed in Jesus: a love that does not give up on others but accepts and advocates for all others just as they are (good, valuable, and lovable), even when they do bad things.

When describing our use of the spark within us, Rogers was not content merely to point to a Bible verse or a theologian who had written about love. Sure, he had his favorite verses, including Mark 12:29–31 (the Great Commandment to love), and his favorite Christian writers, especially Henri

Nouwen and Frederick Buechner. But Rogers's primary sources for explaining our use of the divine spark were "extraordinary, ordinary people" (some he knew, others he didn't) whose everyday actions reflected the advocate. By describing the lives of these "extraordinary, ordinary people," Rogers identified several ways we use the spark.[22]

First, we give expression to the divine spark by reflecting and enacting God's desire to accept all people just as they are, no matter who they are and what they believe or do. For Rogers, this is what human love is all about—accepting others without requiring them to change anything about themselves as a condition for our love. Just like divine love, real love between people is unconditional. "When we love a person," Rogers stated, "we accept a person exactly as is: the lovely with the unlovely, the strong along with the fearful, the true mixed in with the façade."[23]

To explain unconditional love, Rogers often told a story about his childhood. "When I was a kid," he recounted, "I was shy and overweight and scared to death to go to school each day. I was a perfect target for ridicule." And ridicule is what he got when his school dismissed early one day and Rogers had to do something unusual—walk home. "It wasn't long before I sensed I was being followed—by a whole group of boys," he remembered.[24]

Rogers sped up his pace, but the pack started to call his name as they closed in on him. "Freddy," they shouted. "Hey, Fat Freddy. We're going to get you, Freddy." With his heart pounding madly, Rogers dashed to the home of a widow who was a friend of the family, praying that she would be there. Mrs. Stewart was home indeed, and she welcomed Freddy into her house, granting him refuge. The teasing boys went on their way, Rogers stated, "but I resented the teasing. I resented the pain. I resented those kids for not seeing beyond my fatness or shyness."[25] He resented that they did not accept him just as he was, and he was grateful that Mrs. Stewart did—that, like God, she saw him in his essence.

Rogers also pointed to his maternal grandfather, Fred Brooks McFeely, as another adult from his childhood who accepted him just as he was. As a child, Rogers used to love the weekly visits to Grandfather McFeely's farm not far outside Latrobe. The two spent many hours together, talking and walking and enjoying the countryside. Looking back on those days, Rogers remembered his grandfather saying, "Fred, you made this day a special day by being yourself. Always remember there's just one person in the world like you . . . and I like you just the way you are."[26]

Second, employing the divine spark means helping others grow even as we accept them just as they are. Yet again, Rogers's beloved grandfather served as the perfect illustration. In Rogers's own telling, when Fred was just a youngster, his Grandfather McFeely sensed how much he wanted to climb atop the farm's old stone walls. Fred's parents were overly protective and protested this new venture as far too dangerous. But McFeely would have none of it. "So the boy wants to climb the stone walls?" he said to Fred's parents. "Then let the boy climb the stone walls! He has to learn to do things for himself."[27] Fred was thrilled with his new freedom to grow in ways others found unimaginable.

He was equally thrilled as a youngster when Mama Bell Frampton, one of his closest neighbors, taught him how to make "toast sticks." Mama Bell had long welcomed young Fred into her kitchen when he showed up at her back porch. She would invite him in and make him a special treat—four long "sticks" cut from one piece of toast and smeared with butter and jam. When Fred was five or six, Mama Bell invited him to make his own toast sticks. "Seems like a simple thing," Rogers recalled, "but 65 years later, I can still feel it—that neighbor's trust and my own pride at having made those first ones on my own. I think she really did love me. She just somehow sensed what I needed to grow."[28] Like the advocate, Mama Bell and Grandfather McFeely accepted Rogers just as he was while also encouraging him to grow in ways that were right for him.

Third, using the divine spark means seeking to identify with and under- stand those who intentionally hurt us or damage our lives. This requires seeing ourselves not merely as accepted by God but also as just like those we imagine as outside of God's care—the sinners of sinners. As a member of an inner-city church, Rogers once found himself writing some rambling thoughts about individuals who had damaged one of the church buildings. His thoughts, uncharacteristically scattered here, reveal his belief in the need for us to see ourselves as "hoodlums":

> We, as the Church, should be glad when the 'hoodlums' of the neigh- borhood impose on us. How else do we fulfill our mission—as suffering servants what do we do? Throw them out? Of course not. We repair the damage ourselves and solicit their help. When we realize that we're hood- lums too—inside. (That's harder to do. It's easier to spot an outside hood- lum. They leave behind lots of property damage.) Once we see ourselves as hoodlums, we can find more compassion for our brother-hoodlums and be amazed over and over that God would take us all in.[29]

Fourth, reflecting the divine spark means forgiving those who do not accept us as we are or, more generally, anyone who has made wrongful or unwise choices. This point became especially pertinent to Rogers when the infamous Monica Lewinsky scandal rocked the Clinton White House and the entire country in 1998. With the threat of impeachment dogging him, Clinton appeared before a group of ministers on September 12 to share some uncomfortable news. "I don't think there's a fancy way to say that I have sinned," he stated. "It is important to me that everyone who has been hurt know that the sorrow I feel is genuine—first and most important, my family, my friends, my staff, my cabinet, Monica Lewinsky and her family, and the American people. I have asked all for their forgiveness."[30] Two days later, Rogers emailed his friend Tom Junod:

> Last week I woke up thinking how I would like to go on the air and say something like "Whoever is without sin cast the first stone," or "The Lord's property is always to have mercy," or some other outlandish thing, and then ask for a moment of silence to think about forgiveness for those who want it. In fact if our country could dwell on forgiveness for awhile I think that would be the one real positive outcome of the pain which must be pervasive in the White House and beyond. I've already written letters to both the Clintons and the Gores saying that often "enormous growth comes out of enormous pain." I trust that will be so for all of us. The attitude which makes me (sometimes physically) sick is the "holier than thou" one.[31]

After criticizing the self-righteous types, Rogers then commended J. Philip Wogaman, the pastor of Foundry United Methodist Church in Washington, DC, where the Clinton family regularly attended public worship. Throughout the crisis, Wogaman had described the president as contrite, and he steadfastly called for the country to practice grace and forgiveness. A few months after Rogers wrote his email, when Washington was focused on impeaching the president, Wogaman put it this way: "I'm afraid that the punitive attitudes of some people now represent no grace at all. In Christian theology, Grace is actually free—not even cheap. But it does entail responsibility to turn away from sin. I believe the president is working hard on that. Perhaps we can work a little bit harder on the Grace side."[32] In his email to Junod, Rogers expressed appreciation for Wogaman's earlier emphasis on "the fact that we are *all* children of God and God wants what's best for us . . . in all ways . . . always (even when we don't make such wise choices ourselves). God NEVER gives up on any one of us, Tom. To be able to know that and effectively communicate that is sheer grace. That's what history is all about: God's unending waiting for us to return to the Love that created us."[33]

Fifth, and on a related note, Rogers held that we reveal the divine spark by ensuring that our love is constant across the ages, even with people who no longer serve our needs. One of the characteristics Rogers admired most about his father, Jim, was his constancy as a friend to the customers of the

McFeely family brick business. As a child, Rogers knew one of those loyal customers as "Uncle Murph." "When Uncle Murph's wife got sick," he later recounted, "Dad and Mother drove to West Virginia to visit." While Rogers conceded that the visit "may have been part of selling silica brick," he had a strong sense that his father truly loved Uncle Murph and his family. "Even when Uncle Murph's wife died and he retired from the steel business, Dad still kept in touch with him as long as he lived," Rogers noted. Jim Rogers's constancy was inspirational to his son. "I wanted to be like Dad," Rogers wrote. "I wanted to be a trustworthy friend, coworker, person. . . . Perhaps I've always been trying to live up to the example of the Mr. Rogers (Jim) who was my father."[34]

To illustrate this same point, Rogers often told a heartwarming story about a Seattle Special Olympics featuring nine physically or mentally challenged Olympians about to run the 100-yard dash. When the track official fired the gun, one of the boys stumbled at the start line, fell to the ground, and bruised his knee. The other eight children heard the boy's cries, ran back to him, and when he returned to his feet, linked arms with him so that all nine of them finished the race at the same time. The spectators went wild as the children crossed the line, and for a long time afterward. Rogers took the crowd's reaction as evidence that deep down we all know what "really matters is helping others win, too, even if it means slowing down and changing our course now and then."[35]

Sixth, we use the divine spark by seeing *all* others as under the providence and care of God. Rogers made this point numerous times in his life, but one of the more memorable times was in the same year the United States announced plans to deploy cruise missiles. The Cold War was still raging in 1977, and even though the SALT II nuclear disarmament talks were underway, the United States remained wary of the new president of the Soviet Union, Leonid Brezhnev, and Soviet plans for spreading communism across the world. In that Cold War context, Rogers stood in front of his home church and offered this conclusion to his prayer of intercession:

> Last of all we pray for those we do not know or those we find it hard to love. The world seems so vast, and some of its people seem so very different from what we understand and like, we find it hard to imagine that *they* come under Thy care too. And yet we realize that there are those who can't imagine that Thou wouldst ever care for *us*. Help us *all* to understand that any blessing which comes to one ultimately blesses *everyone*.[36]

Finally, and more fundamentally, reflecting the divine spark means that we will undertake the first six practices in relation to ourselves. Using the divine spark does not mean we will love only *others*. In fact, for Rogers, we cannot love others at all if we first do not love ourselves as God loves us. The only way we can love others is by accepting ourselves exactly as we are (good, valuable, and lovable), forgiving ourselves when necessary, and remaining constant in our self-acceptance, even when we seem to have every reason to criticize ourselves without mercy. As Rogers put it, "It's hard to realize but it's true: feeling good about ourselves is an essential thing in our being able to love others."[37] Only when we feel accepted for who we are in our essence can we enjoy the foundation required for loving others.[38]

Holy Ground

Using the divine spark—appreciating and advocating for others and ourselves—is "a holy thing," according to Rogers.[39] To be loved as God loves us is a primary way in which we encounter God, and to love as God loves is to make God real in the lives of others. When we love our neighbor, he or she really experiences God; we experience the same when our neighbor loves us. God is present, incarnate, in the sharing and exchanging of human love. Love is a sacrament.

Again, because he believed in free will, Rogers held that we experience the fullness of God in human love only through our own choosing. If we come to one another without judgment and in need, we will encounter the Spirit of God in our lives. Rogers's primary illustration for this came from an early experience he had during a weekend vacation in New England. He was a seminarian at the time and had gone to hear a visiting preacher in a nearby chapel. "I heard the worst sermon I could have ever imagined," he recounted. "I sat in the pew thinking, 'He's going against every rule they're teaching us about preaching. What a waste of time!'" But he soon discovered it was not a waste for everyone. Sitting next to him was a woman in tears at the end of the service. "He said exactly what I needed to hear," she whispered.[40]

Rogers analyzed the event by saying that a major difference between his response to the sermon and the woman's was that she had come in need and he had come in judgment. Because she had come in need, she had opened herself to receiving the sermon as a gift of love, and because Rogers had sat there so judgmentally, he "heard nothing but the faults." The experience "turned out to be one of the great lessons of my life," Rogers added. The lesson was "that the space between a person doing his or her best to deliver a message of good news and the needy listener is holy ground."[41]

Holy ground is where the Holy Spirit resides. As a conventional Trinitarian, Rogers believed that the Spirit of God—Jesus' gift to humanity at the time of his ascension—sanctifies the ground between those who express love and those who come in need of love. "The Holy Spirit," Rogers said, "uses that space in marvelously wonderful ways," translating the message of love in a way that meets the immediate needs of the listener. The Spirit of God thus exists between us, not merely within us, and if we are to experience the fullness of the Spirit here on earth, it is necessary for us to leave behind our judgmental ways and instead offer ourselves as people in need of love.[42]

Are God and Neighbor Somehow One?

Rogers found holy ground elsewhere too. He saw it especially in places where we experience "little quiet moments." In his own reading of the Bible—he read it devotionally every morning—Rogers was not especially attracted to those writers representing God in "great overwhelming events . . . like the flood and the Exodus." As he put it, "It seems to me that none of the worldly overwhelming events which we so easily ascribe to God speak to God's inner nature."[43]

Rogers was much more fascinated by the New Testament story of the resurrected Jesus walking alongside two of his disciples on the road to Emmaus. At first, the disciples did not recognize him; they found him to be merely a friendly stranger. But when they all sat together to eat, and Jesus broke the bread and shared it, the disciples finally recognized the risen Lord. "It was the sharing of a simple meal," Rogers noted, "a usual kind of thing—not *un*usual—a nourishing gift of love."[44]

The subsequent challenge for us is to find "that place of quiet rest where the real *you* can be ultimately found." God may not be "where the world expects—in fancy structures and loud, noisy displays," but God is "most certainly in unsuspected quiet moments like a manger (outside a crowded inn) and an empty tomb and a walk with two sad friends."[45]

One of Rogers's favorite Bible verses underlay this conviction: "For God's foolishness is wiser than human wisdom, and God's weakness is stronger than human strength" (1 Cor. 1:25). Rogers took this verse as impetus to look for God in other surprising places too, including among the dispossessed: those Jesus refers to as "the least of these" (the poor, the sick, and the imprisoned) as well as those Matthew refers to as "poor in spirit." For Rogers, we can always be sure to find God "in the midst of the needy, the helpless, the sad, the lonely people who are living along every road in every kind of wilderness."[46]

Yet even while he encouraged us to look for God in surprising places, especially among our neighbors in need, Rogers dared not confine God to any particular group of people; God is within and between all of our neighbors. Perhaps most important, later in his life Rogers even dared to suggest that God and neighbor are so closely aligned that they are indistinguishable. "The more I think about it," he wrote in 2002, "the more I wonder if God and neighbor are somehow One. 'Loving God, Loving neighbor'—the same thing?"[47]

This bold suggestion represented Rogers's radical turn from traditional Christian dualism, with its crystal-clear separation of God and humanity, toward the nondualism often found in Asian religious traditions and in Christian spiritual writers steeped in mysticism. One of these spiritual writers was Rogers's dear friend Henri J. M. Nouwen. Rogers appreciated Nouwen's nondualism so much that in the same article in which Rogers posed the question of whether God and neighbor are one, he included Nouwen's own argument that "when we truly love our neighbor as our brother and sister, we will find, right there, God and ourselves in complete unity. . . . All is one; the heart of God, the hearts of all people, and our own hearts."[48]

Although it seems logical that he might have done so, Rogers did not also pose the question of whether God and self are somehow one. Nevertheless, just as he believed that God is in us, so too did he hold that "whether we realize it or not, God is with us always in this life and the life everlasting."[49] God is always with us, no matter who and where we are.

But Rogers did not stop there, either. He saw the love of God as infusing the entire universe. As he put it in 1995, "Life is infused with the divine."[50] God is not just present in, between, and beside us; God is also present in and through the entire creation.

"I believe at the center of the universe there dwells a loving spirit who longs for all that's best in all of creation, a spirit who knows the great potential of each planet as well as each person, and little by little will love us into being more than we ever dreamed possible. That loving spirit would rather die than give up on any one of us."

The love of God is thus not just with and for us; it is with and for all of creation. At last, God is "a loving presence who desires the best for you and the whole universe," Rogers stated.[51] Holy ground, it turns out, is everywhere.

So what does all this have to do with peace?

The Peace of God Emanating from Our Hearts

On May 15, 1984, President Ronald Reagan held a press conference in which he spoke about the need for the U.S. House of Representatives to provide funding for the production of thirty MX missiles. Dubbed by Reagan as "the Peacemaker," the MX was an intercontinental ballistic missile, one of the most powerful nuclear weapons of its time. In that same month, Fred Rogers stood before the new graduates of Washington and Jefferson College, a school founded in 1781 and named for two vigorous proponents of the Revolutionary War, and delivered the following benediction: "May the peace of God, which passes all understanding, fill our hearts and minds and remain with us in all that we do, in all that we say, and all that we think and feel—both now and forever in the nature of Jesus, the Christ, our Lord. Amen."[52]

The contrast could not have been more striking. For Reagan, the peacemaker was a weapon of mass destruction with the ability to kill millions and devastate huge parts of Planet Earth. For Rogers, the peacemaker was the God revealed in Jesus.

Rogers held that God does not force peace upon people unwilling to accept it. Nor does God mold us, forcibly, into peacemakers. But insofar as God is in, between, and beside us, each of us has the capacity to become a peacemaker. We already have the peace of God in our hearts, and if we allow that peace to come to expression, the results can be stunning. "It's only the peace of God emanating from all of our hearts that can ultimately bring lasting peace to our world," Rogers stated.[53]

How can we allow divine peace to emanate from our hearts? Rogers's answer was plain and simple: Love as God loves. Although he never explicitly provided a definition of the peace of God, nuanced or otherwise, Rogers tended to use the words *peace* and *love* interchangeably. In a 1998 email to Junod, for example, Rogers referred to the "Word" within us (that is, God within us) as "Love," "Grace," and "Peace."[54] For Rogers, the love of God, as revealed by the advocate, *is* the peace of God.

So if we put all our pieces together, it becomes clear, given what Rogers understood by the love of God as revealed in Jesus, that we allow the peace of God to emanate from our hearts by *advocating* for people—by affirming all others as good, valuable, and lovable; by accepting all others just as they are and offering forgiveness to anyone, whether or not he or she seeks it; by continuing to care for all others, even when they no longer serve our needs; and by seeing God in, between, and beside all people. Most fundamentally, we allow the peace of God to emanate from us by advocating for ourselves in the exact same ways. By loving ourselves as God loves us, we become peace, and being peace is the first step to creating peace. For Rogers, then, making peace is about reflecting the attitudes and actions of the advocate in our dealings with all others and ourselves.

This means that certain attitudes and actions become unthinkable for those whose lives reflect the advocate. Russian novelist Leo Tolstoy, one of the most famous Christian pacifists in history, claimed that "a whole series of acts becomes impossible" for one who abides by the teachings of Jesus. "Just as it is impossible for a man to lift up a mountain, and just as it is impossible for a good man to kill a child, so it is impossible for a man who lives a Christian life to take part in violence," Tolstoy wrote.[55]

Fred Rogers was Tolstoyan. When a person taps into the divine spark and consciously participates in a relationship with God the Appreciator, "that person would rather die than participate in such things as a Holocaust," Rogers wrote.[56] But it is not just the Holocaust and things like it that become impossible; any sort of annihilation of any person, other than self-sacrifice for another, becomes unthinkable. Why? As Rogers put this in a letter to historian Martin Marty, "There is no chance of redemption if the goal is annihilation."[57]

Rogers could have easily pulled from other parts of his theology of peace too. If the goal is annihilation, there is no chance of *advocating* for those we would kill—of affirming them as good, valuable, and lovable; of accepting them just as they are and offering them forgiveness; of caring for them constantly; and of encountering and honoring God in and beside them. Annihilation makes advocacy impossible, and in Rogers's theology, it is wholly and utterly profane. It kills those who have God in and beside them, preventing them from using their divine spark.

Moreover, if God and neighbor are somehow one, as Rogers suggests, then annihilation of our neighbor, any neighbor, is assaulting the sacred itself. So too is self-annihilation, if God and self are somehow one, and, yes, so is annihilation of the natural world, if God infuses all of creation. Rogers's pacifist theology effectively undermines any rationale for annihilating self, others, and creation.

But his theology implies even more than what he stated explicitly about annihilation. Indeed, *any* human attitude or action that uses violence in judgmental and punitive ways is opposed to the sacred work of advocating for others and honoring God in and beside them. This includes violence we direct at others, ourselves, and the created world. In plain and simple language, Rogers's theology implies that violence is always and everywhere the work of the accuser, not the way of the advocate. Violence is always wrong; this faith-fueled tenet is the hallmark of Rogers's principled pacifism.

For Rogers, then, the antidote to violence is the love of God as it takes shape in everyday lives. When a person "feels at peace and feels loved and valued, the chances are that that person is not going to blow up an airplane or shoot a fellow student or get hooked on drugs or step into the alley of hopelessness and despair."[58]

One final note: Although his mystical notion that we should light the divine spark by becoming advocates and seeing God everywhere left Rogers with no grounds for self-defense, he did not feel helpless or hopeless. He took great comfort in the following words from Frederick Buechner: "And then there is the love for the enemy—love for the one who does not love you but mocks, threatens, and inflicts pain. The tortured's love for the torturer. This is God's love. It conquers the world."[59] After reading Buechner's words, Rogers wrote that they "made me feel . . . well, *strong* is how it made me feel."[60] At last, the logic and convictions of Rogers's peace theology left him hopeful. With the peace of God emanating from our hearts, he believed we can and will conquer the world of violence. Love will win.

Rogers used numerous episodes to show practical ways for us to express anger without hurting ourselves or others. Playing piano is one such way, he told the audience.

Chapter 5

"It's Okay to Be Angry"

A Psychology of Peace

Rogers's pacifism was deeply rooted in his faith in God the Appreciator. But it had extensive roots elsewhere too, especially in Sigmund Freud's notion of sublimation—channeling socially unacceptable instincts or impulses into socially acceptable attitudes and actions. Although Rogers rarely invoked God on his television program, he often spoke about sublimation, though without calling it by name, when addressing one of his favorite subjects: "mad feelings." Believe it or not, Fred Rogers got angry. There's no denying that it seemed "as if peacefulness spun itself around him like a silk-stranded cocoon," as Amy Hollingsworth has written.[1] But like the rest of us, Rogers knew the feeling of emotional fury. He referred to it as "inner violence" and spent much of his professional life trying to make sure we understand the best ways to tame its destructive potential.[2]

From O. J. Simpson to Make-Believe

The subject of inner violence was so important to Rogers that in 1995 he devoted an entire week of programs to "mad feelings." As usual, context mattered. News reports of the O. J. Simpson trial saturated the country throughout the summer and fall of 1995. The former football star had been charged with murdering his former wife, Nicole Brown Simpson, and one of her best friends, Ronald Goldman. The drawn-out trial made for an epic feeding frenzy. Court testimony was graphic, with chilling details about multiple stabbings and Simpson's history of battering his former wife, and the coverage seemed relentless. Despite damning evidence, in early October the Los Angeles jury found Simpson not guilty of murder.

Less than two weeks after the verdict, President Bill Clinton used his radio address to speak about violence against women. While he seemed to have the

Simpson trial in mind, the president also had a personal stake in the subject. As a youngster, he had prevented his stepfather from physically attacking and beating his mother, Virginia Clinton Kelley. Speaking to men in particular, the president stated, "The real solution to the problem starts with us, with our personal responsibility and a simple pledge that we will never, never lift a hand against a woman for as long as we live."[3]

Fred Rogers had a bigger message to share, and on October 16, just two days after the president's radio address, he began a week of programs devoted to one of the most repeated lessons throughout the history of his program: It's okay to be angry, but it's not okay to hurt ourselves or others.

Like Clinton, Rogers had a personal stake in his message. One of his most vivid memories of his own anger centered on the time he ran to Mrs. Stewart's home after the bullying boys called him "Fat Freddy" and threatened to "get" him. In recalling his feelings, Rogers said he "resented those kids for not seeing beyond my fatness or shyness—and what's more, I didn't know that it was alright to resent it, to feel bad about it, even to feel very sad about it." The adults in his life had advised him that if he acted as if he didn't care about the teasing, the boys would stop bothering him. "But, of course, I *did* care," he recalled.[4] With those dismissive adults in mind, Rogers crafted his special series to affirm children who care about such things and to let them know it's okay to feel angry.

Our Right to Be Angry

The week of mad feelings begins with a confession of sorts. "I'm not very good at drawing, I guess because I haven't practiced very much," Mister Rogers says in the first episode. "I remember when I was a boy. If I couldn't do something very well and I got frustrated about it, I'd go to the piano and tell it my feelings in the piano keys." He then walks to the piano and plays angrily, even making a slightly angry look as he strikes the keys.[5]

"Are there things that make you angry?" he says as he faces the camera. It's a question he asks, in one form or another, throughout the week. When neighbor Maggie Stewart shows up at his house the following day, for example, he asks whether she ever gets angry. Her answer is one of the most fundamental points Mister Rogers seeks to instill in us all week. "Oh, sure," she says. "Everybody gets angry."

For Fred Rogers, anger is a natural human emotion, common to all. "There is no 'masculine' or 'feminine' when it comes to anger," he believed.[6] "We all have angry and even violent feelings within us."[7] That "all" included Mister Rogers, although not all of his young viewers were so sure about that; after all, Mister Rogers smiled *a lot*. His typically sunny disposition resulted in more than a few letters asking if he ever got angry. "You wonder if I ever get angry," he replied to a boy named Alex. "Of course I do; everybody gets angry sometimes."[8]

Many children also wrote letters to confess their own anger, as did Taylor, age 3, in this short note: "The baby came to live at my house. I like her sometimes. Sometimes I want to sock her." A curious boy, Taylor also requested a picture of Mister Rogers looking angry. "Taylor," Rogers replied, "you asked if we could send you a picture of me looking angry. We don't have any like that. But I certainly do get angry sometimes; everybody does."[9]

In spite of his incomplete portfolio, Rogers saw anger as a natural part of living and loving. Look at babies, he said. "If a baby's needs are taken care of, he or she feels good, feels loving. If needs are not provided for, the baby feels bad and outraged."[10] This type of anger is simply a natural response to conditions in which our basic needs are unfulfilled.

Because he saw love as a basic human need, Rogers identified anger as a "normal part of loving and being loved."[11] It's our response to conditions in which our capacity for loving or being loved is unrecognized, thwarted, frustrated, or otherwise unfulfilled. Events like divorce and death anger us because we perceive them as taking away something important to our ability to love and be loved. Rogers added that the anger we feel toward those we love is a special kind of anger, fundamentally different from the type we feel toward strangers, "because it is so deeply entwined with caring and attachment."[12] This type of anger is deeply personal, going to the very heart of our hopes and fears.

By emphasizing its role in living and loving, Rogers sought to *normalize* anger—to assure us that we are not freakish or abnormal when we feel inner fury for reasons related to basic human needs, whether they relate to ourselves or others, and especially to love. Like other feelings, anger is simply "part of who we are."[13] As part of our constitution, anger is even a fundamental right, not unlike the rights to life, liberty, and happiness. We have a "right" to our anger, Rogers claimed.[14]

Further, he held that exercising this basic right is essential to human development. "It may be easier for us if, as children, we were allowed to have our angry feelings and if someone we loved let us know that those feelings were a normal part of loving and being loved," he wrote.[15] Had we been allowed to have our angry feelings as children, chances are we would better understand ourselves. Referring back to his childhood bullies, Rogers stated, "If I'm angry with someone, and I say, 'Oh, it doesn't matter, I don't care,' then I probably don't know what I'm feeling. On the other hand, if we can allow ourselves to be gentle with ourselves no matter what our feelings may be, we have the chance of discovering the very deep roots of who we are."[16]

This is one of the main reasons for his special series: to help us recognize anger as permissible—as a right we can, may, and should acknowledge and exercise so that we can better understand ourselves and others.[17] As Rogers often summed this up, it's okay to be angry.

Anger in Make-Believe—and on Television

As Lady Aberlin says during the special series on mad feelings, though, it's not okay to be angry in just any old way. In making this statement, she's commenting on yet another major crisis in the Neighborhood of Make-Believe. This time the mischievous Lady Elaine Fairchilde has used her magical boomerang to turn Grandpère's tower upside down. She did this during a fit of anger at her inability to draw a picture of the tower to her satisfaction. Rather than practicing her drawing skills, Lady Elaine has lashed out—stomping, screaming, punching the sky, spinning on top of her museum, and flipping the tower over.

She's out of control, and her destructive and violent actions have created quite the furor. "Oh, that Fairchilde!" King Friday says angrily. "This unruly behavior must be curtailed!" Neighbor Aber is so concerned that he decides to have a one-on-one chat with Lady Elaine, and after he flat-out states that her anger is no reason for her to turn the tower upside down, she threatens to change him into a doll, just as she has done to Mr. McFeely of Speedy Delivery (or so she believes after seeing a doll resembling him near her museum). She threatens King Friday too when he shows up to register his own protest. Increasingly angry, he says, "It looks as if I may need to muster an army!"

As a writer for children, Fred Rogers normally steered far away from such explosive actions and violent reactions. He detested violence on television, not only on the programs offering up the usual fare—"murders and bombings and gross physical harm"—but also on those that employed "subtle violence": "the so-called 'insult humor' of situation comedies where even the parts acted by children are filled with wisecracks and insults."[18] Subtle or unsubtle, violence filled the airwaves, and Rogers was not pleased. "The children of our country," he stated, "are exposed every minute, every day to hurtful ways of people dealing with their feelings. Just on television alone, they see 200,000 acts of violence by the time they reach 18. It breaks my heart!"[19]

Rogers conceded that television violence may not be harmful to everyone. "For most of us," he wrote, "a violent episode . . . may indeed be cathartic, as some television researchers have claimed." But this was never his emphasis. The more important point, as he saw it, was that for those of us who have not yet learned to recognize and control our feelings, "a violent television episode may touch an inner drama and stir it into violent, outward reality."[20]

Violence on television may cause the immature among us, especially children, to act violently.

Rogers did not hesitate to draw a connection between violence on television and the violent acts of angry children in real life. "The usual response of many children who are angry is to hit and fight, to attempt to resolve things physically and destructively," he wrote in 1990. "Our children certainly see enough adults on television handling problems those ways."[21] This point struck an especially personal note during a visit Rogers paid to his grandsons Alexander, age 10, and Douglas, age 5, in 1998.

> Neither their mom nor dad was there. But their babysitter told me the boys were playing upstairs. So I went up only to find them watching a Batman cartoon on television. The first thing I saw on the program when I walked into the room was a group of people with machine guns shooting everyone and everything in sight. . . . A cartoon to be sure, yet nonetheless these human characters were solving something with deadly violence. I sat beside Douglas, the five year old, and said how scary that all looked to me. And he nodded his head. And after a while of more shooting and hitting and screaming on the screen, I said, "You know, people shouldn't do that to other people." And Douglas said, "But they're the bad people," to which I passionately replied, "There are better ways of treating bad people than killing them and hitting them and screaming at them." Then Douglas looked at me in the strangest way, as if in the Batman environment that he had just been visiting nobody had ever thought of that.[22]

For Rogers, television programs often give our children the impression that violence is necessary and even moral in situations of conflict—that they have to be violent because it's their only good option. Just as problematic is television's abstract depiction of violence. Children see shootings and stabbings, but they don't often see the negative consequences that follow: funerals, burials, long-term grief and suffering.[23]

The issue of television violence was so troubling to Rogers that he made it the main point in the speech he gave at his induction into the Television Hall of Fame in February 1999. "Last month," he stated, "a thirteen-year-old boy abducted an eight-year-old girl, and when people asked him why, he said he learned about it on TV. 'Something different to try,' he said. 'Life's cheap. What does it matter?'" Rogers was appalled by the comment and pleaded with his colleagues to do everything they could to broadcast the message that life is precious.

"I feel that those of us in television are chosen to be servants," he stated. "We are chosen to help meet the deep needs of those who watch and listen day and night." One of those deep needs is to feel as if our lives are good and valuable. "Life isn't cheap," Rogers added. "It's the greatest mystery of any millennium, and television needs to do all it can to broadcast that, to show and tell what the good in life is all about." He carried that main point through to his concluding invitation. "Through television," he said, "we have the choice of encouraging others to diminish this life or to cherish it in creative, imaginative ways."[24] Rogers's choice was already crystal clear.

It's no surprise, then, that back in the Neighborhood of Make-Believe, Neighbor Aber disagrees with King Friday's suggestion that he might have to muster an army. "Oh," Neighbor Aber says, "surely there's a better way to deal with Lady Elaine's anger." As Aber thinks of a better way, the rest of Make-Believe is reeling from Lady Elaine's violent actions. Violence has terrible consequences in the Neighborhood: Ana Platypus is scared and crying, and Grandpère can neither sleep nor eat well. Daniel Striped Tiger says he's frightened too. "I'm scared that Lady Elaine will turn my clock upside down or turn me into a doll," he tells Lady Aberlin.

Lady Aberlin has come to Daniel's clock (where he lives) to borrow his pounding board. When she and King Friday were talking earlier, she came up with the idea that hammering on a pounding board might help Lady Elaine "get over the mad that she feels." After Daniel retrieves his wooden hammer and board, Lady Aberlin gently hammers the pegs while saying that although everyone gets angry "what's *important* is what we *do* with our feelings." Daniel, who no longer seems so frightened, agrees. "Oh, sure," he says. "There are lots of things to do with mad feelings that don't hurt you or anybody else."

What Do You Do? That Good Feeling of Control

Do no harm. This is the first principle of Fred Rogers's ethics of anger. And it's a principle we all can follow, Rogers claimed, because each of us is able to stop ourselves from acting violently. Yes, we all have violence within us, but we also can stop those violent feelings from manifesting themselves in harmful attitudes and actions. While Rogers delivered this message throughout the special series, it's an old lesson from *Mister Rogers' Neighborhood*.

It first appeared in 1968, when Rogers introduced a song—"What Do You Do?"—he had copyrighted that same year. Rogers gave various explanations for the song's title, but it seems a concerned boy had once asked, "What do you do with the mad that you feel when you feel so mad you could bite?" Rogers was inspired by the question and wrote a song about the intensity of children's anger. The lyrics are revealing:

> What do you do with the mad that you feel
> When you feel so mad you could bite?
> When the whole wide world seems oh so wrong

And nothing you do seems very right?
What do you do? Do you punch a bag?
Do you pound some clay or some dough?
Do you round up friends for a game of tag?
Or see how fast you can go?

It's great to be able to stop
When you've planned a thing that's wrong,
And be able to do something else instead
And think this song:

I can stop when I want to,
Can stop when I wish,
Can stop, stop, stop any time.
And what a good feeling
To feel like this,
And know that the feeling is really mine.
Know that there's something deep inside
That helps us become what we can,
For a girl can be some day a woman
And a boy can be some day a man.

By his own account, Rogers wrote this song because he had a sense that
many of us grow up fearing our own anger. "One of the most frightening
things in the world," he said, "is the fear of losing control—that you really
might go out of control and hurt someone you love and then lose that person's love!"[25]

"What Do You Do?" addresses our fear of losing control (and love) by
assuring us "there's something deep inside" that allows us to stop any time
we're angrily plotting something that will hurt ourselves or others. This was
a theological and spiritual point for Rogers. He was convinced that God created all of us with a "healthy deep reserve" that we can tap into and draw
from to stop our angry selves from doing something violent. And all of us,
even those who have already acted violently, have access to this peacemaking tool. The challenge is for us to care "enough about ourselves and others
that we will try to understand and count on that healthy deep reserve that our
Creator has offered to us all."[26]

Rogers also emphasized the point of self-control, though without the
underlying theology, during a special program on violence in the news that
he broadcast in June 1968. "The country was in deep grief," he recalled in
2000. "I mean, President Kennedy had been killed, and then Martin Luther
King was killed, and then Robert Kennedy. And I said, 'I've got to talk to
the families.'"

Rogers used the special to help families understand that "there is just so much a child can take without it being overwhelming to him." Listen to your children, he said, and watch them play. He then gave the example of a little boy who had recently built a precarious structure of blocks and then walked into them as they began to fall. "I'm grumpy," he told his teacher. "Why?" she asked. "Somebody shot my head today," he replied.[27]

Rogers encouraged parents to include children in the family's particular "ways of coping with the problems that present themselves anytime but particularly now in this very difficult time in our nation." But he also addressed the children, teaching them the meaning of assassination, telling them they don't have to play about shooting if they don't want to, and assuring them they can control their own mad feelings. After speaking about "that good feeling of control," Rogers sang "What Do You Do?" for the audience. In context, the point of the song was that, unlike the assassins, we don't have to shoot people in the head when we're angry.[28]

Rogers emphasized the importance of self-control throughout the 1970s too, and the theme enjoyed a strong creative boost in 1980. One of the violent programs that caught Rogers's attention that year was *The Incredible Hulk*, starring the mild-mannered Bill Bixby as Dr. David Banner. While conducting a scientific experiment, Banner, a physician and scientist, had become exposed to a high dose of gamma radiation that altered his body chemistry in a most peculiar way. When Banner grew angry, he would transform into a raging, green, muscular creature with really bad hair—the Incredible Hulk. Played by bodybuilder Lou Ferrigno, the Hulk expressed his mad feelings by busting up things and throwing people around. "You wouldn't like me when I'm angry," Banner told unsuspecting people. But child viewers did, and many of them ran through their neighborhoods acting like the raging green creature.

Concerned about children mimicking the furious Hulk, Rogers visited the show's production set, chatted with Bixby and Ferrigno, and showed children that the Hulk was not real. In his conversation with Rogers, Bixby delivered a message that sounded oddly familiar. "It's okay to be angry," he said, "and it's okay to let it out as long as we don't hurt anybody and as long as we don't hurt ourselves."[29] Ferrigno joined in the peaceful chorus too. When Rogers asked him what he did when he got angry, Ferrigno said, "I'm able to control that."[30]

Why did Rogers focus so much on self-control? Obviously, keeping our angry feelings in check helps the objects of our anger enjoy a basic human need: safety. But more fundamentally, the "good feeling of self-control is yet another facet of self-esteem," Rogers claimed. "It feels really good when we can stop before doing something we shouldn't do."[31] And feeling good about ourselves is so important because it helps construct the foundation we need for loving others—namely, love of self. Unless we show love for ourselves by exercising self-control, we will never be able to love others as fully as possible, and peace—both personal and social—will remain as elusive as ever.

Still, extolling self-control was never a sufficient response for Rogers when responding to "mad feelings." That's because Fred Rogers was Freudian.

A Freudian Channel in Make-Believe

In July 1932, the brilliant physicist Albert Einstein, acting under the auspices of the League of Nations and its International Institute of Intellectual Cooperation in Paris, initiated a public exchange of letters with Sigmund Freud. The institute had proposed that Einstein invite any person of his choosing for a "frank exchange of views" on any problem. Einstein selected Freud as his conversation partner, and the question he posed to the world-famous psychoanalyst was this: "Is there any way of delivering mankind from the menace of war?"[32]

Part of Freud's complex response was that "every living being" has an instinct "to destroy and kill." "The death instinct," he wrote, "becomes an impulse to destruction when, with the aid of certain organs, it directs its action outward, against external objects." The instinct is so much part of our constitution that "there is no likelihood of our being able to suppress it." Nevertheless, although complete suppression of the death instinct is not possible, we do have the power to "divert it into a channel other than that of warfare."[33] That is, we can sublimate our instinct to destroy.

We can divert or channel our aggressive instincts into acts that are more socially acceptable and beneficial than those that destroy and kill. As we do this, we mature as individuals and societies, becoming cultured rather than merely instinctual. And the more our reason rules our emotions, the less likely we will be to embrace warfare as a viable option. We will become repulsed by the horrors of war and attracted to the many benefits of life without war.

Rogers's writings about "inner violence" echo Freud on diversion and channeling (otherwise known as sublimation). Like Freud, Rogers believed we all have violence within us and that most adults have "learned to control our violent impulses, to channel them into safe or even creative directions."[34] Clearly, that's how Rogers interpreted his own life. Reflecting on that scary childhood experience of being chased by the teasing boys, for example, he noted that his anger had transformed into intense sadness. "What I actually did was *mourn*," he remembered.

> I cried to myself whenever I was alone. I cried through my fingers as I made up songs on the piano. I sought out stories of other people who were poor in spirit, and I felt for them. I started to look behind the things that

people did and said; and little by little, concluded that Saint Exupery was absolutely right: "What is essential is invisible to the eye." So, after a lot of sadness, I began a lifelong search for what is essential, what it is about my neighbor that doesn't meet the eye.[35]

In other words, he channeled his anger and sadness into a constructive action that eventually became the hallmark practice of *Mister Rogers' Neighborhood:* radical acceptance.

Like Freud, Rogers also commended sublimation. Just as he thought it beneficial to exercise self-control, Rogers held that it is "great . . . when we come to know . . . that anger can be channeled into creative achievements . . . and dreams that we can make come true!"[36] And because, like Freud, he saw such channeling as a sure and certain sign of personal development and maturation, available to one and all, he considered it his responsibility as a television producer to help us learn concrete ways of channeling our mad feelings and to see this channeling as a sign of our development.[37]

Rogers's Freudianism is the underlying reason that, way back in the Neighborhood of Make-Believe, Daniel Striped Tiger tells Lady Aberlin that when you find things to do with your mad feelings that don't hurt you or anybody else, "that shows you're growing." Still concerned about Lady Elaine's violent actions, Daniel makes sure to add, "I hope Lady Elaine can grow!"

Just then, Lady Elaine's longtime friend Betty Okonak Templeton shows up in Make-Believe. When Betty lived in Make-Believe many years ago, she and Lady Elaine often enjoyed playing music on steel pans and making clay sculptures. "She was always real good at sculpting things and playing pans," Betty recalls.

Betty is hoping to resurrect those fun and creative times of old, and so she's brought along ingredients for making play clay with Lady Elaine. After Lady Aberlin breaks the news about Lady Elaine using her boomerang to flip Grandpère's tower, Betty says, "I always told her to put that silly thing away and do more constructive things with her hands."

Back in his television house, Mister Rogers agrees. In fact, throughout this series, he skillfully shows what he had long been depicting on *Mister Rogers' Neighborhood*—namely, ways in which children and adults can and do express their mad feelings in constructive ways. On the first day of the series, young neighbors Adrian and Anthony Montgomery visit Rogers's house to play a selection from Bach on their violins. Mister Rogers asks whether they ever play when they get angry, and Adrian says, "Sometimes, like when I'm mad or something, I go to my room and I close the door and I play the violin by myself. And it calms me down a little bit."

On the second day, Maggie Stewart says, "The thing that helps me most when I get angry is swimming. I swim and swim and swim. In fact, it does me good just to think about swimming." After she leaves, Mister Rogers tells us, "You know, my main way's with music. I started to make up songs when I was very young." Later on in this same program, he visits with neighbor Jay Styperk, who says he "shoots hoops" and takes deep breaths when he's angry.

The options begin to overflow on the third day of the week. "I like to think of things that people do with their hands—things that don't hurt themselves or anybody else," Mister Rogers says. He then shows us a video of children playing with trucks, kneading dough, playing with puppets, washing cars, finger painting, knitting, building blocks, making lemonade, gardening, building a bird house, playing Wiffle ball, and hugging. "There are lots of healthy things we can do with our hands," he says as the video ends. "Can you clap? How about pounding? How about building with blocks?" Mister Rogers then builds a tower of blocks, only to use the doll of Mr. McFeely to knock them down.

On the fourth day, he tells us he's been "thinking of different things we can pound without hurting ourselves or others." He then clenches his fist and proceeds to pound some play clay. "After you pound it," he says, "it sure makes you feel good!" He also shows a video of a neighbor, Phil Jackson, making and playing steel pans. And on the last day, he visits local artists from *Stomp*, a musical whose youthful performers stomp their feet, clap their hands, and use brushes and brooms and buckets to make music.

With so many options before his viewers, Mister Rogers states clearly what he's been showing so well for so many years. "The important thing to remember," he says, "is that there are many things we can do when we're feeling angry . . . many things that don't hurt ourselves or anybody else, like exercises or breathing or music or sports or crafts—all sorts of things. In fact, they're some of the best things we can ever learn to do."

There's another important thing to remember: Channeling, however vital it may be, does not cancel out the need for us to talk about our mad feelings.

Talking about Mad Feelings

Who knew anger could turn out to be so constructive? Perhaps Lady Elaine Fairchilde knew—at least somewhere deep down. She's not so keen on Lady Aberlin's idea about the pounding board—she's says she's not good at it—but she's thrilled to hear Betty Okonak Templeton's suggestion that they make play clay and play steel pans, just as they did so long ago. "Come on inside," she tells Betty excitedly. "Let's go cook up a batch . . . and play steels. I need to do something better with my hands!" Before she's able to disappear, though, the ever sensitive Lady Aberlin asks her about the possibility of "rectifying" Grandpère's tower. "Ask me next time," Lady Elaine says. "I've still got some worries, Toots. Betty and I are about to create. Hey, this is great!"

But Betty is not so dismissive. "Give us a little while," she tells Lady Aberlin. "You never know what good can come when old friends get together and play a few helpful things." Sure enough, while the two are playing and creating, they talk about feelings, and Betty discovers that Lady Elaine is terribly worried. "There we were," she later tells Lady Aberlin, "playing with the clay and doing a few beautiful tunes on the steel pans and all when all of a sudden Lainey just burst into tears. . . . She's worried that she's turned Mr. McFeely into a doll and she didn't mean to and she doesn't know how to turn him back."

Fred Rogers described his beloved mentor in graduate school, Margaret McFarland, as "the most major influence in my professional life."[38] He first encountered McFarland when he asked his seminary adviser if he might work with children as part of a required course in counseling. His adviser approved the proposal on the condition that he study directly with McFarland, then director of the Arsenal Family Children's Center. Founded by Benjamin Spock at the University of Pittsburgh, the center became Rogers's home base for the academic study of child development.

As a student at Arsenal, he spent countless hours studying children as they talked and shared, played and threw fits, ate and grew. But his time at Arsenal was perhaps most fruitful because it gave him and McFarland an opportunity to form a professional relationship that would endure for decades to come. McFarland soon became a consultant on *Mister Rogers' Neighborhood*, and she and Rogers often met weekly to discuss scripts and other ideas related to the cognitive and emotional development of children. When she died in 1988, she had advised Rogers for at least thirty years. Five years after her passing, Rogers held his hands over his chest and said, "I think I've incorporated so much of who she was in here."[39]

Some of the most important counsel he received from McFarland, if we consider the number of times he referred to it, involved children vocalizing their feelings: "Margaret used to say to us, 'Anything that's human is mentionable and whatever is mentionable is manageable.'"[40] Rogers took that advice seriously and spent the better part of his professional career encouraging children to talk about their feelings, especially their mad feelings.

"When we can talk about our feelings," he said, "they become less overwhelming, less upsetting, and less scary."[41] Talking about our mad feelings in particular helps us understand the deepest roots of our own identity—the very personal reason for those times we fly off the handle. Understanding our deepest fears and loves can make it easier for us to identify the most fitting and constructive choices about what to do with our mad feelings. Understanding can thus be an antidote to anger; it can help us to manage and dominate our anger.

To explain the importance of self-understanding in relation to anger and its origins, Rogers shared a story about engaging in puppet play during his early training in child development:

> One four-year-old little boy would intervene and actually prevent my being able to do much work. I remember how angry that made me. I was angry because of the frustration of my work; but I was angry at another level because when I was a little boy I wasn't allowed to prevent adults' activities like that. It took quite a while to resolve that situation, and I came to realize that one of the most important aspects of working with children is developing the capacity to differentiate between the inner child of our own past and the child we're working with in the present.[42]

Discussing mad feelings can also lead us to a greater understanding of others, including those with whom we are angry. By talking about those who make us angry, we can begin to understand the deep roots of *their* identity—the very personal reasons for their attitudes and behaviors. Once again, rational understanding about their core identity can help trump the emotional fury that so often consumes us. Born in love and care, understanding others is an antidote to violence. Rogers explained the importance of awareness of others in relation to our anger by telling another story from the days of his work at Arsenal:

> One young boy seemed to make me continually angry with him. Those times I felt as though I were acting like someone else. As I thought more about it, I realized that the child with whom I was working was doing his or her best to get me to act that way. The more I found out about the child's family—and particularly the father—the more I understood the fact that young children transfer their feelings about their primary caretakers onto their teacher. And what's more, that child will be very skilled in evoking behavior from adults that's like the behavior of the mother and father.[43]

For Rogers, talking about our mad feelings can also create a sense of psychological liberation, of individual freedom to be the best person we can be. When he was a high school student, Rogers often saw a message on a sign above the auditorium stage: "You shall know the truth, and the truth shall make you free." The words, excerpted from the Gospel of John, meant so much to Rogers that he penned a song titled "The Truth Will Make Me Free." Written in 1970, the song includes these verses:

> What if I were very, very sad
> And all I did was smile?

I wonder after a while
What might become of my sadness?

What if I were very, very angry?
And all I did was sit
And never think about it?
What might become of my anger?

Where would they go, and what would they do
If I couldn't let them out?
Maybe I'd fall, maybe get sick
Or doubt.

But what if I could know the truth
And just say how I feel?
I think I'd learn a lot that's real
About freedom.

Rogers conceded that the meaning might be difficult for children to grasp, but he wanted to plant a seed in them so one day they might understand that repressing their anger would make them prisoners of rage—so constrained, so tight, that they would be able to do nothing except fall down. On a more positive note, Rogers also wanted children to know that talking about their mad feelings would help them feel a sense of relief and release—freedom to live as fully and peacefully as they could. Sharing mad feelings may often be painful, Rogers stated, "but the freedom it can bring is worth the trying."[44]

Finally, talking about our anger is important because the deep awareness it brings, of ourselves and others, is a condition required for love—for accepting ourselves just as we are and others just as they are. If we do not know who we are in our essence, or who others are in theirs, we cannot accept others or ourselves fully. Deep love becomes impossible. But when talking leads to deep understanding, it actually strengthens and advances our ability to care for others and ourselves. Rightly expressed, anger is a tool in the service of love.

Punishing the Violent

Back in the Neighborhood of Make-Believe, Lady Elaine, in conversation with Betty, has discovered that her anger has gotten the best of her. Her violent outbreak is worrying her silly, especially when she thinks about having turned Mr. McFeely into a doll. Lady Elaine even shares her concern with King Friday, who promptly asks her what she's going to do about it. "First of all, I guess I'll say I'm sorry," she says. "That's a fine beginning," King

Friday replies, "but it's just a beginning." Spoken apologies are necessary but not sufficient in the Neighborhood of Make-Believe.

At this point, Lady Elaine shows King Friday and Lady Aberlin a tower she has molded out of play clay. Lady Elaine has worked out her mad feelings by doing something at which she's really good. The tower is beautiful, and it looks just like Grandpère's. Having gotten over her feelings, Lady Elaine is now inspired, with a nudge from Lady Aberlin, to turn Grandpère's tower right side up. "That's easy!" she says as she uses her boomerang to make amends.

Not so easy is turning the doll back into the real Mr. McFeely. Lady Elaine is worried sick, and she begins to cry again. "I don't know how to make him back into himself," she whimpers. But just then the real Mr. McFeely shows up in the Neighborhood to pick up his doll—the Mr. McFeely doll. Lady Elaine was mistaken; she never did turn him into a doll.

As the Neighborhood rejoices, King Friday imposes a consequence on Lady Elaine. "You are to help Lady Aberlin sweep up whatever mess has been incurred by your topsy-turvy behavior," he declares. Lady Elaine accepts her punishment and says she'll apologize to Grandpère and try not to use the boomerang when she's angry. The best amend of all, though, is her decision to give the beautiful clay tower to Grandpère as she apologizes for her violent actions. "Now I guess I'll sweep up the mess," she concludes.

Make no mistake—for all his gentleness, Fred Rogers believed in firmly disciplining those who express their mad feelings through acts of violence. This was clear not only in the series on mad feelings but also in a 1981 special on violence in the news. Rogers broadcast this special not long after the murder of John Lennon and the attempts to assassinate President Ronald Reagan and Pope John Paul II. He mentions all three of these events, plus the murders of numerous children in Atlanta, at the beginning of the special. "The people who are doing these terrible things are making a lot of other people sad and angry," he says.[45] After observing that "one of the most important parts of growing up is learning to talk and play about our feelings," Rogers then takes us to the Neighborhood of Make-Believe, where something terrible has happened.

"Call out the troops!" King Friday shouts. "Everyone on guard!" The king has just learned that "some big thing" has taken Little Walking Talking Tree.

"I'm angry, frightened, and very, very sad," Queen Sara says upon learning the news. When King Friday asks what she's "going to do about those feelings," the queen replies that she'll use them "to help somebody else."

"And so must we all!" he announces.

A search across the Neighborhood begins, but it concludes all too soon when Maurice Edwards, the producer of MGR-TV, appears back at the castle, carrying a lifeless little tree in his arms. Little Walking Talking Tree is dead. "There isn't any more life in him," Edwards says.

Daniel Striped Tiger, tame as tame can be, worries that others will think he killed Little Walking Talking Tree, since he was the last to see him. But Lady Aberlin assures him otherwise. Comforted for just a moment, Daniel then wonders why people "do very bad things."

"I guess it's because they're very sick people," Lady Aberlin says. "They don't know what to do with their feelings."

In a special news flash on MGR-TV, Maurice Edwards reports that while flying over the Neighborhood he spotted a sign carried by a big walking tree. The sign read, "I did it," and the big tree was heading toward the castle.

King Friday, always prepared to use force, announces that "our troops are ready," but it turns out that no more violence is necessary. The big tree surrenders. "I did it, I did it, I did it," he repeats.

"You killed Little Walking Talking Tree?" King Friday asks.

"Yes, I did it," Big Tree confesses. "Help me to stop being bad."

"We will help you," Queen Sara replies. "We won't let you hurt anybody else."

"You may take Big Tree to jail," King Friday adds. "Help him to learn how to stop."

Rogers believed in the need to discipline those whose mad feelings are inappropriate on any level, from slugging a brother to murdering an innocent person. In fact, he saw discipline, rightly done, as a practice of love—caring for others in need and helping them to mature. "Love . . . is at the root of all healthy discipline," he wrote. On the subject of disciplining children in particular, Rogers stated that when we punish them in a healthy way it's because "our continuing love" for them "makes us want them to become all they can be."[46]

Of course, we don't always punish in healthy ways, and Rogers characterized our unhealthy methods as "power punishments." These tend to be entirely negative reactions to something we identify as a "personal challenge" or as a threat to our "sense of security." They often manifest themselves in egotistic shouts of anger and physical punishments (slapping and spanking). By contrast, loving punishments "tend to be firm reminders to the child that there are some limits that, for health, safety, or practical reasons, *have* to be observed." They manifest themselves in corrections and explanations that "have a different sound" than power punishments, and they refuse physical punishments in favor of "restrictions on activity, the curtailing of pleasures, and the revoking of privileges."[47]

Rogers always and everywhere preferred "loving punishments," and not just for children. Look at his decision about punishing the adult tree murderer. Sending Big Tree to the nearest lumberyard, or allowing him to rot in solitary confinement, would have been a form of power punishment. But escorting Big Tree to jail, where he will receive counseling that will help him "learn how to stop," is a form of loving punishment. It envisions Big Tree as redeemable and focuses on his rehabilitation, even as it ensures that he will not be able to hurt anyone else in the Neighborhood.

Making Peacemakers

It should come as no surprise that, far beyond the Neighborhood, Fred Rogers opposed the death penalty. Jeff Garis, a former director of Pennsylvania Abolitionists United Against the Death Penalty, recalls Rogers communicating an anti-death-penalty position through his public relations adviser, David Newell. Garis had invited Rogers to speak at an awards dinner, and Newell called to decline the invitation but also to assure the group of Rogers's opposition to capital punishment. "It just sends a horribly wrong message to children," Newell stated. "For Fred a lot of it comes down to this: 'What are our children learning from us when we model that this is an appropriate way of responding to societal problems?'"[48]

For Rogers, modeling ways of expressing our mad feelings has long-term effects on individuals and societies. "I believe that for many violent adults the start of it all lies in their earliest years of their lives," he stated.[49] When children do not learn self-control, channeling, or even ways to communicate their anger, they often grow up to become violent adults who create violent societies. These children did not have to become violent—they had the God-given ability to practice self-control, channeling, and communication—but adult models in their lives encouraged them to believe otherwise. Violence often begets violence.

Conversely, for many of us who are nonviolent adults, we can point back to our earliest years, when adults showed us the joys and benefits of self-control, channeling, and sharing. Nonviolence often begets nonviolence. In fact, for Rogers, the whole point of a series on mad feelings and of all those other episodes of *Mister Rogers' Neighborhood* that modeled channeling was to create little peacemakers who would grow up to be big peacemakers. He put it this way:

> One of the most important messages we can give our children is, "It's okay to be angry, but it's not okay to hurt ourselves or others." Besides giving children the right to their anger, we can encourage them to find constructive things to do with their feelings. This way, we'll be giving them useful tools that will serve them all their life, and help them to become the world's future peacemakers—the world's future "helpers."[50]

Rogers used the Neighborhood of Make-Believe to share an antiwar, prodiplomacy message shortly after President George H. W. Bush declared a cease-fire in the Persian Gulf War.

Chapter 6

"A Gross Form of Abuse"

From the Persian Gulf War to the War on Terror

*D*riven by his faith in God and by his Freudian perspective, Fred Rogers used his program during the Vietnam War, the invasion of Grenada, and the nuclear arms race to deliver the plain and simple message that war is neither wonderful nor nice. But it's not clear that most of his viewers ever fully embraced this message as they grew into adults who could vote and carry weapons.[1] The majority of U.S. voters certainly did not wave Rogers's peace flag in the 1990s or during the post-9/11 response to terrorism. But even as many of his fellow citizens fiercely supported the Persian Gulf War and the War on Terror, Rogers continued to hold fast to his pacifism, arguing that war abuses children and encouraging us to become "helpers"—peacemakers in violent times.

The Persian Gulf War and Child Abuse

The Persian Gulf War began in January 1991, after Iraqi leader Saddam Hussein refused to abide by UN Security Council demands to withdraw his occupying forces from Kuwait. Hussein had invaded the neighboring country, which was an important oil resource for the United States, in August 1990. Concerned about oil reserves and regional instability, the United States conducted a massive air and land assault from mid-January into February against an ill-equipped Iraqi army. Forty-two days after the assault began, and with the Iraqi army successfully routed from Kuwait, President George H. W. Bush declared a cease-fire. From beginning to end, the war enjoyed widespread public support, but Fred Rogers was not among the cheering masses. As usual, he was concerned about the effects of war on children.

The United States won the war with an all-volunteer army, including a large number of married couples with children and single parents who had turned to the military for stable employment. The run-up to the war saw them staring at a family crisis. Because the Pentagon did not exempt from combat single parents or one member of a military couple, their children faced an uncertain future with no parent at home to care for them.

Rogers called for congressional action on this issue. The possibility of children being separated from their soldier-parents struck a very personal note with him, echoing back to a troubling time when he, Joanne, and their two young sons, Jamie, 3, and Johnny, 1, were living in Canada. Rogers rarely recounted the details of this story in public, but he did so in a 1987 speech to migrant educators.

> Our younger son needed to have a hernia repair and we were told that the procedure could be done with only a few hours in the hospital. He could be an out-patient, and we could take him home the same day. . . . So with the best of intentions we took him to the hospital and went to the out-patient surgery department. When we checked in, the first thing we knew was that a nurse and an orderly came with a crib on wheels that was like a cage, and these people checked to see if we were the Rogers, and then grabbed Johnny and put him in the crib cage and wheeled him screaming down the hall to the operating room—no pre-operative sedation . . . NOTHING!
>
> To this day I have nightmares about it, and I get so angry when I talk about it that I find it hard to be the least bit charitable. If I'd known then what I know now, those people would have never taken our son from us that way. I would have insisted on being with him until he was asleep. We later learned that it took the surgical team 45 minutes to get him sedated and those 45 minutes changed all of our lives. The physical part of the surgery was a success. Johnny's hernia was repaired, but his emotions were severely damaged. From that day on, he was a changed child. Before the hospital, he was a happy, competent 16 month old. Afterwards, he was an anxious accident-prone boy who fell from climbing frames and pulled hot coffee pots over on himself, and got his leg stuck in a basement drain.
>
> And when we got back to this country and had him enrolled in nursery school, there were doctors who saw him who were convinced that he was brain damaged from birth. We KNEW that he wasn't; but, that's the way he acted. He felt damaged all right, but it was because he had been subjected to what one of my colleagues calls BARBARIC MEDICINE! Well, after a decade of intensive psychotherapy, John worked through a lot of the trauma. The analyst told me that all the associations led back to that terrifying hospital experience.[2]

Rogers shared this story to explain his reason for doing a television special on children visiting the hospital and facing surgery. But the horrific memory also no doubt fueled his longtime focus on the crippling anxiety children can suffer when they become separated from their loving caretakers for a host of other reasons too, such as daycare, preschool—and war.

With children and separation in mind, Rogers accused the U.S. government of child abuse during the run-up to the Gulf War. He did so in a "personal and confidential" letter he sent to his good friend, Senator John Heinz of Pennsylvania. After the popular senator had introduced a bill designed to exempt from combat one parent of military couples or single parents who were their children's sole provider, Rogers wrote him a short message:

> Even though I believe that no parent of a preschool child should have to go to war, I strongly applaud your efforts to insure that at least one parent is available to young children, especially in such a threatening time.
>
> We must not perpetuate abuse from one generation to the next—and separation from a young child's security (their loved ones) is a gross form of abuse. Thank you for your continued sensitivity to the needs of children.[3]

Heinz's bill was easily defeated, and Rogers felt stung. "Does the U.S. Congress have little or no understanding of early trauma due to premature separation anxiety?" he asked.[4] The answer was obvious. Like the Pentagon, Congress was evidently full of people oblivious to the abuse they were perpetrating on numerous children. In fact, by February 1991, children from 17,500 military families had been left at home either without both parents or without the parent who cared for them solely.

Rogers continued to explain his position on war as child abuse after the defeat of Heinz's bill. In a May 1991 speech, he stated that the ability to trust—to become mature adults capable of love—"begins with the development of the mothering person in our lives. That image takes about 5 years to develop, so that anything that disrupts it is in 'the worst interest of the child.'" That includes sending parents of young children to war. When we separate children from their nurturing caretakers, we rip apart the "essential bond" children so desperately need for their psychological well-being. At the same time, we also undermine the "emotional health of our country," mainly because the children we abuse today may become the abusers of tomorrow.[5]

That's what was happening in the Gulf War, according to Rogers. As he put this in a letter to his friend Larry Kutner, "To raise a generation which is not abused (by war or any other means) should be our goal. As you can see so clearly the abused grow up to be the abusers—sometimes on a worldwide scale."[6]

Subversive Public Service Announcements

Rogers also told Larry Kutner that "in light of the war itself, there's little we average souls can do besides pray; but, when it comes to our own homes, there's *lots* we can do," such as maintaining familiar routines.[7] Nine days before Rogers penned this letter, his company, Family Communications, had sent a memorandum to PBS managers across the country asking them to help children maintain their familiar television routines. "As the adult world with its Persian Gulf situation continues to provide uncertainty and distress, we in Public Television can help young children by providing their regular and predictable preschool programming," the memo stated. Family Communications believed what children needed during the Gulf War was not another new program on the war but the consistency of Mister Rogers walking through the door, smiling, singing "Won't You Be My Neighbor?" changing his sweater, putting on his blue sneakers, and taking children to the Neighborhood of Make-Believe. "Knowing what to expect comforts preschoolers," the memo argued.[8]

Rogers did more too. While Senator Heinz's colleagues gave their blessings to the Pentagon's insistence on sending parents to war, Rogers counteracted by airing public service announcements about children and war. One spot included Neighbor Aber and Daniel Striped Tiger having a simple conversation about the pain of separation caused by war:

Daniel: Did you ever know somebody who had to go far, far away?

Aber: Yes, I did. And she had to stay a long, long time.

Daniel: How did you feel when she was gone?

Aber: I felt like crying.

Daniel: *Did* you cry, Mr. Aber?

Aber: Of course, Daniel. People often cry when they're sad.

Daniel: Tame tigers do, too.

Aber: Well, it's all right for *all* of us to have feelings. That's what makes us special.

Daniel: I feel better when I talk to you.

Aber: I know that good feeling, too.

Another spot, this one featuring Daniel, Mayor Maggie, and Fred Rogers, focused on the fear war creates in children:

Daniel: I get scared when I hear about the war.

Maggie: Can you tell me what scares you?

Daniel: When people are crying.

Maggie: That's very sad, isn't it?

Daniel: Yes, and I could use a hug.

Maggie (*giving Daniel a hug*): I'm grateful for you, Daniel.

Fred: When we're scared, sometimes a hug is the best thing we can give . . . or receive . . . no matter how young or old we may be.

Taken out of context, these two public service announcements seem caring and comforting, and only that. But when viewed in conversation with Rogers's beliefs about child abuse, the announcements are nothing less than pointed messages designed to counter a government that abuses its children. Contrary to the government's abusive practices, Fred Rogers was attempting to create new bonds of security for children left behind or any child saddened or frightened by the government's actions.

Equally significant, Rogers also used his public service announcements to give children a model directly contrary to the one offered by their violent government. His alternative, subversive model appeared in the following thirty-second spot:

When I was a little boy, I had some neighbors who wanted to play war games all the time. After a while, I got scared of those games, and I didn't want to play. I told my dad about it, and I'll always remember what he said. "You don't have to play anything you don't want to play in life. In fact, deciding about your play and your work is one of the most important things you'll ever do." My dad really helped me by telling me that.[9]

Rogers, in turn, was helping children understand that they did not have to be like the violent government—which made its soldiers use real guns—or the children in their neighborhood who mimicked soldiers. While the government was conveying that it's sometimes good to kill bad people, Rogers offered children his alternative message of nonviolence: You don't have to play war, and you don't have to be a soldier when you choose your lifework.

Rogers was not an idealist on the issue of play guns. He often noted that "at a certain age young children turn almost everything they pick up into a 'gun,' and that if there isn't anything to pick up, a cocked thumb and forefinger will do just as well."[10] He also expressed doubt that children who play with guns will likely "grow up to use real ones."[11] But Rogers found all aggressive toys—guns, swords, even water pistols—to be problematic. On the one hand, they "give children the clear message that the way to handle conflict is to wipe out the 'bad guys' with force."[12] As we've seen, Rogers did not believe that anyone was altogether bad; nor, of course, did he ever concede that killing was an appropriate way to solve conflict. On the other hand, toy guns and other aggressive weapons do a poor job of channeling children's instincts. Children find gun play so compelling, he stated, because of their "need to feel powerful and in control."[13] That need is basic to the human condition, and while it can be used for "creativity and invention," toy guns direct the instinct merely to destroying and killing.

Rogers was thus opposed to buying aggressive toys for children. Rather than equipping our children with toy machine guns, we should stop gun play when it becomes too scary, share our negative feelings about gun violence, explain that there are always better ways to solve a problem than by killing, and let children know "in as many ways as we know how that they are very valuable to us."[14] Better yet, we should encourage our children to play with open-ended toys that allow for creative problem solving—a skill that will help them solve conflicts peacefully the rest of their lives.

However strong his convictions, Rogers did not guarantee that any of these measures, including his public service announcements, would actually succeed in creating little peacemakers. But he was convinced that trying to save children from the abuse of war was the work of God. As he put this not long after the tragic death of Senator Heinz on April 4, 1991, "Just as John Heinz's efforts in behalf of our young children didn't always succeed, ours may not either; but when we've gone to where he is now, someone may well say, 'You thought of the children first. In as much as you did it for them, you did it for me.' "[15] Rogers was referring to the Gospel of Matthew, where the Son of Man announces at the Great Judgment that those who will inherit the kingdom of heaven are the ones who fed the hungry, gave drink to the thirsty, welcomed the stranger, clothed the naked, and visited the imprisoned. "Truly I tell you," the Son of Man says, "just as you did it to one of the least of these who are members of my family, you did it to me" (25:40). For Rogers, trying to save children from a violent government was holy work with eternal rewards.

Dissent in the Neighborhood

In addition to running public service announcements, Rogers also took the occasion of the war to rerun episodes of *Mister Rogers' Neighborhood* from

1986 that had peace among their themes. At the beginning of the war, for instance, Rogers ran an episode in which Lady Elaine covers her museum with plaid quilting that includes the word "peace" in many languages, such as *paix, paz, amani, mir,* and (aptly) *fred,* which happens to be the word for peace in several Nordic languages.[16] In another episode at the war's beginnings, poet May Sarton read a selection from her poem about a gentle cat who will not fight and who encourages all others to disarm themselves and be gentle.[17]

But Betty Aberlin (the actor who played Lady Aberlin) did not find these reruns and the public service spots to be sufficient responses to the war, and she pleaded with Rogers in person, on the phone, and in letters to do much more. In a February 1991 letter, for instance, she criticized Rogers for not rerunning the 1983 special series titled "Conflict Week," with its clear, strong message that "war isn't nice," and she urged him to make a public statement opposing the war. "Dear Ferd," she wrote, using the playful name she often called him,

> I was grateful that the week war was made, May Sarton read the poem about the cat who would not fight, and the backdrop of Lady Elaine Fairchilde's Museum had the word PEACE, including your name, in many languages.
>
> When I was young I remember hearing how the Jews were exterminated in part because good men and women did nothing to prevent it. Now the Iraqi people are being slaughtered, and children in Israel and in the U.S.A. terrorized, traumatized, brainwashed and placated.
>
> Tony Bennett came out on Arsenio Hall against the war. This President with his "kinder, gentler" talk of the New World Order gives me the willies. He seems to have studied your on-air persona. He is considered a sane man.
>
> Your decision not to refer to or air CONFLICT week, and to do all-purpose spots instead, when you might have influenced popular opinion to embrace the New Order of Christ's Kingdom of Peace—stunned me. It was what you did not do and did not say that offended me. I strongly disagree with you. I continue to love and forgive you as I question my capacity to *collaborate* with you.
>
> Your "restraint" will probably insure the longevity of the Neighborhood on PBS. Perhaps when the privilege of free speech has ended in the world Bush intends, dissent will still be permitted in Make-Believe.[18]

Unlike Rogers, Aberlin was an activist who marched and rallied against the war at the end of January 1991 and at other points. She didn't expect Rogers to march with her, but she did want him to use his program and his soapbox to publicize his faith-filled opposition to all wars, including the Persian Gulf War. Aberlin voiced her dissent to the war in letters and mailgrams to other opinion makers too, including President George H. W. Bush, Barbara Bush, and ABC News anchor Peter Jennings. In her mailgram to Jennings, Aberlin informed him about Rogers's programming decision and sent a positive word about Jennings's forthcoming special on children's questions about the war:

> "Mister Rogers' Neighborhood" programs on Conflict . . . deal explicitly with issues of war and peace, but Rogers has chosen not to run these now for many reasons. In my 23 years on the program (as Lady Aberlin) I have described Fred to non-viewers as "the flip side of Big Brother." I now find George Bush's resemblance to Fred Rogers, in delivery and demeanor, a bit too close for comfort. I feel these shows would have been great as catalyst for profound talk at this time, and hope that your show will not only answer children's questions, but hear and heed their thoughts on this real war.[19]

Aberlin had many reasons for opposing the war. She saw it as a war of greed that trampled on the principles of freedom and human rights while terrorizing and killing innocent civilians in Iraq, all for the sake of oil. More fundamentally, however, she found the war directly contrary to the Prince of Peace, whom President Bush professed to follow. "Bush is no Christian," she wrote to a special assistant to the president. "Christ asks us to love our enemies. In this sense I love Bush [and] pray for his conversion to the *real* new order—Christ's Kingdom of Peace."[20]

Although he too was a follower of the Prince of Peace, Fred Rogers did not accept Aberlin's advice to rerun the 1983 special series on war. Was he afraid of even more backlash among viewers? The file of extant anti–Conflict Week letters at the archives in Latrobe is certainly one of the larger files available among those filled with viewer mail. Was he fearful that his sponsors would pull funding? That Congress would do the same? Perhaps the answer to these questions lies in new episodes that Rogers broadcast at the end of February 1991 in a special series on growing. Although President Bush had already declared a cease-fire by the time these episodes aired, they were deep in production during the execution of the war. As wartime episodes, they make an unambiguous case for diplomacy over military force.

Talk, Don't Shoot

In the first Make-Believe segment of the series on growing, Queen Sara tells her husband that while she was in the lookout tower, checking on the crop production, she spotted "this large looking ball or something over in the Westwood area."[21] Worse, the "very big" thing seemed to be rolling toward the Neighborhood. King Friday responds to Queen Sara's troubling report, now a "state secret," by ordering Handyman Negri to encourage everyone "not to be afraid of anything," even though no one other than a few know about the big thing. Negri follows the king's order, but the result is the creation of fear among the unknowing neighbors. X the Owl wonders aloud whether "something bad is going on, and the king isn't telling us."

Meanwhile, King Friday consults with Mayor Maggie and Neighbor Aber (who's the associate mayor) from Westwood. "The news," Mayor Maggie says, "is that this big thing is making its way very slowly from Westwood to the Neighborhood. Now, it did no harm in Westwood, and it may just pass by here." Nevertheless, in spite of Mayor Maggie's positive scouting report, King Friday gives a panicky order as the big thing rolls into Make-Believe. "Call out the troops!" he says.

The royal order immediately prompts Associate Mayor Aber to interject a plea for patience. "Excuse me, King Friday," he says. "That big thing didn't do any harm in Westwood. Couldn't we just wait and see what happens here?" Though reticent, Friday agrees to wait, but only on one condition— that Mayor Maggie, Aber, and Purple Panda "speak to the big thing and see what he plans to do." Just before the "intermediate delegation" leaves, Handyman Negri and Miss Paulificate appear on the scene, dressed as royal soldiers and carrying rifles that look like a cross between a popgun and a plunger. "You may guard the castle, but hold your fire," King Friday says. "Our representatives will speak to the big thing."

The three members of the intermediate delegation cautiously approach the big thing and slowly begin their efforts to ascertain the big thing's motives and plans. "Hello, Big Thing," says Purple Panda. "Are you planning to roll out?" With no reply to the unwelcoming question, Aber shares his own thoughts: "King Friday XIII, who lives over in that castle, has called the royal troops out and considers using force. But we were hoping that wouldn't be necessary." Still, there's no reply from the big thing. "We're really peace-loving people around here," adds Mayor Maggie, "and, as mayor of Westwood, I'm certainly grateful you passed us by." Her peaceful request in turn encourages Purple Panda to make his own: "And maybe you would pass us by, too." Hearing these peaceful overtures, the big thing rolls back and forth—which makes Aber think he'd better run back and give a report to King Friday. "Keep talking peace and passing on," he says to Mayor Maggie and Purple Panda before he leaves. "That seems to get the most response."

Back at the castle, the heavily armed Miss Paulificate asks Aber if he would like "some force." Aber declines right away, telling her and King Friday, "Peace is the word. As soon as we mentioned peace and passing on and things like that, the big thing kind of teeter-tottered, as if it were happy or something. It was nice." Heartened by the report, King Friday says, "It looks very hopeful. There's growth in this situation." Aber agrees: "I really do think so. I mean, if we can talk and think and feel peace, we'll all be the better for it."

With the positive news, everyone breathes a sigh of relief and takes a leisurely nap. Just then, Robert Troll arrives at the castle, spots the big thing, and approaches it in the friendliest manner, as if there's not an ounce of fear in him. After Robert Troll introduces himself to the big thing, it asks him for a warm blanket, even suggesting that he might find one at Daniel Striped Tiger's.

When Daniel learns that Robert believes the big thing is really something like a seed—something that will grow—he expresses surprise that the big thing may not be "something scary." "Oh, no," says Robert Troll, as jovial as ever. "It's not scary at all. It has a very nice voice." Daniel is absolutely shocked to learn that Robert has actually talked to the big thing. "Sure," says Robert. "I like to talk to things."

Back with the big thing, Robert places Daniel's blanket on top of it, prompting the big thing to respond, "Thank you." Much to Robert's surprise, a shoot immediately begins to sprout out of the big thing. "Look at the shoot growing out!" Robert shouts.

His shout of "shoot" is loud enough to wake the royal troops, who, looking dazed and confused, yell, "Prepare for fire!" and even begin firing their weapons in a haphazard way. "Don't shoot!" yells Robert Troll. "Wait! Wait!" He quickly explains that he did not say to shoot at all. "I said, 'Look at the shoot growing out of Big Thing!'" Things quiet down for a second, but then Lady Elaine gets into the mix of things by telling King Friday that "the big thing's been shooting." Shocked, King Friday says, "Then shoot we must!" But Soldier Negri holds his fire, explaining that "the big thing isn't shooting anything like a gun, Sire. It's growing a shoot out of itself."

Robert Troll, as sane and friendly as always, walks over to the big thing to listen to what it's saying. "Big Thing wants you to know he's very grateful," Troll explains, "and he wants to thank you for trusting him. See?"

What the others might not "see" right away is that they trusted the big thing not to harm them when they earlier breathed a sigh of relief and fell asleep. Asleep, they were not in a defensive or fighting mode; they were at peace.

"And he also says . . . he's going to grow something really nice for everybody," Robert Troll adds. Indeed, by the end of the series, the big thing grows a really big flower for everyone in Make-Believe.

Back in his television house, Mister Rogers draws attention to the remarkable work of Robert Troll—"a marvel," as Mayor Maggie described it earlier. Unlike King Friday, Robert did not seek assurance in armed troops when learning about the big thing. Unlike the troops, he did not carry weapons and assume a defensive posture and position. Unlike Mayor Maggie, Neighbor Aber, and Purple Panda, he did not approach the big thing cautiously, as if it were about to attack him. Robert Troll was just his friendly, open, honest self—and, perhaps most importantly, a really good listener. "Robert Troll is an elf in Make-Believe," Rogers explains. "He says he's used to hearing all sorts of things talk. I guess he knows how to be very quiet—and very understanding."

The storyline of the big thing seems like yet another sweet message about personal growth coming through patience and understanding. But placed in context, it delivers a sure and certain message about war. The unambiguous though subtle message is that even in times of invasion, it is best to "wait and see" what the invader is planning. Perhaps an authentic conversation, a nonthreatening give and take, will reveal real and pressing needs underlying the invasion. With an accurate understanding of the invasion, perhaps we will then realize that the best response to it is not the use of force but rather the skills of diplomacy backed by action focused on the needs at hand. In context, the message is that diplomacy, not military action, would have been a far better way to deal with Hussein's invasion of Kuwait.

Yes, Fred Rogers decided not to rerun the 1983 programs on war, but the new ones he aired right after President Bush declared a cease-fire in the Persian Gulf War delivered yet another antiwar, prodiplomacy message. With this strong and clear message, these new episodes offer no evidence to suggest that Rogers was fearful of a backlash among viewers or a withdrawal of funding.

Heroes Are Helpers, Not Killers

Issues of war and peace were on Rogers's mind once again when he penned Scott Simon of National Public Radio a year later. He had just listened to Simon's interview of Hugh Thompson, the U.S. Army helicopter pilot who rescued Vietnamese noncombatants during the My Lai massacre on March

16, 1968, when U.S. troops murdered between 347 and 504 civilians, including many children and infants. The photographs of these Vietnamese peasants from the rural village of My Lai remain among the most horrific ever taken in U.S. history.

After hearing Simon's interview, Rogers wrote a letter stating, "I just have to let you know that your response to Thompson's saying that he wishes he had 'never been there that day' to me was the zenith of journalism. When you told him that because of his being there certain people are alive today I felt a welling up of gratitude for you that I can't describe adequately. What a fine model!" A far better role model, that is, than soldiers who slaughtered innocent children or those who looked the other way during the horrific massacres in Vietnam.[22]

Rogers was frequently on the lookout for role models upon whom he could shower praise. The models he found were often quite different from those the country admired. Rogers was far from thrilled, for example, with the role models director Steven Spielberg served up several years later in the popular film *Saving Private Ryan*. The gripping film tells the story of a squad of soldiers who, after landing in Normandy on June 6, 1944, set out to find Private James Ryan, a paratrooper who is missing in action. The mission comes straight from Washington, DC, where General George Marshall has just learned that Ryan's three brothers have been killed in action. In a moment of empathy for the boys' mother, Marshall orders that U.S. troops find Ryan so that he can return home and ensure the ongoing legacy of the Ryan family. Led by Captain John Miller, played by megastar Tom Hanks, the rescue mission turns out to be a great success (although countless other soldiers get blown to pieces along the way).

Saving Private Ryan was wildly popular with U.S. audiences and film critics alike, becoming the highest-grossing film of the year and winning Spielberg his second Academy Award for best director. But Fred Rogers didn't want to see the film. "No, we didn't see Pvt. Ryan," he wrote to his friend Tom Junod in early September.

> Joanne didn't want to, and I guess I didn't either. I remember so well those days when we huddled around the radio listening to the news of battles and finally the war's end. I remember the V days and the release of the prisoners. In fact I remember crying when I heard about the release of the prisoners. I think we all have certain prisons within us, and such news "releases" are sometimes . . . in some hearts . . . taken very personally.[23]

Junod had asked Rogers how he would have responded to a call to join the war effort—a great question to ask of a compassionate pacifist. In World War

II, young pacifist men of recruitment age had various possibilities. Thanks to lobbying efforts by the historic peace churches (Friends, Mennonites, and Brethren), pacifists could carry out "work of national importance" in Civilian Public Service camps organized and funded by the churches.[24] They could also serve in noncombatant roles in the military, as Lew Ayres did. The famous actor served as a medic in the Pacific Rim and donated all of his earnings as a serviceman to the American Red Cross. Pacifists who found it immoral to undertake any war effort, including the noncombatant work of medics, could choose to spend the war years in federal prison. Bayard Rustin, the brilliant civil rights strategist who later organized the 1963 March on Washington for Jobs and Freedom, chose this option.

Fred Rogers was less like Rustin and more like Ayres. "I have no idea how I would have responded to a call to the war," he replied to Junod. "I may have had to do alternative service . . . as did the Friends. I have a friend (not a Quaker friend) who was in the Ambulance Corps. I would have probably been good at something like that. I would not have been good at shooting people though; I don't think I could have done that."[25]

The government's call to bear arms in World War II did not apply to Rogers. The war had already ended by the time he was eligible for the draft, and when he did take his military physical, he failed it with a classic case of flat feet. But had he passed and had the government actually drafted him at some point, it does seem likely, given his own words, that he would have opted for a noncombatant role. Service in an ambulance corps would have been unsurprising for another reason too: It was the type of work his beloved mother had long extolled. In his 1983 book on parenting, Rogers recounted his mother's counsel:

> Much of what is seen through the mass media is . . . dramatized mayhem, murder, debased sexuality, and an endless succession of real-life disaster, tragedy, and violence that comes to us through news and documentaries. When I was a child and my mother and I would read about such events in the newspapers or see them in newsreels, she used to tell me, "Always look for the helpers. There's always someone who is trying to help." I did, and doing so changed the way I saw them. I began to see the world was full of doctors and nurses, volunteers, neighbors, and friends who jumped in to help when things went wrong. That was reassuring.[26]

In stating his preference for serving in an ambulance corps, Rogers was saying he wanted to be one of those helpers his mother had told him to look for, an individual who helps save lives in war and violence and mayhem. Rogers longed to bestow life, preserve life, help life—not to end it.

The War on Terror

Rogers recounted his mother's hopeful view many times throughout his public career, but never more significantly than after the terrorist attacks on September 11, 2001. Interestingly, Rogers had mentioned terrorism in his 1992 letter to Scott Simon. The topic of international terrorism, usually addressed in relation to Libya and Iran, was common at that point, and Rogers told Simon he'd just spoken with an expert in the field.

> He talked about how countries are taught to hate (first one enemy then another) and when we don't have an enemy we start to hate one another. "All the major religions espouse peace and love," he said. "If everyone made manifest what he or she professes the world would be such a profoundly different place." Sounds simple but he's right.[27]

Given this short note, it's easy to imagine that Rogers was fervently opposed to using religion to justify the terrorist attacks on 9/11 and, equally important, to our own violent response to them. For Rogers, the world's major religions, including both Islam and his own Christian religion, rightly espouse peace and love at all times, not only until one becomes a victim of oppression, violence, or terror.

Rogers had stressed a similar point long before 9/11 when he introduced Tenzin Gyatso, His Holiness the Fourteenth Dalai Lama of Tibet, at a public lecture in November 1998. "Curiously," Rogers stated then, "my personal introduction to the Dalai Lama was by way of television—in a hotel room."

> I was in Washington, DC, preparing for a conference on children and the media and was looking for a certain news program when I happened upon His Holiness saying, "Someone else's action should not determine your response." I was so intrigued, I wrote down those words, turned off the television, and thought about nothing else the whole evening. "Someone else's actions should not determine your response."
>
> It sounds so simple, doesn't it? And yet what if someone else's action should be shouting angry words at us or hitting us with a rotten tomato! That doesn't affect what we do in response? Not if our compassion is genuine. Not if our love is the kind the Dalai Lama advocates.[28]

With the kind of love taught by the Dalai Lama, Rogers did not join the chorus of citizens calling for the United States to exact revenge on the terrorists. He did not allow their violence to make him violent; their actions did not determine his response. Refusing to stoke the rising war fever, and still concerned about child abuse and war, Rogers instead recorded a series of public service announcements designed to assist parents in dealing with children who were frightened, worried, or confused. More particularly, Rogers encouraged parents to help their children find the helpers in violent times, to become helpers themselves, to do everything possible to keep their children safe, and perhaps most important of all, to "help them express their feelings in ways that will bring healing in many different neighborhoods."[29] The last thing the world needed was more people who expressed their feelings through violence. True to his pacifist convictions, Rogers responded to terrorism by calling us to spread peace across the land.

Not everyone followed Rogers's counsel. President George W. Bush favored fighting violence with violence and quickly authorized the War on Terror, promising to hunt down and kill terrorists who threatened the United States. Of course, rather than doing the dirty work himself, he relied partly on the soldier-parents of young children. Given Rogers's convictions about child abuse and war, he must have seen the president as yet another child abuser in a long line of presidents and politicians.

The contrast between Fred Rogers and President Bush became remarkably clear in July 2002, when the president awarded Rogers the Presidential Medal of Freedom, the nation's highest honor for civilians. In his comments at the awards ceremony, President Bush extolled Rogers's teaching of unconditional love. Footage from the event shows the ceremony was a touching event for Rogers and the president, but a speech delivered the very same day suggests that Rogers's message of unconditional love had no real effect on the president or his foreign policy. Speaking to his corporate supporters on Wall Street, the president confidently assured them he was "hunting down the terrorists who seek to sow chaos. . . . We will not relent until the cold-blooded killers are found, disrupted and defeated."[30]

Rogers opposed the president's war, and he did so publicly, though gently. In the month before he received the medal, as the War on Terror was well underway, Rogers stood before the newly minted graduates of Dartmouth College—which he had attended between high school and Rollins College in Florida—and sang them a Neighborhood song "meant for the child in each of us." After singing "It's You I Like," Rogers carefully explained that when he says, "It's you I like," he means "that deep part of you that allows you to stand for those things without which humankind cannot survive. Love that conquers hate, peace that rises triumphant over war, and justice that proves more powerful than greed." It was that deep part Rogers asked the graduates to tap into and draw from as they faced the future—which, of course, included material opportunities to advance the War on Terror. "So in all that you do, in all of your life," he concluded, "I wish you the strength and the grace to make those choices which will allow you and your neighbor to become the best of whoever you are."[31] The language was subtle, but the words were clear: Fred Rogers was yet again subverting the nation's call to war.

Nevertheless, subverting war—any war—was never enough for Fred Rogers. Although he saw the absence of war as a necessary condition for peace, he did not find it a sufficient one. "Peace means more than the absence of war!" he believed.[32] While other pacifists who make this argument typically follow it by speaking of the need for justice, Rogers was not inclined to do so. In fact, the word *justice* does not seem to be present in any episodes of *Mister Rogers' Neighborhood.* Still, Rogers had a highly nuanced view of loving relationships, of treating others with the respect and dignity due them, and so his vision of peace demanded not only the absence of war but also the presence of relationships of deep love—with ourselves, animals, and the world. With this expansive vision, Rogers used his program and other venues to address many other obstacles to peace, such as racial discrimination, poverty, gender inequality, the killing of animals, commercialism, and environmental degradation. As he did so, he revealed his faith-fueled belief that overcoming these obstacles—the subject of this book's next section—will help create the lasting peace that God intends for all creation.

PART 2

Peace as More Than
the Absence of War

François Clemmons debuted as Officer Clemmons a few months after inner-city riots erupted across the nation following the assassination of Martin Luther King Jr.

Chapter 7

"A Black Brother"

Race and Diversity

*F*red Rogers did not march in the modern civil rights movement led by Martin Luther King Jr. Unlike many white liberals of his day, Rogers did not attend the March on Washington for Jobs and Freedom in 1963, sign up for the famous Selma to Montgomery March in 1965, or actively participate in local rallies for the cause. Nevertheless, Rogers's public and private actions over time suggest he agreed with King's belief that shattering racial discrimination was essential to peacemaking, that peace required unity among people of different colors.[1] Although Rogers was not a street protestor, he was certainly a quiet advocate of racial integration.

An Early Role Model

When Rogers was about four years old, his mother and father invited George Allen to live in their home. Allen was an African American teenager whose mother had worked as a domestic for the Rogers family. She had just died, and Allen's father did not feel equipped to rear him. So Rogers's parents arranged for Allen to live at their home in exchange for his help around the house, including work as the family's chauffeur.

"He probably wouldn't have thought of himself as a child-care worker," Rogers recalled, "but he was 12 years older than I was, and I was an only child." Allen spent lots of time with Fred throughout his childhood, introducing him to the wonders of jazz, photography, and airplanes. Allen also had ambitions far beyond his work in the Rogers home. With dreams of becoming a pilot, he used the money he earned as a drummer in local dance bands to take flight lessons at the Latrobe airport. He was so good at flying that he became a flight instructor in the late 1930s, giving lessons not only to Civil Air Patrol students from nearby St. Vincent College, but also to young Fred.

When Rogers was in high school, Allen taught him how to fly a Piper Cub. "I call that care," Rogers later stated. "He was so enthusiastic about flying. I know that's why I wanted to learn. The best teacher in the world is somebody who loves what he or she does and just loves it in front of you."[2]

Despite his pacifism, Rogers never stopped bragging about Allen's service during World War II. Allen was an accomplished pilot by the time the war began, and the Army recognized his talents by sending him to the flight school based at Tuskegee Institute in Alabama. The Army had established the segregated school to train African American pilots for the war effort (much to the chagrin of NAACP attorney Thurgood Marshall), and Allen became one of its main instructors. When he ended his career there, he was serving as squadron commander at the primary flight school, responsible for training many of the pilots who flew so successfully against the Axis powers.

Rogers publicly lauded Allen's accomplishments, most notably during an appearance on *The Arsenio Hall Show*. The talk show host was known for being pleasant, and more than a few individuals, including comedian Robin Williams, observed that Hall even looked like a black Mister Rogers. As for Rogers, he truly liked Hall and used his appearance on the distinctively black show not only to praise Allen's wartime record but also to express his deep appreciation for Allen's presence in his early life. "He turned out to be a real model for me," Rogers said. And with a nod to those who drew "brotherly" connections between him and Arsenio, Rogers added, "So I had a black brother even then!"[3]

For Rogers, Allen was not so much "the help" or "the chauffeur" as he was a playmate. Allen was an employee of the Rogers family, just as his mother and other African American workers had been, but Rogers spoke of Allen as one of his earliest friends and playmates. Significantly, his "black brother," too, had positive memories of his life with the Rogerses. In a 1999 letter to Fred, Allen wrote that he would "never forget all the Rogers family and the inspiration they gave me in molding my life." He also described Fred's parents as "wonderful," and claimed God had placed the Rogers family "on this Earth at the right [time]."[4] Allen and Rogers continued their friendship for the rest of their lives and sometimes visited together on the *Mister Rogers' Neighborhood* set.

Perhaps it was his early experiences with Allen that encouraged Rogers to join and later chair the Interfaith and Race Relations Committee at Rollins College. Like other towns in Florida, Winter Park was home to Jim Crow institutions that were understaffed, underfunded, and unable to meet the needs of the town's African American residents. Nearby Eatonville, an all-black town incorporated not long after Reconstruction, was also unable to meet the needs of its poor citizens. Rogers's committee focused its efforts on Winter Park and Eatonville, addressing race-specific problems not by calling for desegregation but rather by seeking to improve the quality of racially segregated institutions.

This accommodationist approach—working with rather than against the system of segregation—is evident in the annual report Rogers penned for the 1950-1951 school year. Writing as chair, Rogers reported that the committee was involved in helping all-black institutions in Winter Park and nearby communities. For example, the committee visited and provided part-time teaching for the Robert Hungerford Normal and Industrial School in Eatonville—an all-black school modeled on the Tuskegee Institute founded by Booker T. Washington. The committee also "treated 96 little colored kiddies . . . to ice cream and cake for their Thanksgiving party at their Colored Day Nursery," furnished fluorescent lighting for a town library designated for African Americans, and solicited funds for a racially segregated nursing home that would also act as a hospital clinic. "Winter Park is in dire need of such a building since there is no colored doctor in the town," Rogers wrote.[5]

The committee could have chosen different tactics in addressing racial issues at this point. For example, it could have supported the Florida NAACP in its widely publicized campaign to raise funds for the defendants in the infamous 1949 Groveland rape case, in which four young black men stood accused—falsely, it turned out—of raping a white woman. But Rogers's report did not even mention the NAACP or any of its efforts to fight segregation and racial violence in Florida.

Although the Interfaith and Race Relations Committee under Rogers's leadership was far from comprehensive in its approach to racial issues, it advanced work markedly different in tone and content from the college's recent history. In 1947, one year before Rogers arrived on campus, the student council had voted unanimously to cancel a football game with Ohio Wesleyan University because the northern team included an African American player (Kenneth Woodward). Although disappointing to the school's president, the decision to cancel was strongly encouraged by the school's trustees. Rollins was such a bastion of Southern white privilege that the work undertaken by Rogers and his committee must have appeared to some of his fellow students as downright radical.

African Americans in the Neighborhood

Fred Rogers's sensitivity about race issues, partly rooted in his respect for George Allen and in his co-curricular work at Rollins, came to expression the first week *Mister Rogers' Neighborhood* went national, not long after the summer of 1967's devastating riots in Detroit. The raging violence in Detroit captured the nation's attention for five long days, beginning on July 23, when white police officers conducted a raid on an after-hours club located at the corner of Twelfth Street and Clairmount Avenue in one of the city's predominately black neighborhoods. Inside the club were eighty-two men and women celebrating the return of two soldiers from Vietnam. As the officers attempted to arrest the group, a crowd gathered outside to protest the raid. Local residents had long resented the rampant police abuse in their neighborhood, and this time the tension erupted with acts of vandalism followed by looting, arson, and gun violence. With local police unable to reestablish order, Governor George Romney sent the Michigan National Guard, and President Lyndon Johnson ordered the deployment of Army troops on city streets. When the riots ended, forty-three people lay dead; most were African American residents, the youngest of whom was Tonya Blanding, age 4, who was killed by gunfire from a National Guard tank.

The Detroit riots provided part of the backdrop to the first week of *Mister Rogers' Neighborhood*, and so too did white backlash. By the time the program went national, white backlash against the civil rights movement, Malcolm X, the Nation of Islam, the Black Power movement, urban riots, and related issues and events had already taken the form of "white flight." Fearful for their lives and property, white residents fled their city neighborhoods in unprecedented numbers and relocated to bourgeoning suburbs, where they believed safety and stability awaited them.

As whites were bolting from African Americans, Mister Rogers opened the front door and welcomed them into his television home. In the first week's fourth episode, he enjoys a visit from Mrs. Saunders, an African American teacher in the Neighborhood, and a small interracial group of her students. "I'm glad to see you," he says as he greets them with a welcoming smile. "Come on in!"[6] They sit together at the table, talk a bit, sing a few songs, and then say goodbye. It's a simple visit that, when placed in context, delivers a hard-hitting message: Whites and blacks live and play together in the Neighborhood. Although the Neighborhood may have a suburban or small-town feel—and it does feel like much of white suburbia—whites don't run away from blacks there; they welcome them into their homes as friends and neighbors. Importantly, the reverse happens too. In later episodes, African American neighbors welcome Mister Rogers into their homes and (racially integrated) schools. The Neighborhood built by Fred Rogers, it turns out, is a long way from Winter Park, Florida.

Fighting Riots with Officer Clemmons

Less than two months after the broadcast of Mrs. Saunders's visit to Mister Rogers's television house, James Earl Ray murdered Martin Luther King Jr. at the Lorraine Motel in Memphis. In the wake of the assassination, riots erupted in black neighborhoods across the nation, from Newark to Los Angeles. Stores, homes, and entire neighborhoods went up in flames as troops from the Army and the National Guard sought to reestablish order. Some of the worst rioting took place in Washington, DC, where President Johnson deployed over 13,000 federal troops and local residents saw twelve of their own killed, mostly in burning buildings. Pittsburgh, where *Mister Rogers' Neighborhood* was filmed, was not immune to the violence, and riots broke out in the city's Hill District, once one of the nation's most prestigious African American neighborhoods.

As televised images of police officers beating and shooting blacks flooded U.S. households during the summer of 1968, Fred Rogers began to develop a completely different image for his viewers: a startling image of a black police officer keeping everyone safe in the Neighborhood. Rogers's radical idea came to fruition on August 1, 1968, when François Clemmons debuted as Officer Clemmons on *Mister Rogers' Neighborhood.*

Rogers and Clemmons had met a year earlier at Third Presbyterian Church in Pittsburgh. Clemmons was the solo tenor in the choir, and Rogers's wife, Joanne, was in the alto section. Like Joanne, Fred quickly grew to appreciate Clemmons's rich musical talents. "Fred came to everything I sang at in Pittsburgh," Clemmons recalls. "He loved my singing."[7] Impressed by his talents, Rogers decided to get to know Clemmons personally, inviting him to lunch at Stouffers in downtown Pittsburgh and then back to the television station. "He introduced me to everyone as if I were the King of England," Clemmons says, adding that the lavish attention was "disconcerting to someone from the ghetto."

Clemmons had grown up in a black ghetto in Youngstown, Ohio, after his mother had left behind her husband (and their abusive relationship) in Tuscaloosa, Alabama. He remembers his mother singing all the time and encouraging him to sing for visitors who came to their house. One of those visitors, Mary Lou Davis, was so struck by Clemmons's raw talents that she arranged for him to take music lessons for several years. The lessons paid off handsomely when Clemmons earned a music scholarship to Oberlin College in Ohio, but the move to the highly selective liberal arts college was not without its challenges. "Growing up in a black ghetto, where your neighbors were black, your minister was black, your doctor was black, the apothecary was black," Clemmons found that "coming to Oberlin was quite a cultural shock."[8] But he endured the shock and eventually flourished in the music program, even winning acceptance into a master's program in music at Carnegie Mellon University in Pittsburgh. It was while he was a student there that he joined the choir at Third Presbyterian and met Fred Rogers.

At the end of their first visit together, Rogers invited Clemmons to come back to the studio any time. After Clemmons failed to return in a timely manner—a trip back to the studio had not struck him as enticing, let alone promising for his career—Rogers called him on the phone and asked him where he had been. "Franc [pronounced "France"], is something wrong?" he asked. Clemmons assured him nothing was wrong, that he had just been busy and would swing by the station sometime soon. But he was not quite sure how to interpret Rogers's attention and persistence. "I don't think he's gay," he remembers thinking at the time. At the very least, Rogers seemed "very fatherly and a little presumptuous in his care," and Clemmons was unaccustomed to such behavior.

Rogers would not let the talented Clemmons disappear, and by the summer of 1968 he invited Clemmons to appear as a regular on *Mister Rogers' Neighborhood.* "You have a beautiful voice," he said, "and I think you could find a positive place here in the Neighborhood." Clemmons accepted, but not without a condition. "Fred," he replied, "I will be very happy to do your program as long as it doesn't interfere with my singing." These days Clemmons laughs at his youthful hubris. "What in the hell was I thinking of?" he says.

Before his debut, Clemmons and Rogers talked about the role of Officer Clemmons in light of the riots, the problem of race relations in the United States, and the negative image many black children had of police officers in their neighborhoods. As a child of the ghetto, Clemmons had experienced the police as corrupt authorities who dealt mostly in bribes, so he told Rogers he was skeptical that a police officer was the best way to introduce him as a regular cast member. But Rogers's view prevailed—he could be surprisingly inflexible—and Clemmons soon appeared in a police uniform in the Neighborhood.

"I have a friend by the name of Officer Clemmons, who is a policeman," Mister Rogers says in the debut episode. "He helps take care of people. That's what policemen do. He's a very special person." It is indeed clear that Officer Clemmons is not your everyday patrol officer. He's a "special patrolman"— it says so on his side patch—and his general assignment is to "instruct other policemen how to help people be safe," especially when crossing the street and driving cars. He has other duties too, and in the first episode he shows up in the Neighborhood of Make-Believe to issue a permit for a street fair. Remarkably, he also sings while working his beat; in this first episode, he sings "You Are Special" not just once, but twice.[9]

Reflecting back on his neighborhood beat, Clemmons says, "My friends used to tease me that I was an officer without a whistle, without a bully club, and without a gun, and that I sang all over the place." That was a fair point to make: Officer Clemmons is always more of a singing peace officer than a street police officer. He helps neighbors remain peaceful and quiet; he never beats, clubs, shoots, or even blows his whistle at anybody; and he often smiles and sings.

While all this may suggest a certain fluffiness to Officer Clemmons, the role delivered yet another sharply pointed message for its context: Through Officer Clemmons, Rogers showed his white viewers that, contrary to the message in the constant barrage of news reports about race riots in 1968, not all blacks were rioters and looters, just moments away from being shoved into a waiting paddy wagon driven by white officers. More positively stated, Rogers used Officer Clemmons to demonstrate that African Americans could and did occupy trusted positions of authority on which all of us rely for welfare and safety—and, more generally, that African Americans like Officer Clemmons were really good neighbors: trustworthy, helpful, and reliable. No doubt, there was a lesson here about police officers in general (they were not always shooting people), but the stronger message was about race and ethnicity.

A Wade-In

The role of Officer Clemmons took another highly symbolic turn the following year when Mister Rogers showed up at his TV house carrying a wading pool. Once again, context matters: Five years earlier, wading had attracted national headlines when a pro-integrationist and interracial group staged wade-ins at a public beach, a "whites only" area, in St. Augustine, Florida. Formerly home to a famous slave market, St. Augustine had long known racial strife, and June 22, 1964, added to that ignoble history when an angry gang of whites used their fists and clubs to assault the interracial group holding the wade-in, sending more than a handful to the hospital. Although the violence halted the integrationists' efforts, they returned again seven days later, this time with protection from state police officers and their dogs, and held another wade-in.

Mister Rogers held his own wade-in on a program that originally aired on May 9, 1969, just after the first anniversary of the death of Martin Luther

King Jr. In the memorable episode, Rogers enters his television house hold-ing a wading pool (he calls it a "pond") and explains that on hot days he enjoys soaking his feet in cool water. Outside in the yard, as he is using the hose to spray his feet, he spots Officer Clemmons nearby and invites him to sit down and join him. "It looks enjoyable, but I don't have a towel or any-thing," Clemmons says. Rogers suggests they share the same towel. "Okay!" Clemmons replies. "This is going to be a beautiful day!" As he takes off his boots and socks, the camera focuses on four feet soaking in the pool—a strik-ing image of pasty white and light black.[10]

The symbolism of the moment would have been clear to racially sensi-tive and discerning adult viewers. It was certainly clear to Clemmons at the time: "I saw it as integration—Fred showing blacks and whites doing things together." Rogers was also demonstrating that the color of people's skin was not as important as "how people feel about each other." Rogers had a black friend, Clemmons had a white friend, "and we were friends because we cared about each other, not because of our color." For Clemmons, "that's what people putting their feet in the water meant."

The message of the wade-in was thoroughly integrationist, and it marked Rogers as squarely positioned in the then-contested tradition of Martin Luther King Jr. and other mainstream civil rights leaders and organizations. A raging battle for the soul of the civil rights movement at the time saw Black Power activists, with their embrace of racial separatism and the use of "any means necessary," pitted against the old guard, which still favored integration and the use of only nonviolent means. Rogers took sides in the battle, favoring not the young separatists in the Student Nonviolent Coordinating Committee (SNCC) and other groups, but rather the traditional integrationists in the Southern Chris-tian Leadership Conference (SCLC) and the NAACP. The wade-in suggests that Rogers was a mainstream civil rights advocate opposed to the militant agenda set forth by individuals such as Stokely Carmichael, H. Rap Brown, and others.

The wade-in's integrationist message was also embodied and reflected in the close personal relationship that François Clemmons and Fred Rogers cultivated as the years rolled on. An odd couple of sorts, the two spent lots of time together away from the set, talking about everything from politics (both opposed the Vietnam War) to family problems (Clemmons shared his estrangement from his biological father, and Rogers spoke of his loneliness as a child). Clemmons also offered Rogers insight into the lives of African Americans, the poor, and urban ghetto dwellers—lives foreign to the wealthy white man from small-town Latrobe. In turn, Rogers provided Clemmons with a deep sense of personal security and a relationship that was "healthy, wholesome, intense . . . loving, supporting, nurturing, and long-term."

"He was my surrogate daddy," says Clemmons, who had his own key to Rogers's office. "He really had a way of making me feel very special." It took a few years for that special feeling to sink in, but Clemmons experienced it in a dramatic, perhaps mystical, way shortly after he moved to New York City in 1970. During a trip back to Pittsburgh, Clemmons visited the set just in time to watch the closing of an episode, as Rogers was saying, "I like you just the way you are, and you make every day a special day for me just by being you." Clemmons remembers the moment: "I was standing on the other side of the studio, but I swear he was looking into my soul. And I stood there and I looked and I looked, and he kept looking at me. . . . When he was out away from the camera, I said, 'Fred, were you talking to me?' He said, 'Franc, I've been talking to you for two years; you finally heard me today.' That was how we bonded. I knew I was special to him."

Clemmons had experienced that same feeling—a deep personal connection—when he met Martin Luther King Jr. at Oberlin in 1965. King was on his way to deliver the commencement speech, the high point of the academic year, when Clemmons and his friend spotted him walking across campus. The students dashed over to the famous civil rights leader and immediately engaged him in conversation. "He was so patient, receptive," and he had "the warmest, deepest, most blessed eyes," Clemmons recalls. Clemmons told King he was a tenor on a full music scholarship, that he wanted to sing one day at the Metropolitan Opera, and that he and the Oberlin choir had recently visited the USSR. "When I finally came up for air, he said, 'Well, keep on keeping on, young man. We need what you're doing. I'm very proud of you.'" It was an empowering moment, says Clemmons, "because I did not always get that message from Oberlin."

That's the way Clemmons experienced Fred Rogers too—as inspiring and encouraging when other important figures in his life were failing him. "When he was alive, in some ways he was like Dr. King to me," Clemmons states. "We found a commonality that was a soul grip." The "soul grip," formed in part by their gifted creativity and shared love of music, led to jealousy and resentment among some staff members who longed for a similar relationship with Rogers, but the bond between the two friends continued uninterrupted.

The Limits of Interracial Life in the Neighborhood

Nevertheless, Clemmons did not always find Rogers inspiring and encouraging. Even in matters related to race and ethnicity on *Mister Rogers' Neighborhood*, he feels Rogers did not accomplish as much as he might have.

"I think he should have done a lot more," Clemmons says. "For example, almost every time Lady Aberlin did an opera and a love scene, I was never her love partner."

The topic of interracial love and marriage was popular in U.S. society and culture in the 1950s and 1960s. It was so significant in 1958 that journalist Mike Wallace made sure to include it in an interview about race relations with Martin Luther King Jr. When Wallace asked King to comment on interracial marriage ("the underlying fear of white Southerners," as Wallace put it), the civil rights leader replied that, while he doubted the possibility of "mass intermarriage," human freedom includes the right to marry whomever one chooses. "When any society says that I cannot marry a certain person, that society has cut off a segment of my freedom," King stated.[11] That was a radical position in significant parts of the United States in 1958, but just nine years later, the Supreme Court delivered a famous and widely publicized ruling in *Loving v. Virginia* that essentially agreed with King's earlier position. On June 12, 1967, the court unanimously ruled that the right to marry a person of another race "resides with the individual and cannot be infringed by the state."[12]

A few years after this ruling, Clemmons began to imagine the possibility of depicting interracial love on *Mister Rogers' Neighborhood*. More particularly, he thought it would be "helpful and realistic" for Rogers to show him and Betty Aberlin as an interracial couple in one of the program's colorful operas. "I mentioned it [to Rogers] several times," Clemmons recalls. "I mentioned it several times to Lady Aberlin, and she was *totally* open to it."

But Rogers, who wrote all the operas, never dared to couple the two. "Fred was always receptive," Clemmons says. "He was never hostile. He just never did it." Clemmons assumes that Rogers was overly concerned about alienating socially conservative viewers who still held negative attitudes toward interracial relationships.

Rogers did, however, accept Clemmons's invitation to visit him in his racially diverse neighborhood near the edge of Harlem. He had moved there in 1970 to sing with the Metropolitan Opera Studio after winning an audition back in Pittsburgh. Clemmons extended the invitation to Rogers partly out of concern about the breadth and depth of racial diversity on *Mister Rogers' Neighborhood*, a concern he heard from numerous parents as he traveled the country for *Neighborhood*-related events. "You don't really have a diverse community," they told him. The Neighborhood was like "being in the suburbs," far distant from the racial diversity in many inner-city neighborhoods.

The criticism was partly true. *Mister Rogers' Neighborhood* was certainly no *Sesame Street*, whose 1969 debut program featured Gordon, an African

American teacher sporting a hip suit and a cool beard and mustache, as the main human character in an urban neighborhood populated largely by adults and children of color. Perhaps even more remarkably, the debut of *Sesame Street* showed a puppet family whose mother and father appeared to be an interracial couple—at least as interracial as puppets can be. With its urban, hip, and racially inclusive sensibilities, *Sesame Street* seemed light years away from the show hosted by a white gentleman who was always clean-shaven and wearing a respectable sweater, tie, and gold collar clasp.

Yet to be fair, even in its first year of production, before Officer Clemmons appeared for the first time, *Mister Rogers' Neighborhood* had included segments depicting a black schoolteacher, a black master drummer, black preschool and elementary school children, an interracial school, a black salesman, a black tap dancer, African folk dancers, a Chinese American scientist, a black florist, a Japanese origami artist, and Native Americans. It's not that *Mister Rogers' Neighborhood* did not have a diverse community even in its earliest days; it's just that viewers had to look for it harder than they did when they watched *Sesame Street*. This was true especially in the first year because all of the *Neighborhood*'s main human characters—Mister Rogers, Lady Aberlin, Chef Brockett, Handyman Negri, John Reardon, and Mr. McFeely—were white.

With this comparatively shallow diversity in mind, Clemmons encouraged Rogers and the *Neighborhood* film crew to visit him at his apartment on West 101st Street in New York City. He lived on a richly diverse block and thought it important for Rogers to experience and show the depth of life beyond the Neighborhood. Rogers accepted the invitation, brought his film crew, and handed out balls and roller skates to neighborhood children. With permission from the city, Rogers's production team also roped off the street and opened up the fire hydrant. "I wanted to show something different from a small town with a brook running through it," Clemmons recalls. Rogers later used the film of children at play on *Mister Rogers' Neighborhood*, and Clemmons could not have been more pleased with this additional attention to issues of racial diversity and urban living.

Clemmons continued to appear on the program throughout his longtime residence in New York City, cementing his role as the first person of color to become a regular, major, long-term character on a children's program. There were other persons of color in the early years of the *Neighborhood*. Joey Hollingsworth—a talented African Canadian tap dancer, actor, and singer—made at least ten appearances between 1968 and 1973. But his role never blossomed into a major character like that of Officer Clemmons. The same is true of Marilyn Barnett, an African American physical education teacher and, later, school principal; Jose Cisneros, the top assistant at Chef Brockett's bakery; Keith David, an African American carpenter from Southwood; and Yoshi Ito, whom François Clemmons had recommended Rogers hire. Not until 1975 did the next person of color join the ranks of the Neighborhood at Clemmons's level. But when that happened, Rogers made another (subtle) splash.

An African American Mayor

One of the biggest advances in the civil rights movement at the time centered on the elections of African Americans to political office. On November 7, 1967, Carl B. Stokes, then the first black Democrat elected to Ohio's state legislature, became the first African American mayor of a major U.S. city. The city was Cleveland, a mere two-hour drive from Pittsburgh, and his election attracted national attention. Richard Hatcher of Gary, Indiana, was also elected on the same day, and blacks across the nation became inspired all the more to run for political office. Arguably the most exciting event occurred in June 1973, when a city clerk in Compton, California, beat the incumbent mayor in a fiercely contested election. As the successful candidate, Doris Davis became the first African American woman mayor of a smaller city. It would take fourteen years before an African American woman would become mayor of a major city. But the glass ceiling had been broken.

In 1975, Fred Rogers had in mind his own mayoral election or appointment—one far more radical than those in Ohio and Indiana, and one more in line with the radical voters in California. Rogers introduced viewers to his jolting idea in an episode originally broadcast on March 4, 1975, not even two years after the election of Doris Davis. In the historic episode, we meet Maggie Stewart, a light-skinned black woman, for the first time; she's making flowers out of foam at Elsie Neal's craft shop. Rogers carries a few flowers back to his television house, and as he begins his transition into the Neighborhood of Make-Believe segment, he says that King Friday and his family will be visiting Queen Sara's hometown of Westwood. "Maggie Stewart could be the mayor of Westwood," he adds. "That would be nice."[13] With those simple words, Mister Rogers arranged for a black woman to be mayor of Westwood, a friendly community just to the west of the Neighborhood of Make-Believe. There was no election, no announcement of an appointment, and no swearing-in; Rogers drew no attention to the significance that Stewart was black and female. However understated, the arrival of Mayor Maggie delivered another powerful message about race.

As her character develops through the years, we learn that Mayor Maggie is a very important woman; she's in charge of Westwood, just as King Friday XIII is in charge of the Neighborhood of Make-Believe. Indeed, although they come from different body politics—she from a democracy, he from a patriarchal monarchy—Mayor Maggie is King Friday's political and social equal. So just one of Mayor Maggie's lessons, as developed by Rogers, is that black women are as important, smart, capable, and reliable as white men. That was not a standard message in 1975, on television or anywhere else.

Another important dimension of Mayor Maggie's storyline is that her community of Westwood is full of good people who embrace and serve her as their chosen leader. With Mayor Maggie as a beloved figure, Rogers's message is loud and clear: Despite news about the prevalence of racism, the country includes good people, even white people, who have the ability and wisdom to see black women as political leaders deserving of love and respect. This message takes fascinating form when we learn that Mayor Maggie's assistant is a white man, Associate Mayor Aber (played by the blond and blue-eyed Chuck Aber). That coupling, of course, suggests not only that Aber is a good guy but, more pointedly, that black women could be professionally superior to white men—no doubt a difficult message for some viewers still steeped in the unneighborly ways of racial prejudice and discrimination.

Diversity after Mayor Maggie's Arrival

For about two decades, Rogers did not add any other persons of color to the roster of major and long-term cast members of *Mister Rogers' Neighborhood*. But one of the most significant additions in the late 1990s was the Hispanic actor Tony Chiroldes, who was cast first as the owner-manager of Tony's Costume, Book, and Toy Shop in the Neighborhood, and later as Hula Mouse, the royal mouse in the Neighborhood of Make-Believe. Chiroldes was not the first Hispanic cast member, but especially significant about his characters, Tony and Hula Mouse, was the way they spoke Spanish. As Chiroldes remembers, he and Rogers "treasured the fact that the conversations with the Hula Mouse . . . and Tony . . . would flow in English and Spanish without an overt need to translate every phrase or word." Flowing freely from Spanish to English and from English to Spanish, the conversations sounded truly authentic. "In fact," Chiroldes says, "*that* was another reason why I wanted to be in the show: it never spoke down to its multicultural audience."[14]

Rogers consistently showed and celebrated racial diversity in other ways throughout the remaining years of *Mister Rogers' Neighborhood*, especially through arts, crafts, and food. From 1975 until the end of the program, Rogers highlighted Indian dancing, Chinese pottery and calligraphy, Japanese origami, African American jazz and spirituals, and Native American dancing and pottery among so many other things. One of the most creative, or peculiar, nods to diversity was the appearance of the Spanish-speaking Fortune Cookie Man in the Neighborhood of Make-Believe in 1998, and one of the most amusing occurred in 1985, when Rogers tried his hand at breakdancing.

In episode 1543, originally broadcast in February 1985, Mister Rogers enjoys a visit from Jermaine Vaughan, a twelve-year-old African American who lives in the Neighborhood. Vaughan arrives outside Mister Rogers's home carrying a boom box and a large piece of cardboard—essential ingredients for demonstrating his expertise in breakdancing. Before he shows off his moves, he tries to teach Mister Rogers how to do "the wave" and the "moonwalk," popularized by Michael Jackson two years earlier. Unsurprisingly, Rogers's wave doesn't really wave, and his moonwalk is downright earthbound, but he enjoys watching Vaughan execute his moves with fluidity and precision. "You're a mighty special neighbor of mine," he says as Vaughan finishes his routine. "I'm glad to know you!"[15]

Another Type of Diversity—and Love

Episode 1543 is especially striking because it also demonstrates Rogers's commitment to a type of diversity that includes individuals with physical challenges. Rogers had a deep and wide understanding of diversity—he did not see it as race-specific—and he used his program to show and celebrate differences in race and ethnicity, religion and class, and age and abilities (mental, emotional, and physical). With this rich understanding of diversity, Rogers designed episode 1543 to include not only Jermaine Vaughan's exploits in breakdancing but also Chrissy Thompson's plans to become a medical secretary.

Thompson is physically challenged; she wears braces on her legs and walks with crutches as a result of spina bifida. Longtime viewers first met her in the mid-1970s, when she and her sister appeared as the granddaughters of Mr. and Mrs. McFeely. In one of those appearances, she sits on Mister Rogers's porch and shares a moving story about a little girl who grew so angry with her own leg braces that she put them away in the attic. But after seeing Chrissy walk so well on *Mister Rogers' Neighborhood*, the little girl crawled up to the attic, retrieved her braces, started walking again, and even began to run. Near the end of this episode, Mister Rogers asks whether any of us become angry when we discover there are certain things we cannot be or do. He does too, he says, but then adds, "There's only one person like you in all the world, and I like you just the way you are."[16]

That familiar message appeared in yet another moving episode focused on a physically challenged child. In the February 1981 episode, ten-year-old Jeff Erlanger, sitting in his wheelchair, visits with Mister Rogers as he sits on the porch steps of his television house. Jeff demonstrates great skill as he takes tight turns with his electric wheelchair, and Mister Rogers tells him how proud he is before asking Jeff to share his story. In an unscripted and unrehearsed conversation, we learn that Jeff became quadriplegic following surgery for a spinal tumor and that he continued to experience physical issues, such as stomach problems, requiring surgery. "You have a lot of things happen to you when you're handicapped—and sometimes when you're not handicapped," Jeff says. He and Mister Rogers talk about what Jeff does in those times when he's feeling down and out, and the two end their time together by singing "It's You I Like." Authentic beyond authentic, the scene of Jeff and Mister Rogers looking at each other and gently singing ("It's you I like . . . the way you are right now, the way down deep inside you") is one of the most powerful moments in the entire history of *Mister Rogers' Neighborhood*.[17]

The message "I like you just the way you are" is also front and center when the adult Chrissy Thompson makes a return visit to Mister Rogers's front porch. As they sit there and chat together, Chrissy, still wearing her braces and using her crutches, says that people look at her in "different ways." "Some people are ready to accept you," she says. "Other people aren't. But what people have to remember is that everybody has limitations, and it doesn't matter if some are more obvious than others." In talking about what's most helpful to her, she quickly suggests that people who care about her are the best help available. "One person who cares about you just the way you are," Rogers adds.[18] If we can find one person like that, we can flourish despite our challenges.

Love is what Chrissy and Mister Rogers are talking about—and love, in the final analysis, is the underlying philosophy and theology of Fred Rogers's long-term embrace of diversity. To reiterate: As an attitude and practice, love simply means accepting others just as they are, including, not in spite of, all the ways they are different from us.

The inextricable connection between love and diversity for Rogers becomes explicit in a week of 1987 episodes devoted to the theme of "alike and different." In the first program, just after Mister Rogers has talked about alike and different things, Maggie Stewart visits him in his television house. The unstated but obvious point is that while Stewart is like Mister Rogers (they both have heads and bodies, for example), she's also unlike him (she's female, and her skin color is darker than his). But the most important point of this particular segment, and indeed the entire week, emerges when Stewart uses her lovely alto voice to sing about love: "When your heart has room for everybody, then your heart is full of love."[19] At its finest, diversity is not the result of a court order or an administrative mandate; it's the natural result of loving others just as they are.

A Final Wade-In

In 1990, Fred Rogers, armed with his understanding of love and diversity, joined his company, Family Communications, in successfully suing the White Knights of the Ku Klux Klan and three men to stop them from using tape-recorded telephone messages that imitated *Mister Rogers' Neighborhood* music and Rogers's own speech patterns. The messages, which callers heard when dialing a number that had been circulated among children and youth in the Kansas City area, were blatantly racist and antigay. "The messages are of racism, white supremacy and bigotry—the antithesis of everything Rogers and Family Communications Inc. stand for," said Rogers's attorney, Cynthia Kernick.[20] It was one of the few times Rogers took legal action against individuals and groups who used his popularity to advance their own agendas and causes. The rarity of the action revealed the intensity of Rogers's commitment to diversity and his opposition to hate groups and their racist, homophobic, and exclusive actions.

Three years later, François Clemmons, no stranger to the horrors of the Klan, made his final appearance on *Mister Rogers' Neighborhood*. He appeared during a special series centered on love, and his second-to-last scene included a wading pool, echoing back to the wade-in of 1968. Donning his police officer suit one last time—he was just "filling in" at the local precinct—Clemmons joins Rogers in the front yard as he is soaking his tired feet in a wading pool and thinking of different ways people say "I love you." Rogers invites Clemmons to soak his feet too, and the gentle police officer accepts the offer. There they are again—white and black feet, alike and yet different, soaking in the same pool and reminding us once more that what matters most is a little bit of love between two people.

In Clemmons's last scene, he stops by Mister Rogers's house to sing a song he'll perform at a concert later in the day. But it's not just any song— it's "Swing Low, Sweet Chariot," a spiritual about going home to be with Jesus. Standing on his porch, Rogers beams and sways as Clemmons, now dressed in a suit and tie, sings the spiritual just for his friend:

> If you get there before I do,
> Coming for to carry me home,
> Tell all my friends I'm coming too,
> Coming for to carry me home.

His performance is so compelling that Rogers even joins in singing the spiritual as it comes to a close. "Oh, I love your singing," he says as Clemmons waves goodbye and walks away.[21] In real life, he was leaving the program partly so he could devote more time to a musical ensemble he had founded in 1984—the Harlem Spiritual Ensemble. He had earlier brought his two worlds together when *Mister Rogers' Neighborhood* featured the ensemble in a 1991 episode in which Mister Rogers visits the singers as they practice several selections. But the pressures of directing the group, which traveled across the globe, finally led Clemmons to step away from his work on *Mister Rogers' Neighborhood*. As he departed, the legacy he had created meant that there would be no more wade-ins in the Neighborhood. Instead, there would be a Neighborhood marked by racial diversity—a diversity that added rich substance to Rogers's depiction of the peaceable reign of God.

At the beginning of 1984, the Presidential Task Force on Food Assistance, appointed by President Ronald Reagan, reported that it could not find evidence of rampant hunger in the United States. By the end of the year, Rogers broadcast episodes addressing the need to combat hunger.

Chapter 8

"Food for the World"

Tears for Hungry Children

While the Poor People's Campaign was lobbying for antipoverty policies in Washington, DC, in 1968, Fred Rogers remained ensconced in his Pittsburgh studio, churning out programs that included no images of children or adults suffering from the ravages of poverty. Although committed to racial and ethnic diversity throughout the early years of *Mister Rogers' Neighborhood*, Rogers did not seem inclined to show poor people, let alone the devastating effects of poverty. It's likely he did not want to burden his young viewers with such graphic depictions, though he never stated as much. As the years advanced, however, Rogers began to take up the issue of poverty, not so much in abstract or general terms, but largely by addressing concrete needs of the poor: clothing, shelter, and above all else, food. In focusing on hunger in particular, Rogers's emerging words and actions uncovered his faith conviction that feeding the hungry is essential to the practice of peacemaking: Peace on earth requires food in our bodies. As he advocated for the hungry, Rogers also gave voice to a faith that called for living simply and opposing consumerism.

Early Charity

More than any other cast member, François Clemmons educated Rogers about the lives of the poor. "He and I talked mostly about ghetto life— the importance of taking care of those who are less fortunate," Clemmons recalls.[1] Of course, the talented singer's long and deep roots in the ghettos of Youngstown meant that he was the one teaching Rogers about the harshness of poverty in urban ghettos; vice versa was impossible.

Clemmons's early life of poverty stood in stark contrast to Rogers's comfortable upbringing in the upper-class life of Latrobe. Fred Rogers came from wealth—lots of it. His father, James Hills Rogers, had bought the McFeely Brick Factory from Fred's maternal grandfather, Fred McFeely, another man of considerable means. Fred's father increased his wealth all the more by later purchasing the Latrobe Die Casting Company. The financially successful businesses allowed the Rogers family to live in a huge, stately, red-brick home in town, and to hire local African Americans to take care of the cooking, gardening, driving, and other chores inside and outside the property. Like other members of the upper class in the North, the Rogers family also held property in Florida, where they could escape from the bitter winters of western Pennsylvania. It was an all-around bourgeois life.

Although as a child he never wanted for basic goods such as food, clothing, and shelter, Rogers was well aware of individuals and families with such needs, partly because of his mother's community work. "My mother was the original 'Meals on Wheels' person," he said. "Whenever she heard of someone who was sick or hungry, she'd show up wherever they were with a covered dish. She was always asking 'What can I do?' "[2]

Rogers was exposed to poverty at a young age also because his parents were directly involved with the social outreach mission of their local Presbyterian church. He remembered his father insisting that the church was not caring for its neighbors well enough if it finished the budget year with too much in the bank; the church's funds were for taking care of people in need, not for wasting away in a bank. As significant donors to the church, the Rogers family gave serious heed to the words of Jesus in the Gospel of Luke: "From everyone to whom much has been given, much will be required; and from the one to whom much has been entrusted, even more will be demanded" (12:48).

Perhaps it was this biblical expectation that fueled Rogers's own charitable acts in leading the Interfaith and Race Relations Committee at Rollins College. As we've already discovered, the committee under his leadership offered material assistance to African Americans stuck in an especially dire form of poverty fueled by Jim Crow. But whatever the case might have been, Rogers's sense of the importance of charity was validated all the more when he became a student at Western Theological Seminary in Pittsburgh. It was there that he experienced an inspiring charitable act he would recount numerous times throughout the remainder of his life. Unsurprisingly, it was a good deed undertaken by his theological mentor and favorite professor, William Orr. As Rogers recalled,

Dr. Orr would be quick to remind me that we're all saints, we believers; nevertheless, when you see someone go out to lunch on a winter's day and come back without his overcoat because he had given it to a person who was cold, you have a growing understanding of "living theologically." When we asked Dr. Orr about the coat, he said, "Oh, I have one other at home." And that was all he ever said about it. . . . What I discovered was that William Orr took Jesus of Nazareth seriously—very seriously.[3]

While he did not unpack this point, Rogers no doubt had in mind Jesus' teaching in Matthew 25: Those who will enter "the kingdom of heaven" are the ones who, right here on earth, clothe the naked, feed the hungry, give drink to the thirsty, and visit the sick and the imprisoned. Taking Jesus seriously, as Rogers understood it, meant enacting the social gospel in our economic lives—the good news that the spirit of Jesus is with "the least of these" and beckons us to join him there.

Beyond Charity in Make-Believe

By the time *Mister Rogers' Neighborhood* went national, Rogers had long embraced the conviction that his faith required acts of charity for those stuck in poverty and suffering from material need. One of the earliest times he expressed this belief was in 1972, during Make-Believe segments about a financially struggling magician named Mr. Appel. This poignant storyline originally aired in March, during the same week that 30,000 demonstrators marched on Washington, DC, to protest the Nixon administration's policies on welfare, education, and child care. The protestors, many of whom were children, depicted President Nixon as an irresponsible politician who paid insufficient attention to poverty and the need to eradicate it.

Unfazed by the protestors, Nixon suggested there were moral differences between the poor and the nonpoor. For instance, during his Labor Day speech in 1972, he drew the sharpest of distinctions between workers and welfare recipients. "We are faced this year with the choice between the 'work ethic' that built this nation's character—and the 'welfare ethic' that could cause that American character to weaken," he said.[4] Nixon and those who believed in this so-called choice held that the poor operated with values markedly different from those embraced by workers. Unlike those who believed in the traditional work ethic, the poor were lazy, slothful, irresponsible, and altogether unwilling to labor for a day's living.

As Nixon and his supporters were advancing this thesis, Leonard Goodwin, a research associate at the Brookings Institution, was doing his best to undermine it. Using a survey of over 4,000 individuals (poor and nonpoor), Goodwin argued that "poor people—males and females, blacks and whites, youths and adults—identify their self-esteem with work as strongly as do the non-poor."[5] One of his related points was that it was inaccurate to suggest that the poor embraced laziness, slothfulness, and irresponsibility as moral virtues.

Even before Goodwin's study appeared in national reviews, Fred Rogers had already staked out his position in the debate. He did so primarily (and subtly) through the Make-Believe character Mr. Appel, who fears he will have to divest the tools of his trade because he cannot sell enough tickets for his shows. "I guess that does it," he says. "I'm going to have to sell all of my equipment and my magical clothes so that I can buy food and clothing for my family."[6]

Always sensitive to those in need, Lady Aberlin protests, but Mr. Appel is adamant. "I'm out of money, and my family's out of food," he says. Lady Aberlin remains gently insistent, however, and says that she and Daniel Striped Tiger will find a solution that will allow the poor magician to keep working and feed his family.

Back in his comfortable television house, Rogers takes the opportunity to share a compassionate, empathetic lesson about parents who cannot always provide for their children. "Dads and moms sometimes want to do special things for their children, and they can feel really disappointed when they don't have enough to do those things, or they don't have the right things," he says. Given what just happened in Make-Believe, Rogers is referring especially to parents who, though they work hard or try to do so, don't have enough money to buy food and clothing for their children. These types of parents are not irresponsible; they're hardworking, diligent, and concerned mothers and fathers who grow disappointed when they cannot satisfy their families' basic needs.

Through Mr. Appel, Fred Rogers advanced a position directly opposed to President Nixon's efforts to depict the poor as lazy, irresponsible, and unwilling to work. In doing so, Rogers subtly offered the progressive point that poverty is not always the fault of the poor individual. In Rogers's view, it's inaccurate to reduce poverty to issues of moral character or individual choices and actions, because social forces larger than the individual sometimes conspire to keep him or her in poverty.

Back in Make-Believe, Lady Aberlin decides to take her concern to King Friday XIII and Queen Sara. "It's really a desperate situation," she reports. But King Friday—a man of wealth who enjoys his velvet robes, gold crown, and sprawling castle—is skeptical about the situation. "Are you sure you're not just talking dramatically, my dear?" he says, revealing a bit of sexism along the way. "No," Aberlin replies, "I mean it. The magician said he might have to sell all his equipment just to get food for his family."

Just then, Mr. Appel, sporting a blazer and showing no obvious signs of poverty, runs onto the castle grounds while carrying a bag full of groceries. He's in a hurry, he explains, because he has to take breakfast to his family. "Breakfast at this hour of the day?" asks King Friday, perplexed because it's the middle of the afternoon. "Well, it's the first thing they've had to eat all day, so it's just like breakfast," replies Mr. Appel before rushing on to feed his hungry family (and thereby showing us that poverty can consume daily schedules, including those of children who treasure routines and rituals).

After Mr. Appel leaves the scene, King Friday and Lady Aberlin get into a bit of a tiff. The king suggests that because Appel was carrying a bag of groceries and wearing a decent jacket, he really doesn't seem to be in need. But Lady Aberlin does not accept her uncle's snooty and dismissive analysis. "Just don't go making mountains out of molehills, Lady Aberlin," he warns. To which she indignantly replies, "Uncle Friday, I just don't think you understand!"

Does the king not understand because his wealth blinds him, because the weight of his gold crown affects his ability to see beyond his purple robes? Does he have no class-consciousness? Rogers does not reveal the reason for the king's dismissiveness, but he does show Lady Aberlin proving King Friday to be flat-out wrong. After their little tiff, she goes looking for Mr. Appel and soon discovers he has already sold his cape and used the money to buy that breakfast for his hungry family. Appalled by the news, Lady Aberlin begs him not to sell anything else until she has a chance to talk with her uncle.

Back at the castle, she reports her findings to King Friday. "His cape?" Friday replies, shocked that Mr. Appel had to take such extreme measures to feed his family. "This is ridiculous!" More important, though, Friday takes decisive action by delivering a royal order: "No magician is going to go hungry in my neighborhood! Lady Aberlin, I hereby form the King Friday–Queen Sara Saturday Royal Foundation for the Performing Arts. It's my way of helping people like Mr. Appel." Lady Aberlin is pleased with the decree, but she's not entirely sure what it means. "All of the citizens of Make-Believe may contribute what they can to artists who come to be with us," the king explains.

On one level, this is a creative storyline about "starving artists" and the importance of supporting the arts. As King Friday puts the matter, "It's very difficult for some artists to make a living." For Rogers, Mr. Appel's poverty is not a matter of an insufficiently formed moral character; it's partly a matter of the way society assigns values to certain types of work. Kings might typically pull in high salaries, but magicians normally do not. On another level, the storyline is simply about poor parents who cannot provide their children with basic necessities. Even though he does not depict them graphically, Rogers wants us to understand the devastating effects of poverty, especially on children who don't have access to something as basic as breakfast. Poverty hurts kids and disappoints parents. On still another level, the story is about the best ways we can help poor individuals and families as they struggle to meet their basic needs. The royal foundation established by King Friday is a creative public-private venture emphasizing private charitable giving. By the end of the story, it's clear that for Rogers the problem of poverty requires the support of political leaders and everyday citizens working in concert to effect a redistribution of basic goods.

True to her promise to help, Lady Aberlin spearheads the work of soliciting contributions for the royal foundation and the Appel family—not just money but other material things. The neighbors, of course, give generously: Donkey Hodie donates water, Corney makes a table and chairs, Elsie Jean Platypus bakes homemade bread, Dr. Bill Platypus offers free medical care, and even little Daniel Striped Tiger helps out by giving his "second-favorite" toy—a little truck. After expressing suspicions about King Friday's motives, Lady Elaine contributes beds. King Friday, unsurprisingly, grants the grandest gift of all: a beautiful new gold-laced magician's cape.

Back in his house, Rogers makes clear that Make-Believe's effort "is a way of expressing love." Properly done, the practice of caring for our neighbors in need is rooted in and reflective of the love we have for one another. Love—caring for others just as they are—casts out poverty.

Hunger as the Worst Physical Problem

As the 1980s arrived, Rogers focused yet again on the problem of poverty. Hunger in particular was the one social problem related to poverty that at this point captured his attention, empathy, and imagination. He focused on hunger especially in 1984, a time when the subject also captured the nation's attention.

At the beginning of the year, the President's Task Force on Food Assistance, appointed by President Ronald Reagan, reported that it could not find any evidence of rampant hunger in the United States. But just a month later, the Citizens Commission on Hunger in New England, chaired by J. Larry Brown of Harvard University's School of Public Health, issued a 112-page report concluding that hunger in America was indeed "widespread and increasing," and "the result of clear and conscious actions taken by government leaders"—for example, cuts in unemployment insurance and welfare and food stamp benefits. "When one thinks of malnutrition, generally the image of a Third World child with a swollen belly and limbs comes to mind," the report stated. "Malnutrition associated with hunger in America is less dramatic, but it does exist." The committee reported that it had found evidence of hunger everywhere, in every state: "We found hunger and it wasn't hard to find."[7]

But the dramatic event of hunger in 1984 was in faraway Ethiopia, where a drought-related famine left tens of thousands dead and millions in desperate need of food. The famine even prompted pop musicians (among them, Paul McCartney, Sting, U2, and Annie Lennox) to join Band Aid, a group organized by Bob Geldof of the Boomtown Rats, to record a single whose proceeds and royalties were to be used for food and medicine for the famine victims. "Do They Know It's Christmas?" became a lucrative hit at year's end.

Fred Rogers was right in the mix too, supporting a position that resonated less with Ronald Reagan and his task force and more with those finding and fighting hunger in America and famine in Africa. "Did you know that some people are hungry and they don't have enough food to stop their hunger?" Mister Rogers said during Thanksgiving Week in 1984. "That's a terrible feeling. And even if they wanted to, they wouldn't have enough to share with anybody else. Having enough to eat and to share is a very special feeling."[8] Mister Rogers knows that very special feeling because, as he's telling us about hungry people, he's also making homemade granola for Betty Aberlin, Bob Trow, and Mr. and Mrs. McFeely. Mister Rogers, like all the main characters on *Mister Rogers' Neighborhood*, has enough to eat and to share.

In this same episode, the topic of hunger also appears in the Neighborhood of Make-Believe, where Queen Sara is telling Lady Aberlin that in the last thirty-six years thirty-two countries have solved the problem of hunger within their borders. The queen seems firmly convinced that hunger is an eminently solvable problem; there's nothing necessary about hunger, and it does not need to be a long-term problem. (Rogers appears to be using Queen Sara to inform us that, contrary to what the Bible may say, poverty need not always be with us.)

For the women of Make-Believe, a solution to hunger is desperately needed because it's such an extremely grave problem. "Not having enough to eat is certainly the worst physical problem that there is," Lady Aberlin declares. Pleased with Lady Aberlin's expert analysis and compassionate interest, Queen Sara shares some good news: X the Owl has planted "speedy seeds" designed to sprout and grow super fast. This technological advance may turn out to be beneficial for the queen's work with Food for the World—a progressive organization dedicated to eliminating world hunger.

The inspiration behind Rogers's imaginative creation of Food for the World might have come from his familiarity with a real-life organization called Bread for the World. In the early 1970s, Arthur Simon, brother of U.S. Senator Paul Simon, formed the idea of starting "a Christian citizens' movement on hunger to build public support for policies more responsive to the needs of hungry people." Simon's idea eventually turned into Bread for the World, a voluntary organization that appealed to people "on the basis of their faith in Christ and biblical entreaties to help those who hunger."[9] Unlike charities focused on short-term help, Bread for the World "emphasized structural changes more than assistance, and long-term strategies more than emergency aid, so that people would have the opportunity to work their way out of hunger and poverty."[10]

Because it was an ecumenical group with national leadership, Bread for the World attracted significant attention among mainline churches like the one Rogers attended in Pittsburgh. Perhaps more significantly, an early board member of Bread for the World was Thomas J. Donnelly, a Pittsburgh-based attorney who lived just three blocks away from Rogers. Donnelly and Rogers occasionally met at social events, and given their respective interests, it seems possible that Donnelly introduced Rogers to his work with Bread for the World.

But whatever the case, hunger had indeed come to the Neighborhood of Make-Believe in 1984. We know this because as Queen Sara and Lady Aberlin are chatting about Food for the World, a hungry old goat is devouring the plants that sprouted from X the Owl's speedy seeds. Though the Neighborhood residents don't know this yet, the old goat has also eaten Lady Elaine's garden in Southwood (which has good earth for planting and growing).

Eating someone else's garden is a downright shocking act in the otherwise peaceful Neighborhood of Make-Believe. It's even criminal behavior, which means the old goat is a thief, a crook, a bandit. But back in his television house, Mister Rogers does not depict the old goat this way. Remarkably, he does not judge or condemn the old goat for eating gardens that don't belong to him; nor does he point his finger or dare to suggest the old goat should get a job so he can buy his own food. He simply says, "That old goat must have been very hungry. Can you imagine how hungry some people must be to take somebody else's garden?"

For those with ears to hear, this nonjudgmental question offers the simple lesson that hunger sometimes creates conditions that encourage people (or goats) to act in ways they otherwise would not, even in criminal ways. Mister Rogers does not state this explicitly, but his question certainly leads us to the point that hunger can fracture peaceful living. In addition, the implication here is that the best way to address the fracture is not by retaliating, especially with violence, but rather by meeting the underlying need—by helping to feed the hungry. We can restore peace by helping to feed people who might otherwise act in desperate ways.

Back in Make-Believe, as informal detectives Lady Aberlin and Bob Dog attempt to solve the mystery of the missing plants, they come across the old goat red-handed (or, better stated, full-stomached). In his special way of talking, the old goat says that all of Northwood, where he comes from, doesn't have any food and that he's been taking plants back home in order to help the people there. We viewers are left unclear about how exactly the old goat takes the plants back home (Doesn't he eat them?), but we do know that the old goat has confessed to his crime.

"Instead of taking our gardens, why don't you ask us?" Lady Aberlin gently says.

The old goat apparently then does exactly that, because Bob Dog chimes in, "Of course we'll help you!" King Friday delivers a similar response when he learns of the horrible famine in Northwood. "Of course we will help!" he says, as if there could not possibly be another answer. The benevolent king then enlists Make-Believe residents as "all-outers" and calls for "an all-out effort" to plant the entire Neighborhood with speedy seeds that will quickly grow into plants for Northwood. "You need not steal again," Queen Sara says to the old goat. "Simply ask, and you will receive."

Like Bread for the World, then, Fred Rogers saw an important and indispensable role for political leaders in alleviating hunger. The problem of hunger was so big and urgent that it required King Friday to enlist his minions as "all-outers" who will go "all out" in planting seeds; voluntary assistance was simply not sufficient. Like Bread for the World, Rogers also used Christian Scripture to communicate his beliefs about fighting hunger. "Simply ask, and you will receive," for example, is straight from the Synoptic Gospels. The version in the Gospel of Luke describes Jesus as saying, "Ask, and it will be given you; search, and you will find; knock, and the door will be opened for you. For everyone who asks receives, and everyone who searches finds, and for everyone who knocks, the door will be opened" (11:9–10). Finally, like Bread for the World, Rogers also stressed sustainability as a strategy for defeating the problem of hunger. The all-out effort he envisioned for Make-Believe was far more than a mere act of charity, far more than simply giving food as a once-and-done deal.

This last point becomes clear back in the Neighborhood, where the all-out effort sees the whole Neighborhood planting corn, lettuce, pumpkins, apples, oranges, tomatoes, and even cans of vegetable soup. Importantly, though, this is not a paternalistic approach to hunger.

It turns out that Northwood residents are making every effort to become self-sufficient even as they rely on much-needed help from Make-Believe. "I'd like to meet those people from Northwood," Lady Aberlin says. "They're really smart to want us to send seeds and plants so they can grow their own food." The people of Northwood are not unintelligent, lazy, and passive recipients of charity offered by people who work hard and know better than they do. Northwood residents might be hungry, yes, but they also possess the gift of intelligence and, with an idea they themselves have developed, they seek to become self-reliant. They have no desire to become dependent on King Friday XIII and his land; they want to plant and eat their own food.

It's no surprise that paternalism is nowhere to be found in this series. That would have been counterproductive to Rogers's longtime efforts to extol people who work with their hands. "Part of Mister Rogers' mission," as Jonathan Last rightly notes, "seems to have been to honor people who work with their hands. In nearly every episode he toured some workplace—a metal-working plant a factory making rain slickers, a mushroom farm, a paper mill. He approached the workers as though they were artisans, performing interesting and valuable work."[11] Rogers was captivated by manual labor and sought to depict it as of immense value throughout the run of *Mister Rogers' Neighborhood*.

As the weeklong series on food and hunger concludes, Mister Rogers underscores the importance of hunger for his viewers. "When a person is very, very hungry, he or she can't think of any other kinds of food," he says. "But there *are* other kinds. Music, for instance, is food for the hearing. And paintings and beautiful scenes are food for the seeing. And books are food for the soul. And loving other people is food for the spirit." Rogers's creative list of other types of food suggests the gravity of the problem of hunger. Hunger prevents people from thinking of, let alone appreciating, music, paintings, landscapes, books—and even love. Hunger, that is, devastates a child's ability to learn, experience, and value so much of what Mister Rogers shows and tries to teach and instill. And now we know the reason that Fred Rogers considered hunger to be "the worst physical problem that there is."

Hungry Children, Giving Children

Hungry children moved Fred Rogers to tears. In 1986, Rogers was attending an awards ceremony honoring him and other authors for their recent books. The honoree who spoke just before him was none other than J. Larry Brown, now chair of the Harvard Physician Task Force on Hunger in America. Brown's speech, based on his book *Living Hungry in America,* struck a deep chord in Rogers. "When he told about his teams of doctors canvassing our country and finding more hungry people than they found a decade ago, when he told stories about hungry children in school not being able to learn (not being able to think about anything but their gnawing hunger), when he gave his hard-earned statistics about hungry people, I noticed that the tears were going down my cheeks," Rogers recalled. "By the time it was my turn to talk, I was still in tears, and I admitted it's the only time I've ever had to give a public speech when I was crying." Rogers explained his tears to the rapt audience. "I told those people in the audience how I wished I could reach through every television set in the country and offer whatever nourishment was needed. I wished I could help feed hungry people. When my five minutes was over they told me practically everyone in the ballroom was in tears."[12]

Rogers also explained his tears a bit more fully. "Why am I so deeply moved by the thought of someone being hungry—too hungry even to learn?" he asked. His answer suggested that his sensitivity was rooted in an experience he had had while studying child development at the Arsenal Family and Children's Center at the University of Pittsburgh:

> I think of one child at lunchtime. (Everyone ate lunch there: those who came from homes with plenty of food and those who came from poverty.) The little girl I think about (Ellen) lived in a home with 12 brothers and sisters. At their mealtimes whatever was put in front of them was theirs, and that's all they got. Well, I remember one day at the Center, Ellen was handed the basket of toast for her table and she took a piece and ate it and held on to the basket. When her teacher asked her to pass the basket on to the other children, Ellen began to sob. She cried and cried, and at first her teachers just didn't understand why. But after a while—after several days,

they realized that Ellen just never understood that the basket would ever come back to her. In her culture—up to that moment—there was no such thing as "seconds." It's mighty hard to share when you're hungry and you don't think you'll get enough.[13]

As the memory of a hungry child moved Rogers to tears, the image of a giving child—a child who has enough to share—gave him great joy, and in August 1996 he used the Neighborhood of Make-Believe to share his belief that children, not just adults, are fully capable of becoming caring and compassionate neighbors who feed the hungry. In these extra-creative episodes, the Neighborhood of Make-Believe and Westwood are experiencing a peculiar phenomenon: a storm that drops cereal rather than rain. In Make-Believe, the downpour buries Daniel Striped Tiger's clock.

Although these episodes focus on Daniel's fear of falling cereal and his efforts to be brave and strong, they also address the issue of sharing food. After the downpour, the Neighborhood does not scoop up the cereal and place it in the trash; the good neighbors put all the fallen cereal in cereal boxes. With hundreds of boxes of cereal now packaged, Daniel says he wishes he could "give a box to anyone who's hungry." This wish in turn spurs Prince Tuesday to run back to the castle and ask his mother, Queen Sara Saturday, about using the fallen food. "I just thought we could give this cereal to Food for the World," he says.[14] It's a simple scene with a basic point: Adults aren't the only ones who can feed the hungry; children can be caring and compassionate neighbors too.

In 2000, Fred Rogers returned to the theme of charitable giving by publishing a little book called *The Giving Box*. The purpose of the book is to help parents show children the importance of being a caring neighbor. As it does this, *The Giving Box* offers a bit of insight into Rogers's ethics of charity.

Just a few pages into the book, Rogers advises parents that they should not be too grand in their efforts. "I don't think it's helpful to give young children the sense that they are responsible for feeding and clothing all the poor and healing all the ills of the world," he writes. "Children need to know that grown-ups are in charge and that many grown-ups are doing what they can to make this world a better place. We can, however, help children feel they have a part in being a caring neighbor."[15]

A key part of being a charitable neighbor is refusing to divide people into givers and receivers. To make this point, which is another effort to avoid paternalism in giving, Rogers reflected on a sweater drive he had encouraged local public television stations to undertake as part of the thirtieth anniversary of *Mister Rogers' Neighborhood*. "I knew how tempting it could be to encourage generosity by asking people to help 'the needy' or those who are 'less fortunate.' " But Rogers opposed the labels. "That kind of thinking divides people into 'us' and 'them,' and doesn't necessarily contribute to a sense of 'neighborliness.' "[16]

Driven by his vision of neighborliness in charity, Rogers held that "it's far better to say to our children that we are gathering sweaters for people who are cold and don't have the money to buy warm clothing, rather than 'for the needy' or 'less fortunate.' "[17] Rogers and his team thus added this special message to the request for a sweater drive: "All of us at some time or another need help. Whether we're giving or receiving a sweater, each of us has something valuable to bring to this world. That's one of the things that connects us as neighbors—in our own way, everyone is a giver and receiver."[18]

On a related note, Rogers instructed parents to help children see that everyone has strengths and needs. It's inaccurate, in his view, to suggest that the givers are strong and the receivers are weak. Children should learn that "people who have money to donate or who have a sweater to give to a clothing drive have other kinds of needs. And those who receive the money or sweaters or food have other strengths." The "most essential" message we can offer children as they become caring neighbors is that "as different as we are from one another, as unique as each one of us is, we are much more the same than we are different."[19]

Of course, charity is required because of the harsh reality "that some people need more help than others" at certain times and in relation to certain basic needs.[20] Rogers's book, like his television program, tends to focus its discussion of poverty on the issue of hunger, and it does so by sharing several multicultural folktales about helping people who don't have enough money to buy food. Poverty and hunger, we learn, are all over the world—and so are charitable neighbors.

Always practical, Rogers also moves beyond his nonpaternalistic advice about proper vision—seeing all people as givers and receivers—to specific advice about the practices of charity. The main suggestion of the book (but not the only one) is for families to make a "giving box" a central part of their life together. On the one hand, the box offers us an opportunity to develop a ritual for charitable giving—a regular practice of offering our money to people with specific needs such as hunger. On the other, it acts as a constant invitation for us to engage in conversations about giving and receiving. The overall point of the box is for us to think, talk, and act with a spirit of charity toward those who need more help than others.

Unsurprisingly, for Rogers, practices associated with the giving box are essentially about religious faith. While the book does not preach the need to believe in God, it does note that the giving box has roots in similar boxes long associated with Judaism and Christianity: the tzedekah box and the mite box. "*Tzedekah*, the Jewish word for charity, comes from the Hebrew word *tzedek* which means 'righteous person,'" Rogers writes. "According to Jewish law, a person is obligated to be generous." Like the Jewish tzedekah box, the Christian mite box is a way of giving thanks to God for the gifts of life—and not just a little bit of thanks. "The mite box," Rogers explains, "is often linked to the story of the widow's mite, in which Jesus saw some rich people putting their gifts into the treasury. He also saw a poor widow putting in two copper coins. Jesus said that the widow put in more than all the others because she was very poor and gave everything she had."[21]

Rogers and Charity

Fred Rogers was not like the poor widow. He was wealthy in his childhood, wealthy in his adult years, and wealthy in his senior years. His house in the Squirrel Hill neighborhood of Pittsburgh, where he lived for most of the years he and Joanne were rearing their sons, was a stately mansion of sorts, more extravagant than even the huge brick home in Latrobe. With its six bedrooms, the Squirrel Hill home was an ostentatious sign of wealth, far different from the modest cottage that acted as his television house. Indeed, Rogers's Squirrel Hill neighborhood, full of sprawling mansions, bore no resemblance at all to the middle-class modesty of *Mister Rogers' Neighborhood.*

As a rich man whose faith beckoned him to give, Fred Rogers practiced charity in his private life. On the one hand, he gave of his presence and time, often visiting children with physical disabilities. Some of the most moving of the hundreds of photographs of Rogers are those in which he is with a mentally or physically challenged child—or just a child in obvious need. Weekends would also see Rogers traveling to a nearby prison and visiting with children whose parents were imprisoned.

On the other hand, Rogers donated money to his local faith community and to favorite charities. Betty Aberlin remembers that Rogers's annual holiday gift to her was a card with a message indicating he had donated to a charity in her name. There is a bit of complexity to this point. Like other struggling actors, Aberlin was struck by Rogers's apparent inattentiveness to the financial needs of his own staff, especially during the holiday season.

She sensed within Rogers an indifference or ignorance to the material needs of his actors and crew—an attitude that became all too real when they looked at their meager salaries or felt the sting of no special bonuses at holiday time. While in 1972 Rogers had extolled the remarkable effort to care for the financially struggling magician named Mr. Appel, it seems he did not attend as well to his own team of artists.

Rogers did have favorite charities, and these included the Human Kindness Foundation, which supported a prison ministry founded by Bo Lozoff, a nationally prominent spiritual guru and activist before sexual abuse charges later tainted him. Lozoff's Prison Ashram Project was a religious commune in which volunteers lived and worked with ex-offenders completing their parole requirements. Rogers valued and supported Lozoff's work with prisoners and even occasionally sought his advice, especially about how best to deal with the problem of children affected by prison culture. For instance, when he heard about an eight-year-old who said he wanted to go to jail because "you get three hots and a cot," Rogers penned Lozoff about the possibility of broadcasting public service announcements designed to subvert the influence of prison culture on children.[22]

Another favorite charity was L'Arche Daybreak community in Canada, where Rogers's good friend Henri Nouwen had moved after leaving Harvard University. Part of the L'Arche organization in France—which was founded by Jean Vanier in 1964 when he invited two men with intellectual disabilities to live with him—L'Arche Daybreak is a community in which people with intellectual disabilities live, work, and learn with volunteers and staff members. Rogers loved L'Arche's celebration of the lives of those with intellectual disabilities and visited the community while Nouwen was still living and working there. The Fred Rogers Archive includes some wonderful extant photographs of him and L'Arche community members enjoying one another's company.

As a man of charity, Rogers did not take part in rallies, marches, or other campaigns designed to pressure the government to shift more of the nation's resources into social programs benefitting the poor. Although he occasionally lobbied members of Congress—he did so to ensure funding for PBS and the success of the video recorder, among other things—there is no evidence to suggest he ever lobbied any politician to sponsor or support policies benefitting those suffering from poverty. This is not to suggest that Rogers supported charity to the exclusion of government action in addressing poverty; the Neighborhood of Make-Believe episodes discussed in this chapter suggest he favored a public-private coalition in efforts to eradicate hunger and poverty.

But it is important to note that in his personal life, Rogers focused more on charity and less on social justice policies designed to eradicate poverty.

A Move to Simplicity

As he grew older, Rogers valued a life of economic simplicity. This is arguably most evident in his and Joanne's decision to downsize from their huge home in Squirrel Hill. Rogers did not base his part of the decision on the mere fact that he was growing older—their second son was still in high school when Rogers developed the itch to downsize—but on the desire to live more simply than they had up to that point. It seems that Rogers had long been ill at ease with opulent displays of his wealth. Video and commercial director Joe Pytka, perhaps best known for commercials touting products such as Pepsi and Nike, recalls that when he was making a documentary of Rogers during the early years, Rogers admonished him "not to show the tasteful opulence of his home during our filming."[23]

Although the attitude of living simply came to concrete expression in his personal life especially in his later years, Rogers had long encouraged his viewers to be content with basic necessities and the simple, inexpensive pleasures of life. Year after year, even as Rogers himself was living among "tasteful opulence," as Pytka puts it, *Mister Rogers' Neighborhood* lauded attitudes and actions that prioritized needs over wants, simplicity over extravagance. Rogers stressed simple living, the importance of right priorities, and the need to make personal sacrifices, particularly in a 1984 episode that depicts the Neighborhood of Make-Believe facing an economic crisis.

In this striking episode, Make-Believe's water pipes have broken, and for reasons that remain unclear, there's not enough money in the bank to fix the problem. Faced with the crisis of no running water and apparently no money, the adults are left wondering aloud what to do. But the children of Make-Believe, creative as usual, come up with the idea of tapping into funds already earmarked for the construction of a swimming pool. The idea is particularly good, because even if they were to build the swimming pool, they would not be able to fill it with water. "I'm so proud of our children," Queen Sara says. She's proud that the children have recognized the important value of sacrificing wants, especially extra-special ones like swimming pools, in order to satisfy basic needs, like the need for flowing water.

Back in his television house, Mister Rogers caps off the lesson. "Nobody can have everything," he says. "That's why it's important for us to learn to make good choices—learn to choose the things we really need." Using a serious tone, Rogers also notes that making financial sacrifices is hard work. "It's often hard for Mom and Dad to decide how to spend the money to care for the family, but they do decide. You see, they love you and want to take good care of you." Before the episode ends, Rogers delivers his most important economic lesson of all: "Things like friendship and love don't cost any money at all."[24] The most important things in life are free.

Rogers returned to the lesson of sacrifice, though in a different form, two years later. This time he dealt with the very difficult issue of one family having more economic resources than another—and the disappointment that children feel when they see their friends having more or newer things than they have.

In an episode that originally aired in 1986, Ana Platypus is crying in the Neighborhood of Make-Believe because her parents are unable to buy her a bike. The issue is complicated because her friend Prince Tuesday recently got a brand-new bike with a fancy key. "Tuesday got the kind of bike I wanted," she says while fighting back tears. Her father, Dr. Bill, tries to deal with the disappointment as best as he can—gently and reasonably. "You know what I told you, dear," he says. "You said we can't afford one right now," Ana sniffles in reply. "That's right, dear. There are other things we have to use our family's money for right now." When Ana suggests that her parents would get her a new bike if they loved her as much as Prince Tuesday's parents love him, Dr. Bill stays the course. "It's a matter of money, Ana. It's not a matter of loving."[25] Again, by the end of the episode, we know that love—priceless love—is what's most important in every sector of life—even the financial one.

Rogers had long touted not only financial sacrifices but also economic ethics opposed to consumerism and its excesses. One of the most important facts about Fred Rogers is that he started his company, Family Communications, not long after he woke up one morning to discover his face plastered on the side of a milk carton. "Here was the milk at the door," he recounted. "My picture was on the milk carton, and I didn't know anything about it. I was advertising something or promoting something that the station didn't bother to ask me [about]."[26] Disturbed by the thought of appearing as a huckster, Rogers responded to the incident by founding Family Communications, in 1971, as the nonprofit producer of *Mister Rogers' Neighborhood* for PBS.

Rogers consistently refused to identify children and their parents as consumers ripe for buying items associated with his program. He never made a commercial throughout his entire tenure as the host of *Mister Rogers'*

Neighborhood, and he blocked others from using his work to pitch their own products. When advertising giant J. Walter Thompson used a rip-off of Mister Rogers to pitch Burger King burgers in a 1984 television commercial, Fred Rogers successfully demanded that the fast-food chain stop running the spot. "Mr. Rogers is one guy you don't want to mess with, as beloved as he is," a Burger King spokesman explained. "So that particular commercial goes on the shelf. Hopefully, we now have peace in the neighborhood."[27] Rogers also wished others involved in children's programming would halt the commercialization of their products. "I disapprove of hosts of children's programs pitching anything," he said, "because they are to be trusted by the children and they're not to use that trust to be hucksters."[28]

Consumerism in any form irritated Fred Rogers as few other things did. We are not primarily consumers, in his thought, and we should avoid the temptation to measure our lives by our consumption. Rogers cited Martin Luther King Jr. on this point in 1997. Although it was one of the few times he ever cited the great civil rights leader, it was a remarkable tribute to King's economic ethics.

> We've all had voices that we've carried with us as we grew. I remember the voice of Martin Luther King, Jr. warning against judging success by the value of our salaries or the size of our automobiles rather than by the quality of our relationships to humanity. That voice always reminds me of a tyranny that we and our children are subjected to: in subtle—and not so subtle—ways we are taught to look for meaning outside ourselves rather than inside ourselves. Dr. King would strongly object to that tyranny and would ask each one of us to do what we could about it.[29]

Not long before he died, Rogers explained part of his own actions in relation to consumerism and materialism. "Some people get so caught up in the trappings of life that I feel they lose what is real," he stated. "My desire is to help children realize that deep and simple are far more important than shallow and complicated and fancy."[30]

Although he didn't say so in this particular interview, he also sought to help adults, including his fellow Christians, realize the same. A little more than a year before the interview, for instance, Rogers gently criticized a Presbyterian minister who had asked him to support plans to build a new church in Celebration, Florida—a master-planned community originally developed by the Walt Disney Company. "I worry that the Church will appear exclusionary if it is related too closely to such a Disneyutopian concept," he replied in a letter. "The Church's mission—it seems to me—is to do all it can for the disenfranchised. . . . It's only when we follow

Jesus (and Mother Teresa and all like them) that we offer real hope (to the poor *and* the rich)."[31]

At last, for Rogers, deep and simple relationships of love are most important. In terms of economics, that means being with those who are poor and hungry, practicing charity and seeing the importance of political efforts in the battle against poverty and hunger, opposing the shallowness of consumerism and materialism, and living simply.

A model of male sensitivity, Rogers often used his program to teach boys and girls that they could act in ways not typically associated with their gender.

Chapter 9

"I'm Tired of Being a Lady"

Tough Girls, Sensitive Boys

*A*lthough it's impossible to find the words *feminist* or *feminism* in *Mister Rogers' Neighborhood*, there's no doubt that Fred Rogers used the program to teach and celebrate feminist principles and practices. True to form, he did not join picket lines, marches, or demonstrations seeking equality for women. Rogers was no Pauli Murray, Betty Friedan, or Bella Abzug. But in his own quiet way, he taught girls and women that they did not have to be tied to the identities typically associated with their gender. At the same time, he encouraged boys and men to adopt qualities not normally identified with their gender, especially tenderness, sensitivity, and love. Doing so was Rogers's way of helping boys and girls combat inner turmoil and achieve an inner peace essential for human flourishing. It was also his way of showing that peace on earth required gender equality, of seeing boys and girls as equal in value and refusing to discriminate against either because of their gender.

Early Gender-Bending

Fred Rogers was the opposite of macho. He showed no hint of physical brawn; his chin was weak, his muscles toned but underdeveloped, and his face eternally smooth. A model of male softness and sensitivity, Rogers cut a striking figure on and off television. He was not aggressive in any way. He talked softly and carried no stick; his spirit was gentle and tender, patient and trustworthy, and receptive and loving. He truly loved children, and loved connecting with them on their own level.

Just the thought of a middle-aged man coming into a child's home in the middle of the day was countercultural in the 1960s. Most adult males were absent from their homes at that point; they were at work, talking about adult things with other adults. But there was Mister Rogers, taking time before his own workday, or so he told us, to come to his television house and spend thirty minutes of quality time with boys and girls across the nation. Also striking, given the customs of the day, was Mister Rogers's depiction of himself as the children's "television friend." He wasn't a teacher, and they weren't his students; he was their friend, and they were his. That's no small point, and it was directly subversive of gender-related expectations of its day.

The first week of the national edition of *Mister Rogers' Neighborhood* included another jolting image—that of a woman leading a campaign against King Friday's preparations for war. Male-dominated institutions executing the Vietnam War were an integral part of the context of that first week. From the White House, President Johnson, an alpha male like none other, directed packs of male soldiers at the Pentagon. Even the major personalities behind the mainstream peace movement were men—Martin Luther King Jr., Benjamin Spock, William Sloane Coffin Jr., Robert F. Kennedy, Eugene McCarthy, and George McGovern. Like the modern civil rights movement, the peace movement reflected many patriarchal organizations of the 1960s.

Disturbed by their inferior roles, some women broke away from the mainstream peace movement to join or form female-centric organizations—for example, Another Mother for Peace, Women Strike for Peace, Women for Peace, and the Women's International League for Peace and Freedom. Fred Rogers broke away too—from the cultural expectation that men should be in charge of dissent. So in the first week of *Mister Rogers' Neighborhood*, we discover it's not the males of Make-Believe who oppose King Friday's fighting mood and his ill-advised plans to militarize the castle, fire the cannon, and call out the paratroopers; it's the fiercely principled Lady Aberlin. From the epicenter of the public square, she's a bold strategist, a daring activist, and a successful challenge to King Friday's authority. Compared to the soft-minded Friday, Lady Aberlin is one tough woman.

Men with Yarn, Women with Hammers

There's a fascinating twist in the emerging gender roles of the Neighborhood: Within the month, Lady Aberlin appears in Make-Believe as a knitter who wants to be "just like mom." The peace activist, it seems, has become a domestic goddess.

In the same March 1968 episode, Mister Rogers grabs a hammer and begins to pound nails into a piece of wood. He does not seem especially adept at the task; he chokes up on the handle—an odd move for experienced hammerers—and fails to hit the nails with conviction. Nevertheless, he seems to enjoy himself as he arranges a family of nails, some larger than others, in a semi-circle of sorts. While doing this, he asks, "Who does most of the hammering in your house? Your *dad*?" Mister Rogers seems to like that answer, and he follows it up by saying, "I know a lot of boys who'd like to be just like their dads."[1] And with that gender-specific declaration as his cue, he breaks out in song:

> I'd like to be just like my dad.
> He's handsome and he's keen.
> He knows just how to drive the car
> And buy the gasoline.
> And mommy likes the things he does,
> The way he looks and, Gee!
> I'd like to be just like my dad
> And have someone like me.

The message that males are the ones who hammer is reinforced in the episode's Make-Believe segment, in which Virgil Cantini, a Pittsburgh-based sculptor, talks with King Friday about his sculptures. After Friday asks whether he enjoyed using nails as a boy, Cantini says, "Well, I think *all* boys like to play with nails and hammers and hatchets."

We learn about girls and women a little bit later, in another Make-Believe segment in the same episode, when we see Lady Aberlin using needles to knit a very cute sweater for Henrietta Pussycat. While she's knitting happily, she too breaks out in song:

> I'd like to be just like my mom.
> She's pretty and she's nice.
> She knows just how to make the beds
> And cook things out of rice.
> And daddy likes the things she does,
> The way she looks and, Gee!
> I'd like to be just like my mom
> And have someone like me.

Fred Rogers thus peddled in the standard gender expectations of 1968: Boys want to be like their dads, who know how to hammer nails, drive cars, and buy gas, and girls want to be like their moms, who know how to knit sweaters, make beds, and cook rice. What could be more convincing than learning that even the strong-willed Lady Aberlin—who just recently led political dissent in Make-Believe—wants to knit and clean and cook? Despite the first week of episodes, it seems traditional gender identities and roles are safe and secure in the Neighborhood.

But just when we think this episode is merely reinforcing the expectation that gender should correlate to certain tasks (*only* men should hammer, and *only* women should knit), Mister Rogers, back in his television house, retrieves a ball of yarn from the couch. And as he wraps the yarn around the nails on the board, creating a picture he plans to give to a neighbor, he shares the most important lesson of the day: "Some men use yarn very well, too. Some ladies use nails very well." No one breaks out in song to deliver this countercultural message; it just comes quietly, almost in a whisper, as Mister Rogers finishes his picture.

This quiet message, simply stated and yet profoundly complex, shares what many of us didn't know so clearly in March 1968: Women can hammer, and men can knit. There's also unspoken nuance to the lesson about men. Through his own abilities and limitations, Rogers shows us that some men are actually *better* at weaving yarn than hammering nails. Not all males are John Henry types who can swing hammers so hard they break their hearts; some, like Mister Rogers, are far more adept at sitting down quietly and weaving yarn. Further, with the appearance of the Pittsburgh sculptor Cantini—a man with massive hands—Rogers shows us that some men who excel at hammering use their hammers not for building the usual guy things (houses and furniture), or even for knocking things down, but for making gorgeous pieces of art.

Did Rogers also mean to suggest that some women are better at hammering nails than at weaving yarn? That seems obvious by implication, but, unfortunately, we don't see any women wielding a hammer, expertly or inexpertly, in this particular episode; nor do we see women weaving yarn to build guy things or to tear things down. But *Mister Rogers' Neighborhood* has just begun.

Rough-and-Tumble Girls, Boys Taking Care

From 1968 until the end of its run, Fred Rogers used his program to give girls and boys permission to think and act in ways that seemed atypical for their genders. Another excellent example of this from 1968 is an episode in which Mister Rogers tells us that when he was a boy he loved playing with steam shovels and pretending to use a jackhammer. This seems a bit surprising for regular viewers who have been watching him play with dolls, but the news acts as an introduction to the Neighborhood of Make-Believe, where Dr. Marchl, a male medical doctor, has just seen a machine at Grandpère's that can produce anything that someone asks for in French. After hearing him talk about the machine, Henrietta Pussycat tells Dr. Marchl that boys are "so lucky" because they can play with "all sorts of machines"—an opinion that results in a cocked head from the good doctor.[2]

Never far from Henrietta, her trusty neighbor X the Owl then pops out of his tree and asks what's going on. "Henrietta and I were just talking," Dr. Marchl says. "I was telling her about a machine that I saw at the tower, and she was just saying that sometimes she wishes that she were a boy and she could play with machines and do kind of rough-and-tumble things like boys do."

X is quite taken by the conversation. "Well, that's funny," he says, "'cause like in that opera, when I saw Henrietta taking care of the baby, you know what? I thought it would be nice taking care that way." X then begins to sing the song Henrietta performed in the opera—"I Like to Take Care of You"— and she joins along. "Yeah, that's the one," Owl says. "Boy, I think it must be nice being a girl sometimes and being able to take care that way." Stated without embarrassment, the honest and authentic expression earns a similar one from Henrietta: "Meow, meow, rough and tumble sometimes."

Dr. Marchl offers his studied opinion of X the Owl's comment, leaving Henrietta's to dangle alone. "Well," he says, "I'm a doctor, and I'm not a girl, and still I take care of people." A sweet and dear cat, Henrietta agrees, adding some evidence of her own. "Meow, and daddies, too, meow," she says. Although not the brightest owl in the trees, X nevertheless gets the point: "That's right! Man doctors and daddies can take care, can't they?"

Poor Henrietta is left unsatisfied. "Meow, hard, meow, girl, meow, be, meow, meow, digger," she meows. The males are silent, as if they're clueless and directionless about how to respond to her frustration. But Henrietta is a smart cat, and on her own, without the help of any male, she comes up with an idea. As she goes looking for something related to her idea, X offers helpful analysis: "Guess it's kind of funny that boys wish they could kind of do things that girls do, and on the other hand, girls wish they could do things that boys can do." Henrietta, still focused on digging and rough-and-tumble things, then returns with her idea in full view. Although she's just a little cat and cannot don a construction hat and climb aboard a roaring backhoe, she has come up with the idea of grabbing a shovel and digging in her garden. It's the roughest, toughest option available to her, and she's delighted with the prospect of doing something tough.

Back in his television house, Mister Rogers adds to the lesson just played out in Make-Believe. "Sometimes girls would like to try out some boy kind of games, and sometimes boys would like to have some 'play house' kind of games," he says. "You don't have to play the same thing all the time." Rogers is not trying to encourage girls to leave behind "taking care" so they can become diggers alone; his point is that girls who nurture can also be diggers. Nor is he attempting to transform boys from diggers into caretakers alone; for Rogers, boys who dig can and should also be those who "take care." "Everybody . . . has a chance to take care," he states.

Qualities and actions normally bound to one gender—nurturing and digging—thus become fluid in Rogers's countercultural Neighborhood. Girls can act like boys, even as they remain girls, and boys can act like girls, even as they remain boys. Rogers taught this lesson consistently throughout the run of *Mister Rogers' Neighborhood*, expanding on its meaning at times and allowing it to evolve with developing thoughts about gender. The first part of this transformative lesson—that girls can act like boys—was no doubt reflective of Rogers's appreciation for the emerging feminist culture in the United States.

Rough and Tumble with Lady Elaine Fairchilde

By the time *Mister Rogers' Neighborhood* went national, Betty Friedan had already published *The Feminine Mystique*. The groundbreaking feminist book had drawn attention to "the problem that has no name"—a growing discontent among suburban women with their limited and yet idolized roles as stay-at-home moms and wives. Schooled and steeped in "sexual passivity, male domination and nurturing maternal love," these housewives sought fulfillment in a "strained glamour" that bound them all the more to an identity grounded only in their sexuality. "Our culture," Friedan wrote, "does not permit women to accept or gratify their basic need to grow and fulfill their potentialities as human beings, a need which is solely defined by their sexual role."[3]

Fred Rogers agreed with that feminist thesis and sought to counter the wider patriarchal culture by creating and re-creating a neighborhood where girls and women could fulfill their need for an identity not tied to their traditional roles. More fundamentally, he also often gave voice to the frustration of females who felt trapped in their male-engineered lives.

Enter Lady Elaine Fairchilde and the winter of her discontent. In a remarkable episode broadcast in February 1970, ten months before the launching of *Ms. Magazine,* the female puppet, played by Fred Rogers himself, lets out a deep sigh reminiscent of Henrietta's in 1968. "I'm tired of being a lady," Lady Elaine says.[4]

By "lady," she cannot possibly mean "prim and proper," because by early 1970 she has already done quite a few things to disqualify her from wearing that role lightly. For example, she has taken a painting from King Friday without first asking his permission, fought with the mild-mannered Edgar Cooke over borrowing his special pillow, used her magical boomerang to turn King Friday and the entire Neighborhood upside down, borrowed Handyman Negri's tools without permission, tuned her piano while knowing her neighbors slept, and littered during an anti-littering campaign. Far from prim and proper, Lady Elaine is the Neighborhood's troublemaker-in-residence.[5]

She's also the Neighborhood's most independent character—she's her own puppet—and it turns out she wants to be free of the domestic practices typically associated with ladies. "I'm tired of being a lady," she says. "I want to be a *handyman* and *do* things all the time."

Lady Elaine expresses this frustration to her good friend Handyman Negri, an employee of King Friday who is highly skilled at fixing, assembling, and building things. By early 1970, he has already served as a border guard, installed punch clocks, assembled a windmill, fixed a water fountain, and helped rebuild Corney's factory, among other things. Handyman Negri is the Man of Make-Believe—*and* he's deeply sensitive. "But Lady Elaine," he says. "Ladies do things!"

Skeptical about these "things," Lady Elaine replies, "What? Besides washing and ironing and sweeping and scrubbing?" Although Lady Elaine is not exactly like the suburban housewives interviewed by Betty Friedan—she's neither a wife nor a mother, and there's nothing overtly nurturing or glamorous about her—she's certainly unhappy with the domestic duties typically associated with the stay-at-home moms and wives of the 1960s. Tired of the demands of domesticity, she gives voice to "the problem with no name."

"Awwww," Handyman Negri says, displaying his characteristic sensitivity. "It's true they do those things. But ladies have jobs, too, you know. Ladies are teachers and they're doctors and storekeepers. And they're mothers. And all kinds of workers." The good handyman is reminding Lady Elaine of something she already knows (Make-Believe, after all, has already shown ladies as border guards, musicians, wise teachers, and proprietors) and foreshadowing what is to come on *Mister Rogers' Neighborhood*—namely, numerous segments on women working as doctors and dentists, factory workers and farmers, mayors and machine operators.

Reminded of Mrs. Saunders, an African American teacher in the Neighborhood, Lady Elaine is delighted with the possibility of doing a new thing. "Teacher," she muses aloud. "If I were a teacher, I could get other people to do what I told them to do. Do this! Run over there! And write this down! Add this up!" There's nothing passive about Lady Elaine; she likes to be in charge, directing her destiny as well as the destinies of those around her, especially King Friday XIII, whom she refers to as "Friday," never "Your Majesty."

"Slow down, slow down," Handyman Negri says, seeing that Lady Elaine has gone off point. "The best teachers find out what their students like." That wise response earns only a moment's hesitation from Lady Elaine. "Oh," she replies. "I think I'd rather be a bus driver!" Handyman Negri chuckles—he knows he can't squelch Lady Elaine's fierce desire to be in charge—but agrees that she could easily drive a bus. "Well, I guess you could do that, too," he says. "But you know what? When people would come here to the Museum-Go-Round to visit and you wouldn't be here, they would really miss you."

Lady Elaine has been curator of the Museum-Go-Round since February 1969. Her occupying the top curatorial spot was no minor point in the 1960s, when women working in museums tended to get stuck in assistant positions. Despite her frustration with domesticity, then, Lady Elaine has already shattered the glass ceiling in her professional field.

Handyman Negri not only reminds Lady Elaine of her important role as curator; he also calls her "a real handy lady," which leaves her absolutely delighted. "A handy lady!" she repeats. "Just like you're a handy man!" Negri smiles a huge smile, affirming her growing realization that she's already not captive to the traditional roles associated with being a "lady." He also returns to his bigger point: "And you know something? There are lots of handy ladies in the world. I mean, ladies do lots of things!" And with that celebratory point, he and Lady Elaine belt out a song called "A Handy Lady and a Handy Man." Back in his television house, Mister Rogers reiterates Handyman Negri's bigger point. "I bet you know a lot of things that ladies do," he says. "A lot of jobs."

Fred Rogers worked hard at creating a neighborhood where girls and women could fulfill their need for an identity not tied to their traditional roles. There were some blips along the way, and feminist viewers sometimes protested what they took to be antifeminist roles on the program. For instance, they weren't pleased with a new character Rogers introduced in February 1971—Audrey of Audrey Cleans Everything (A.C.E.).

In her first appearance in the Neighborhood, a perfectly coiffed middle-aged woman named Audrey, played by Audrey Roth, wears a light blue dress, red lipstick, and earrings while cleaning neighbor Bob Trow's workshop. She explains to Mister Rogers that she owns a "professional cleaning service," and that her motto is "Audrey cleans everything." Busily moving around the workshop, dusting all around Mister Rogers, she smiles and says, "I really do love to clean." She also describes her cleaning of Bob Trow's workshop as helpful to "his wife."[6]

Feminist viewers did not find Audrey endearing, and they sent Rogers letters of protest. Even though he had made sure she was the owner and operator of her business—she wasn't working for "the man"—Rogers decided to relent, dropping the character completely by the mid-1970s. Arguably more interesting, though, is that actor Audrey Roth remained on the program and that her ongoing role in Make-Believe (as telephone operator Miss Paulificate) became increasingly focused on maintaining security. She too was one tough woman.

Blips like A.C.E. were relatively minor, and Rogers continued to use Lady Elaine to demonstrate that girls and women were perfectly capable of doing things beyond their traditional roles—that they could be someone others might not expect or want them to be. Like Lady Elaine, they could be noisy and mischievous, angry and competitive, athletic and confident, entrepreneurial and inventive, single and self-assured.

Time and again, Lady Elaine demonstrated that females were able to occupy top positions in a wide variety of professions—and simultaneously. While curator of the Museum Go-Round, Lady Elaine opened a pie restaurant and a syrup business, founded her own television station (MGR-TV), and started her own dance school (the Sometimes Happy Dance Studio), all without relying on any boys or men along the way. She also demonstrated that girls and women could pioneer in fields long closed to them. In April 1972, more than ten years before Sally Ride became the first American woman in space, Lady Elaine flew to Jupiter and discovered Planet Purple along the way. In May 1974, two years before Barbara Walters became the first woman anchor of an evening news program, Lady Elaine began anchoring the news at MGR-TV.

Moreover, Lady Elaine modeled female resistance to imperious males. She led a protest march against King Friday's demand that everyone watch his educational television program, and she also fiercely resisted his decisions to stop playtime, to prepare for war, and perhaps most ludicrous of all, to make everyone wear three-cornered hats. Rough and tough, Lady Elaine also let girls know that not all females were natural-born nurturers. In 1970, she expressed frustration that Elsie Jean Platypus took time off from work at the pie restaurant to care for her egg and, later, her baby Ana. And in 1971, when Dr. Bill Platypus used a baby doll to give lessons on patting a baby on the back, Lady Elaine hit the baby with so much force that Dr. Bill had to teach her to be gentle.

The Beauty Myth

In addition to modeling resistance and a natural toughness, Lady Elaine also schooled girls in the importance of self-love. "You can't love anybody else if you don't love yourself," she said.[7] And equally important, she embodied a profeminist message about physical beauty.

In an episode during the last year of *Mister Rogers' Neighborhood*, Lady Elaine hurts the feelings of neighbors preparing works for the royal art show. These neighbors include a trio rehearsing Scottish music for the awards show: Handyman Negri, Dr. Bill Platypus, and King Friday. "You fellas will never win!" Lady Elaine says, evoking the wrath of her archnemesis. "Why must you stick your big nose into everyone's business, Fairchilde?" King Friday angrily asks.[8]

Lady Elaine does indeed have a long red nose; it resembles a thick carrot or, as others have noted, an engorged penis. She sports a bowl cut, and her short-cropped hair is red and straw-like. From certain angles, her eyes appear beady, as if she's squinting to recognize faraway prey. Lady Elaine is no Queen Sara, and now, thanks to King Friday's cruel remark, she's so sensitive about her nose that she shows up at Elsie Jean Platypus's mound-home wearing a small colorful quilt over her head. When asked why she's wearing it, Lady Elaine explains, "So nobody will see my carrot—I mean, my nose."

Lady Aberlin is also visiting Elsie Jean, and she slowly pulls the quilt back from Lady Elaine's face. "It certainly is an artistic covering," Lady Aberlin says, "and one of my favorite people is under it." Surprised, Lady Elaine asks her to repeat her words and then seeks confirmation from Elsie Jean, who assures her that a lot of people like her. "Even with my big nose?" Lady Elaine asks. "With every part of you!" Elsie Jean says. The validation makes Lady Elaine melt, and she cries and cries.

"People don't say kind stuff to me very much," she says. "Maybe people don't say kind things to me because I don't say kind things to them." With this new realization, prompted by the inner beauty modeled by Lady Aberlin and Elsie Jean, Lady Elaine offers a kind remark about Handyman Negri's idea to take a picture of her, Lady Aberlin, and Elsie Jean, all of them beautiful on the inside, for the royal art show.

Back in his television house, Mister Rogers reinforces Make-Believe's lesson about beauty. "No matter what your face looks like, people can like you exactly as you are," he says. "Yep! It's what's inside you that matters most. Our thoughts and our feelings, the way we treat other people, the way we love one another—that's what matters much more than what we look like. Well, I like you exactly as you look right now."

There's no need for girls and women to look like movie stars on *Mister Rogers' Neighborhood*—no pressure to look thin, young, and gorgeous. Naomi Wolf might have been right to argue in *The Beauty Myth* that the 1990s witnessed a backlash against feminism that used female beauty—or, more exactly, pressure for women to be stunningly attractive—as a means to undermine earlier feminist advances. But her thesis did not hold everywhere. In the Neighborhood created by Fred Rogers, the beautiful truth was that physical appearances bore no relationship to the dignity and worth of girls and women. Real beauty was inside, not outside.

Equality and More

Rogers fashioned Lady Elaine Fairchilde as a puppet embodying the feminist belief that women do not have to be domesticated ladies, especially gorgeous ones, and he used Queen Sara to further advance the feminist principle of gender equality. This became especially clear when Sara Saturday and King Friday wed in 1969.

In the 1960s, traditional Christian wedding liturgies saw the groom vowing "to love and cherish" his bride, and the bride vowing "to love, cherish, and obey" her husband. The vows enshrined gender inequality in marriages; wives were to obey their husbands, as the New Testament admonished them, but husbands were not obliged to obey their wives. On the contrary, they were to be the chief authority in their marriages and their families.

One of the most publicized acts to buck that patriarchal expectation occurred when Princess Diana wed Prince Charles in 1981. In a decision that attracted worldwide attention, Diana flat-out refused to vow obedience to Charles; instead, she vowed to "love, comfort, honor, and keep" him.[9] Her bold decision, which foreshadowed many more to follow, evoked the wrath of religious conservatives but earned the praise of feminists long opposed to gender inequality in marriages.

Princess Diana's decision was not without precedent. Whether she realized it or not, she had a role model in Queen Sara of Make-Believe. In 1969, twelve years before Diana wed, Sara Saturday made a vow to King Friday that included no reference to obedience to one's husband. As the two held hands on that joyous occasion, she and King Friday exchanged these vows:

I, King Friday XIII, take thee, Queen Sara Friday Saturday, to be my lawful wedded wife, to have and to hold, in sickness and in health, in joy and in sorrow, for richer or for poorer, as long as we both shall live.

I, Queen Sara Friday Saturday, take thee, King Friday XIII, to be my lawful wedded husband, to have and to hold, in sickness and in health, in joy and in sorrow, for richer or for poorer, as long as we both shall live.[10]

As these vows expressed equality, so too did the substance of their relationship. Although King Friday was wont to command his subjects according to his whims, he did not do so with Queen Sara, and when he made error-ridden decisions, such as his plan to begin an arms race, she did not submit to them, willingly or unwillingly; she fought against them with quiet ferocity—and success eventually heralded by her error-prone husband. While respectful of King Friday, Queen Sara never played the role of subservient wife.

It was clear early on that Sara Saturday would remain her own person throughout her relationship with Friday. Her profeminist appreciation for both independence and mutuality came to the fore especially when she was deciding which name to adopt after her marriage. While in 1969 most women still dropped their birth names in favor of their husbands' surnames, Sara did not follow suit.

In a February 1969 episode, Marie Torre, a reporter for *Neighborhood News*, asks King Friday about Sara's name: "We'd like to know what you plan to call Sara Saturday when she becomes your queen?" Yes, it's an undeniably sexist question; Torre suggests that Sara will belong to Friday and that he will enjoy naming rights over her.

But Friday does not take the bait. "Well, interesting question," he says. "My name is Friday. Her name is Sara Saturday. She could be Queen Friday or Queen Sara Saturday. That should be up to her!"[11] By this point, King Friday had already learned that treating Sara well meant not commanding her to do things. But just as significant here is Friday's acknowledgment that women should enjoy the right to keep their birth names, even while married. Had there been a Lucy Stone League in the Neighborhood—Stone was a nineteenth-century feminist who fought for her legal right to keep her birth name—Friday would have been an enthusiastic member.

Faced with a choice, Sara is troubled; she likes both names. But with help from her friend and personal assistant Robert Troll, she settles on a name that bears witness to both her independence and her deep love for King Friday: Queen Sara Friday Saturday. In turn, King Friday (who, by the way, does not consider changing his name) suggests that the shortened form be Queen Sara Saturday—a creative (and Stone-esque) idea Sara likes very much.

Still, a problem remained. However mutual their relationship was, and however independent Queen Sara strove to be, she and King Friday were not political equals; Friday, not Saturday, was the formal ruler of the Neighborhood of Make-Believe. This intransigent inequality posed a problem for the feminist Rogers, and so in 1975 he selected a woman to be the mayor of nearby Westwood. Mayor Maggie (see chapter 7) arrives in the Neighborhood as the political equal of King Friday. She holds her office from 1975 until 2001, demonstrating over that long period of time that women, just like men, can be political rulers of the highest order.

Permission to Be Sensitive: Crying Corney

As Rogers used *Mister Rogers' Neighborhood* to support profeminist identities and roles for girls and women, he also created many episodes through the years that celebrated boys and men as sensitive and nurturing. Rogers himself modeled the softer side of the male gender in many and varied ways. It's not uncommon to see Mister Rogers playing with baby dolls and rag dolls, making clothes for them, wearing female wigs and hats, cooking and cleaning, and sewing and knitting. In 1996, right in the middle of "Brave and Strong Week," Mister Rogers walks through the door with a bag of knitting supplies and shows us his skills in knitting. "Do you know anybody who knits?" he asks, refusing to suggest that only girls and women knit.[12] It doesn't take too long before we learn that Mister Rogers has learned to knit from Brad Brewer, an African American puppeteer who knits all sorts of clothes for his puppets.

Rogers also sought to school boys and men in the softer, gentler side of the male gender by telling them it's okay to cry. Granting permission to cry was something that Rogers's own father had done for him. "My father was a strong, confident, caring man," Rogers explained in 1988. "His father, my granddad Rogers, was a steel worker and he died when I was only six years old; but, when he died, I saw my father cry." Watching his father cry made a huge impact on young Fred, and it freed him to cry in turn. "Many years later, when Dad himself died, I remembered his tears years before and it seemed like it was OK by him if I would cry then, too."[13] Rogers did cry upon his father's death, and it was one of the few times he felt it difficult to sing about the beautiful day in the neighborhood.

Rogers shared his father's lesson in an April 1971 episode in which Corney S. Pecially, owner of the Rockit Factory in Make-Believe, rushes to set up a new lathe that will allow him to make "fancy chairs." He's so excited to get it running that he dismisses Mr. McFeely's suggestion that they read the directions before turning it on. As the new lathe begins to hum, Corney reaches out to touch it and gets his finger pinched in the process. He fights off tears, but when he retreats inside his factory, he cannot help but cry out loud.

At this point, Nurse Miller walks by the factory, hears the cries, and calls out to ask if Corney is okay. At first he denies he's been crying—he thinks only babies should cry—but he later comes out of the factory, revealing the tears he's been trying to hide. Nurse Miller dries them with her handkerchief, puts a bandage on his finger, and gently leads him to acknowledge that "it's okay . . . for people to cry when they're hurt"—even strong men who own factories.[14]

Rogers returned to this lesson in 1989, sharpening the male-gender angle all the more. In a series of episodes devoted to working parents, Prince Tuesday becomes angry when both his parents face work-related demands causing them to be away from the castle more than usual. After initially ignoring Tuesday's feelings, King Friday confesses that he got angry at his parents when they worked too much during his own childhood, and that they were sad about being away from him so much. "In fact, I remember seeing my father cry one day when he had to leave us," Friday says. Tuesday is shocked. "Your father? Grandfather Tuesday cried?" he replies. Queen Sara then steps in and implicates her husband too. "Sometimes we cry when we have to leave you, Tuesday," she says.[15] And so it is that in the Neighborhood of Make-Believe there is a royal line of men who cry—Grandfather Tuesday, King Friday, and Prince Tuesday—a line that invites the rest of us boys and men to step in, grab our own handkerchiefs, and let the tears flow. Manly stoicism, with its explosive consequences, has no place in the Neighborhood.

Permission to Nurture: Good Fathers

Rogers also wanted men and boys to be nurturers, and he extolled male nurturing primarily by sharing his vision of good fathers. In a March 1968 episode, Mister Rogers walks through the door carrying a baby doll wrapped in a blanket. He tells us he's just passed by some friends, girls *and* boys, who were playing house; they were pretending to be moms and dads and were using baby dolls as their pretend babies. "I asked if I could borrow one," he explains. Sitting down, he pulls a handkerchief out of his pocket, folds it into a diaper, and begins to diaper the doll, using safety pins to finish the job. If that weren't mesmerizing enough, Mister Rogers then slides little rubber pants over the baby doll's diaper. "Daddies have to know these things, you know?" he says.[16]

With this simple statement, Fred Rogers publicly staked out his position among child-rearing experts of his day. Unlike many post–World War II experts, Rogers did not focus on the maternal-child bond to the exclusion of the father. And although he sided with those who believed that a distant or absent father might cause psychological damage in the life of his children, Rogers broke rank from experts who sought to correct the exclusion by calling upon fathers merely "to become buddies with their sons, share sports and hobbies with them, provide them with sex education, and serve as models of masculine maturity."[17] With their focus still on traditional masculinity, these experts "did not expect fathers to change diapers or take an active role in childcare or housework, arguing that this would make it difficult for boys and girls to develop a clearly defined sex role identity."[18]

By contrast, Fred Rogers commended fathers who changed diapers, kissed their babies, helped to rear their children, and even cleaned the house along the way. In a March 1968 episode, Mister Rogers celebrates this image by welcoming a young father, Mr. Swenson, into his television house and chatting with him about his newborn son and the role of fathers in their children's lives. Dressed in a suit, Mr. Swenson arrives with five-month-old Eric wrapped in a baby blanket. As the three of them sit on the couch, Mister Rogers offers little Eric a rattle, noting that he likes to keep one handy in case babies visit. When Eric reaches for the rattle with his mouth, Mister Rogers shares his knowledge about babies by telling us "the way you learn about the world is through your mouth when you're little."

"Where's Eric's mommy today?" Mister Rogers asks. "Eric's mom is helping one of her friends," replies Mr. Swenson. "So I'm sort of in charge of taking care of little Eric for the day." The answer leads Mister Rogers to deliver the message he's been pointing to throughout the episode: "Often dads can be in charge."

As Mr. Swenson shows he's in charge by wrapping up Eric for the departure—an image that also lets us imagine him as capable of diapering—Mister Rogers talks directly to Eric. "Can I give you a kiss before you go?" he asks. The content little boy just looks at him, but Mr. Swenson says yes and so Mister Rogers gives Eric a sweet little kiss on his baby cheek. It's a nurturing moment, full of love and care.

In *Mister Rogers' Neighborhood*, fathers are tender. They wrap their babies in blankets, change their diapers, and surround them with warmth and physical affection, including kisses. In this same episode, Rogers advances this image all the more by showing us a video of him playing with his own son Jamie when he was just fourteen months old. In the dated footage, he sits with Jamie on an organ bench and then plays rocking horse with him, tenderly bouncing him up and down on his leg.

Jamie even shows up for a quick visit in Mister Rogers's television house at the end of the episode. Now eight years old, Jamie joins his father in singing the closing song, and then they walk out the door, with Mister Rogers carrying the wrapped baby doll. Is he oblivious to the embarrassment he might cause Jamie as they walk the streets together? Whatever the case, the image of Mister Rogers carrying a baby doll while walking with his eight-year-old son is stunning. Less striking, of course, is the image of a father diapering his baby son and kissing him on the cheek. But in the 1960s, that image too was countercultural, and it served Rogers's overall mission of showing a softer, gentler side of males.

Family Roots

The image of a nurturing male was one with which Fred Rogers was long familiar. His own father was hands-on in ways that were perhaps uncommon for his era. Rogers mentioned this in 1990, when his son Jamie (now called "Jim") returned to the program with his own toddler son, Alexander. Rogers had spoken about the birth of his grandson in a December 1988 speech at Yale University, devoting the first part of the talk to the different ways generations of Rogerses had experienced childbirth:

> Eight weeks, two days, and 23 and a half hours ago our married son, Jim, and his wife, Tory, had their first child: Alexander Hughes Rogers. I couldn't help but think what a difference two generations had made. Jim was in the delivery room the whole time with Tory; and, since Tory had a caesarean section, Alexander went directly from the womb to his father's chest. Jim was the first person in the whole world to hold that baby in his arms.
>
> Things certainly weren't like that when Jim himself was born about 30 years ago. I wasn't invited to the delivery; and, the first glimpse I got of him he was all wrapped up in a blanket in a nurse's arms behind a glass window. And what's more, when *I* was born, *my* father's only job was to give out the cigars and candy: cigars for the men, and candy for the women. It was all clearly defined. Two generations have made a difference for men and women in the Rogers family.

But Rogers also made sure to note the continuities too, which bespoke a thick family thread of co-nurturing. "I'm glad to report that Alexander is doing very well and his mother and father both take care of him: feeding, rocking, diapering, cooking, laundry . . . the works," he stated. "That doesn't mean that I didn't do that, too, when Jim was little—and my father, too, when I was little. It's just that 50-some years ago, you didn't talk about it beyond the cigars and candy." Rogers was proud of his father's active role in his upbringing and shared "an old family story" that one of his parents' friends had told him: "She'd say, 'You know, Freddie, you were a colicky baby, and you cried a lot and it was hard to get you to sleep; but, when your father would get home from work, he'd take you in his arms and go to the rocking chair and in a matter of minutes you'd be sound asleep—and *he* would be, too.' "[19]

The episode in which Jim and Alexander appear gives a renewed focus to the nurturing male, as well as to the model of a man who cleans. Before the younger father and son arrive, Mister Rogers decides to vacuum his television house, explaining along the way that just as children will not go down drains, neither will they be swept into vacuums, however loud and scary they sound.

As he finishes vacuuming, Mister Rogers asks, "Who does the sweeping in your house?" The question echoes back to 1968, when he asked who does most of the hammering in your house, but this time there is a significant difference. Rather than supplying an answer, as he did in 1968, he simply says,

"Lots of different people can do that."[20] There's not even a hint of suggestion that moms are the ones who do the sweeping or most of the sweeping in our houses, and that dads will be hammering away somewhere else.

After the family visitors arrive, little Alexander sits between his father and grandfather on the piano bench, and he and Mister Rogers plunk the keys a bit before they slide off to play peekaboo with the trolley. The most compelling moment happens when Jim is holding Alexander just before they leave. Mister Rogers stands close to his son and grandson, and he gives Alex a sweet kiss. This tender scene is reminiscent of the 1968 episode in which Mister Rogers kisses little Eric as his father, Mr. Swenson, is holding him close. But there's a difference. This time, Mister Rogers hugs the other adult in the scene—his son Jim. It bears no resemblance to a warm embrace; it's one of those awkward expressions in which the huggers pat each other on the back in a really quick and uncomfortable way. But even so, we can clearly see that Mister Rogers still insists on showing his adult son care and affection, and that Jim does the same in return. These are men who love each other.

Fathers and Music

The family visit is part of a special week focusing on fathers and music. It's of no small significance that the theme is not fathers and sports. Rogers was not opposed to sports—rough sports just weren't his thing—but he had no interest in depicting fathers (or any other males) as rugged individualists climbing unforgiving mountains, or grunting teammates tackling one another on football fields, or pugilists pummeling each other bloody in a boxing ring. When he did focus on a male athlete, especially one in a traditionally rough, male sport, Rogers made sure to show the athlete's artistic side too. In 1981, for instance, Rogers introduced Lynn Swann as not only a star receiver for the Pittsburgh Steelers but also an accomplished ballet dancer.

Swann's presence, which most likely shocked more than a few Steelers fans, cleared the path for a delightful 1987 episode in which Lady Elaine refuses to invite boys and men to her new dance studio. "My theory is that men can't dance," she announces. After King Friday protests by dancing a little tap dance of sorts, Lady Elaine responds, "You simply confirmed my theory, Friday!" But then professional tap dancer Sam Weber, playing the role of a sales representative, arrives at the studio, and he dances his shoes off, forcing Lady Elaine to admit he must be a "real exception." Weber protests, saying he knows "many men who dance really well," and Lady Elaine is so impressed that she decides to discard her theory and open her studio to boys and men too.[21]

For Rogers, ballet, music, painting, photography, and other artistic expressions are ways we nurture our souls. By showing Swann and Weber, and coupling fathers and music in 1990, he supported his longtime mission of showing a softer, gentler side to the male gender. Unsurprisingly, the coupling also reflected his personal background and history: Rogers played the piano for his sons, and his own father had introduced him to the nurturing power of music. "My father used to sing to me when I was a baby," Mister Rogers says in an episode during the special series on fathers. "That helped me to feel so good."[22] He says this shortly after pretending that a rag doll in his care—a little black boy doll—is sick. Mister Rogers covers him with a blanket, puts his head on a pillow, and sings "I Like to Take Care of You."

Some viewers might rankle at an image of the Great White Father taking care of the poor little black boy, but because of the prior episode, it's clear that such an interpretation would be inaccurate. In this earlier episode, Rogers showed members of the Marsalis family (father Ellis and sons Branford, Delfeayo, and Jason) playing several numbers of what they're known for worldwide—great jazz. Seated at his piano bench in the middle of the group, Ellis is the image of a strong black man playing a close and direct role in the lives of his sons. That's also the image confirmed by Branford, who says, "The most important thing about Dad is really not that he drilled us in music, music, music, but more so that he made us see life in a certain way. We have a certain outlook on life—how we're supposed to carry ourselves in the world and how we should see and treat other people."[23] Given the way they're treating Mister Rogers—with a respectful, caring, and fun-filled attitude—we understand the outlook he has in mind. Viewers familiar with the sociological studies about the absence of strong male role models in black families also understand that Mister Rogers wants us to know that African American fathers like Ellis Marsalis stay close to their sons and nurture them with love and care—and school them in the arts.

And if Ellis Marsalis weren't enough, Rogers uses "Fathers and Music Week" to introduce us to another famous and sensitive father: Yo-Yo Ma. We get a glimpse of the cellist's sensitivity when he talks about the "sad piece" he's playing at the time Mister Rogers arrives. Ma says that playing the sad music makes him feel better when he misses his children during his many trips to concerts. His face lights up, though, when he tells Mister Rogers that his children have taught him so many things about himself and his music. "One of the things I've found that I'm able to do is to love everything more—to love what I do more, to love them more," he says, adding that he draws so much from "the incredible joy and the fun we have." After describing his own parents as "loving," Ma breaks out in a huge smile as his young son, Nicholas, runs into his arms. Ma greets him with a huge hug and a warm kiss, and he puts his arm around him as the two of them play "Twinkle, Twinkle, Little Star" on the cello.[24] It's such a tender moment, and Nicholas seems truly at home in the arms of his dad.

Through Jim Rogers, Ellis Marsalis, Yo-Yo Ma, and his own Mister Rogers character, Fred Rogers has shown us that good fathers hold and hug, kiss and care, nurture and love—and are daring enough to dance and play music.

Working Mothers

Rogers also used his program to set forth his vision of good mothers. In 1983, Rogers published a parenting book in which he urged each mother who has "a choice about working during her baby's first years . . . to think long and hard about what that choice will mean."[25] While the choice might mean professional advancement, it might also deny children and mothers so much joy, loving, and learning. Rogers also sternly warned against fathers who work so much that they neglect to participate closely in the lives of their children.

"From what I've seen and heard and read," Rogers wrote, "I have come to believe that a child is most likely to thrive emotionally when he or she, for the first three years of life, has the fulltime care of a consistent motherperson and the close participation in that care of a consistent fatherperson."[26] The fulltime "motherperson" is indispensable because the "baby needs *one primary caretaker* with whom to take those first early steps toward selfhood—one person to feel part of and then grow separate from."[27] The "fatherperson" is so important because he can allow the baby to experience "differences in smells and voices, different ways of being held or hugged, different ways of being diapered and fed, different ways of being comforted—in other words, different ways of experiencing love."[28] Experiencing these differences through both a motherperson and a fatherperson "is a large part of the way we learn about our world and ourselves."[29]

It seems as if Rogers's position in this book is simply sounding the deafening bells of tradition. A mother and child, he writes, "are both vastly enriched if there is a loving, supportive, and participating father in the home." A good father can also help a mother feel more secure by providing "food and shelter during the time of her healthy preoccupation with her baby," and by offering emotional support along the way.[30]

But the reader's sense that Rogers favors only the old model of working father and stay-at-home mother changes a bit upon reading that "a male can be a mothering person."[31] Yes, males, not just females, can be the stay-at-home partner—the primary caretaker who forms the closest of nurturing relationships with the baby. "Mothering," like knitting and cleaning, is thus not bound to a specific gender; nor is "fathering." Rogers's claim about the "motherperson" invariably means that females can be the "father-person," the one who works eight hours a day to provide food and shelter for the family. "Fathering," like hammering and digging, is not confined to a specific gender.

Rogers devoted sustained attention to the issue of working mothers in the 1989 episodes in which Prince Tuesday learns about crying. The storylines from that week depict women who work outside the home for reasons related to finances, personal fulfillment, and service to others.

Rogers's treatment of the issue is remarkable for its sensitivity toward a point that early middle-class feminists seemed to miss—that some women have to work. Feminists such as bell hooks corrected the early error by arguing that whereas liberation for some middle-class women might mean leaving domesticity behind and entering the work world, liberation for poorer women might mean leaving work and staying at home with their children. Rogers recognized the distinction and addressed the issue of mothers who have to work in his series on working parents.

In the first episode of the series, we see Helena Ruoti, a young mother who runs the front counter at Joe Negri's music shop, speaking on the telephone with her son's babysitter. Helena learns that her son Matthew is screaming and cannot be consoled. When Joe hears about the situation, he encourages Helena to go home. "Oh, I'd like that," she says, "but I also want to do my job for you."[32] Like many mothers who have to work, Helena feels an awful pull between job and family.

While acknowledging the pull, her boss Joe also reminds Helena of the top priorities in the Neighborhood. "First things first," he says. "I mean, you're a wonderful worker. But Matthew needs you at home right now more than this store does. . . . There's one thing about *this* Neighborhood—families and children come first." After Helena departs for home, Mister Rogers compliments Joe's decision. "Well, I know how I like people to treat me, and I know how much she cares for her child *and* her job," he says.

A few days later, Mister Rogers returns to the music shop and sees Helena back at the counter. The plain and simple dialogue between them is far from a lament about mothers who work; it's a powerful acknowledgment that it's important for some mothers to work.

Rogers: You're a very caring mother.

Helena: It's hard when you need to be in two places at the same time.

Rogers: You probably think about him wherever you are, don't you?

Helena: I think about him more times than I could count. After all, I go to work because I want to be able to take care of him.

Rogers: That's hard for children to understand.

Helena: Oh, I know it. But it's true. After all, when I work, I earn money that we use to buy food and clothes and other things that we need.

Something similar is going on in the Neighborhood of Make-Believe, where factory owner Corney needs a lot of help. "One of our Rockit makers in the factory here brought her baby to work because she couldn't get a sitter," he says, "and now we're so busy we need somebody to look after the baby." The need is so great that Corney, a sensitive boss like Joe Negri, asks Lady Aberlin if she would be willing to take care of the baby. Lady Aberlin is more than pleased to help out, and factory worker Hilda Dingleboarder soon appears with her baby, Daphne, who's sleeping ever so peacefully.

"It's pretty noisy in the factory, and I just didn't know what to do," Hilda explains. After entrusting sweet little Daphne to Lady Aberlin, Hilda goes right back to work. "Thank you for taking care of Dee Dee," she says on her way back. "I'll see you as soon as I finish work."

Lady Aberlin knows her friend Henrietta Pussycat loves little babies, so she decides to take Daphne across the Neighborhood for a short visit. As Henrietta is meowing with delight over Daphne, Lady Aberlin tells Henrietta about the problem that led to her babysitting job. Because Henrietta excels at taking care of others—that's what she's known for in the Neighborhood—she wonders about the other babies and children whose parents work at the factory. Better yet, when she learns that there are many others, she comes up with the idea to build a "caring center" at the Rockit factory. Corney loves the idea—"A caring center at *this* factory!" he says—and agrees to find not only space for the new center but also to donate Rockits for rocking all the babies.

Fred Rogers did not use his program to support all the policy demands of the women's rights movement. Understandably, he never addressed a woman's right to abortion, nor did he advance the demand for publicly funded and operated child care facilities. But he was deeply sympathetic toward working mothers who sometimes felt torn between their jobs and their families, and he strongly believed that child care should not be an obstacle for working mothers. He also believed that employers should show sensitivity to working mothers by granting them time off when family needs arose and even by creating and maintaining on-site child care facilities.

More fundamentally, Rogers respected and supported a mother's right to work outside the home. He believed in this right not only for working-class mothers who needed money to support their families, but also for middle- and upper-class mothers who opted to work for reasons related to personal fulfillment or the desire to help others. Rogers's support for the right of financially secure mothers to work is also evident in the 1989 series on working parents, particularly in a storyline in which Queen Sara goes to work full time for Food for the World. She does so not because she needs to add to the royal bank account, but because of her passionate belief that no one in the world should go hungry.

Through Queen Sara, Helena Ruoti, Hilda Dingleboarder, and others, Rogers has shown us that good mothers can be either full-time caretakers of children (and their emotional development) at home or full-time workers outside the home whose wages and benefits provide the physical conditions (food and shelter) that enable their children to be safe and to flourish. Like Mister Rogers himself, good mothers can leave their children during the workday and return home at day's end to love and care for their children all the more.

God and the Rhetoric of Sexuality

There is one final, and ultimate, point to note about the gender-bending Neighborhood: Fred Rogers grounded it in his belief that God has both feminine and masculine qualities.

In 1983, Phyllis Trible, a professor of sacred literature at Union Theological Seminary in New York City, published *God and the Rhetoric of Sexuality*, a groundbreaking work in feminist biblical scholarship. The book received widespread attention for the expert ways in which it traced female imagery for God throughout the Bible. Conservative Christians criticized Trible's feminism, but progressive Christians like Rogers began a concerted effort to incorporate female imagery in their thoughts and language about God, including prayers and hymns. Mainstream progressives did not eliminate male language for God; they simply supplemented it with female imagery long hidden in Scripture and tradition.

This is exactly what Fred Rogers did on *Mister Rogers' Neighborhood* in the same year Trible published her feminist study. In a 1983 episode, as nighttime descends on Make-Believe, Lady Aberlin and Daniel Striped Tiger engage in a quiet and peaceful conversation regarding Daniel's thoughts about the rhythm of life and the wonders of the world. Daniel then softly sings the first part of "Creation," a song familiar to longtime viewers:

Who made the rainbow and the sky?
Who made the bird and let it fly?
Who made the hour?
Who made the day?
Who had the power to make the flower?
And who made the rain and made the snow?
Made us and made us want to know?

Lady Aberlin listens intently before saying, "I can sing you what I believe."
She then sings the second half of "Creation," but with a new twist:

God made the rainbow, the bird, and the summer sun.
God made the mountains, the stars, each and every one.
God made the sea.
And She made the land.
God made the mighty and God made the very small.
God made the world, made the people.
He made it all.[33]

The new twist, of course, was the reference to God as "She"; older lyrics
used only "God" and "He." The feminist imagery did not sit well with Rogers's more conservative viewers, and many of them wrote letters accusing him
of heresy. One writer claimed that Rogers had allowed the American Civil
Liberties Union and liberal feminist groups to set the agenda for the show.
Another accused him of embracing humanism and letting go of his traditional
way of thinking about family and God. Still another stated that it was unforgivable for Rogers to teach children such blasphemy. But Rogers did not relent,
and in a handwritten note to his assistant Hedda Sharapan, who found herself
having to explain Rogers's beliefs to angry viewers, he penned, "Since God is
all, both fathering and mothering aspects must be included in God's being."[34]

For Fred Rogers, God is Father and Mother, He and She, Love in all its
forms. And this means, by implication, that Rogers would have understood
Lady Elaine Fairchilde, his own TV character, and all who embrace identities
and roles not typically associated with their genders, as bearing witness to the
image of God—an image in which both maleness and femaleness reside at
the same place. For Rogers, gender-bending is ultimately a spiritual practice.

François Clemmons recalls that shortly after he began appearing on *Mister Rogers' Neighborhood* Rogers warned him against coming out publicly as a gay man.

Chapter 10

"He Understood"

Homosexuality and Gay Friends

*T*he Rev. Fred Phelps of the Westboro Baptist Church of Topeka, Kansas, did not mourn the passing of Fred Rogers in 2003. The self-styled minister had a notorious history of picketing the funerals of gays and their allies, and anyone whose funeral would attract a crowd. Upon learning of Rogers's death, he instructed his church members to picket a tribute to Rogers at Heinz Hall in Pittsburgh. "Well, I don't know if he's gay or not, but he's one of the foremost proponents of 'It's okay to be gay,'" Phelps stated at the time. "And the church he goes to in Pittsburgh . . . is one of the few boldly fag-promoting churches."[1] The antigay minister's daughter, Rebekah Phelps Davis, carried two signs outside the tribute. One read, "GOD HATES FAGS," and the other, "ROGERS IN HELL." "[Rogers] had the bully pulpit for 30 years and did nothing to talk about this message," she said.[2]

She was partly right; Rogers never delivered antigay messages either on or off television. But his stance toward homosexuality was far more complicated than that shallow point. Rogers knowingly hired gays to appear on *Mister Rogers' Neighborhood*, and he counted two of them—John Reardon and François Clemmons—among his close personal friends. Rogers also attended a Presbyterian church known for welcoming gays and lesbians, supported the minister's gay-friendly ministry, and befriended gay church members. Nevertheless, Rogers was never a public advocate of gay rights, and in the early years of *Mister Rogers' Neighborhood* he even encouraged François Clemmons to remain in the closet.

The story of Clemmons and Rogers in relation to the topic of homosexuality is particularly revealing. It shows that while Rogers was willing to address some moral issues publicly—for example, war—he was unwilling to grant similar public attention to others, especially homosexuality and gay rights. Unlike his antiwar stance, there was a private-public split in Rogers's approach to these issues. Privately, he tried to accept and love gays just as they were—as beloved children of God. Publicly, he assumed a pragmatic approach that adamantly refused to address homosexuality and gay rights so that he could avoid alienating certain viewers and continue to reach as many children as he possibly could. Because he did not have these same concerns when dealing with war, it's accurate to say that Rogers was inconsistent in his approach to creating a peaceful Neighborhood that admitted no discrimination. For Rogers, peace in the Neighborhood did not require an open closet.

Spotted at a Gay Bar

François Clemmons had his first gay sexual encounter in his sophomore year at Oberlin College. "I talked with Fred quite a bit about the fact that I was gay," he recalls.[3] He could not talk about his sexuality in a positive way with his mother when growing up in Youngstown, Ohio. She was a fundamentalist Christian who considered homosexuality a sin against God and nature, a judgment reiterated many times in Clemmons's home church and community. They all made it "very clear" that homosexuality was not only a sin but also a symptom of weak-mindedness. "They gave the impression that nobody with a strong mind or strong morals could be gay," Clemmons recalls. "Great artists were not gay—that's what they said. Great thinkers were not gay." Consequently, "nobody in his right mind wanted to be gay, and I didn't want to be either."

Facing the disapproval of his family, church, and community, Clemmons decided to "keep the closet doors closed." But his perspective began to shift when he enrolled at Oberlin and met openly gay students. Among them was the dashing and erudite Glover Parham, another African American chorister, who introduced Clemmons to the works of James Baldwin, Langston Hughes, and others, to help him understand that homosexuality did not mean that one could not be bright or even brilliant.

Parham and Clemmons grew to be close friends, though never lovers, and visited with each other's families. Predictably, the visit in Youngstown did not go well. "My parents recognized . . . that he was gay, and there were some words that were spoken," Clemmons says. Worse than that, he continues, "my mother threw him out. . . . It broke my heart, and it served as a kind of real breach between me and my mother."

The visit to Parham's family just outside of Birmingham, Alabama, proved to be a far different experience. Parham's parents "really treated me like family," Clemmons remembers, and so too did the rest of the extended family. "His family was the dream family I had hoped for. I'm sure his mother knew he was gay, and everyone thought we were lovers. But we weren't—we were literally best friends."

Back at Oberlin, Clemmons wasn't out of the closet. "And I did all these things to throw people off my trail," he remembers. "I dated occasionally, and I said proper things about women because there was a certain amount of terror associated with being gay." He was especially fearful of repercussions from disapproving faculty members, such as an unwillingness to offer positive recommendations for jobs or additional studies. But watching Parham act so openly emboldened Clemmons, and he came out to a few close friends, went to a few gay bars, and began what would be a three-year sexual relationship with a black man from Pittsburgh.

Nevertheless, Clemmons continued to feel that living as a gay man "was not an open life choice," and he still felt obliged to please his mother, who remained resolute in her opposition to homosexuality. "No son of mine is going to be gay," she once announced when he tried to broach the subject during a visit home. "That was like a pronouncement from the Old Testament God," Clemmons says.

Another pronouncement was on its way too. Not long after he began appearing on *Mister Rogers' Neighborhood*, Clemmons found himself in a private meeting with Fred Rogers. "Franc, we've come to love you here in the Neighborhood," Clemmons recalls Rogers saying. "You have talents and gifts that set you apart and above the crowd, and we want to ensure your place with us." Once again, and without surprise, Clemmons was hearing words of love and affirmation from his fatherly boss.

But the conversation took an unexpected turn. As Clemmons recalls, Rogers said, "Someone, we're not able to say who, has informed us that you were seen at the local gay bar downtown with a buddy from school. Now I want you to know, Franc, that if you're gay, it doesn't matter to me at all. Whatever you say and do is fine with me, but if you're going to be on the show, as an important member of the Neighborhood, you can't be 'out' as gay. People must not know. . . . Many of the wrong people will get the worst idea, and we don't want them thinking and talking about you like that."[4] Rogers emphasized that his reason for setting this choice before Clemmons was the potential backlash in viewers. "If those people put up enough fuss, then I couldn't have you on the program," he said.

However gently delivered, the message was blunt: If Clemmons came out publicly, Rogers would fire him for the sake of *Mister Rogers'*

Neighborhood. Of little consolation was Rogers's insistence that he person-ally took no offense at homosexuality. "It's not an issue for me," Clemmons remembers him saying. "I don't think you're less of a person. I don't think you're immoral."

That statement might not have been consoling at the time, but it was sig-nificant nonetheless, reflecting progressive thinking about homosexuality. Although Clemmons cannot pinpoint the exact date of the conversation, it occurred not long after his August 1968 debut and thus most likely before the Stonewall riots in Greenwich Village—and certainly before the American Psychiatric Association stopped diagnosing homosexuality as a mental ill-ness, before mainstream Protestant churches began to ordain homosexuals, and long before the Supreme Court ruled that homosexual behavior was not a criminal offense. Contrary to the many Christians who condemned homo-sexuals as sinners, or the numerous laws that identified them as criminals, or the establishment psychiatrists who labeled them as sick, Rogers's state-ment staked out a countercultural position; it countered the wider culture's identification of homosexuality as a serious problem requiring confession, imprisonment, or reparative therapy.

Nevertheless, even though Rogers might not have believed homosexual-ity was sick, sinful, or criminal—the tripartite judgment that homosexuals often faced at this time—the threat he dangled revealed Rogers to be one who believed that homosexuality should be a private matter, not for public consumption, especially a public that watched his television show. The threat stung Clemmons terribly. "It was devastating," Clemmons recalls. "I felt so bad I wanted to die."

Clemmons sobbed uncontrollably during the confrontation, and Rogers walked around his desk and cradled him in his arms. That fatherly act made him sob even harder, and he wondered aloud whether the end of their rela-tionship had arrived. According to Clemmons, Rogers protested: "Now just wait a minute, young man. Who says that our relationship has to come to an end? You need to decide just what it is you want in life, Franc. . . . Tal-ent can give you so much in this life, but that 'sexuality thing' can take it all away. Faster than you can ever imagine. . . . You can have it all if you can keep that part of it out of the limelight." Clemmons also recalls Rogers sharing a concrete idea about keeping his homosexuality out of the public eye. "Have you ever thought of getting married? People do make some com-promises in life."[5]

Yes, Clemmons wanted a career badly. "I was the first African American regular on a children's television program, and it was . . . a little bit of a heavy weight to carry," he says. "And I couldn't afford to just throw it away. It's like you have to be a credit to the race." And because he truly believed that Rogers's diagnosis and assessment were accurate, he eventually dried his tears and left his boss's office determined to marry a woman who was in love with him at the time.

Acting on Rogers's Advice

Clemmons's decision to marry was also fueled by his ongoing inability to maintain a critical distance from his judgmental mother and stepfather. "I specifically married to please my parents," he says. "I was so profoundly unable to make a decision against their wishes in that area, because I thought I was a sinner and I'd go to hell. And I didn't want to die and go to hell, so I thought that taking my parents' advice was the only course to have a happy, healthy life." Coupled with his parents' harsh judgment, Rogers's suggestion thus made all the more sense, and not long after the office incident he married a "gentle, intense soul."

François and Carol Clemmons got along well, and Carol even appeared twice on *Mister Rogers' Neighborhood*—as Mrs. Clemmons. But François couldn't shake off his identity as a gay man. Marriage was certainly a compromise, but it did nothing to eliminate his desire to be with men. François was gay, period, and it didn't take long for the relationship to falter. He talked openly with Carol about his sexuality and struggles, and though she wanted to remain married, mostly because they still loved each other, he insisted on breaking apart so he could be free to live publicly as a gay man. "I could not be the husband she deserved," he now says.

Clemmons kept Rogers apprised of his personal struggles along the way. To be sure, their earlier conversation had scarred him. "It was something that I mourned about for months and maybe that flowed into years," he says. But the incident "didn't ruin my relationship with him because he was the one person I could talk to about being gay."

In their ongoing chats, Rogers recognized that his earlier idea—that Clemmons consider marrying a woman—had failed miserably. It created inner turmoil rather than inner peace. Clemmons did not complain, though, and in retrospect he feels that Rogers's initial advice was mostly a "reality check" about discrimination in the wider world. Even now he does not sharply criticize Rogers for asking him to remain in the closet. "Fred loved me as I was," Clemmons says, "but the rest of the world was not ready."

Clemmons does not dare ask whether the rest of the world was ready when Rogers preached pacifism during the Vietnam War, or when he sought to undermine racism during the modern civil rights movement; he just insists that Rogers loved him as he was. Beyond this, he also defends Rogers as someone comfortable in the presence of gays—and who welcomed gays with open arms. "Fred wasn't homophobic at all," Clemmons says. "His best friend was John Reardon, and he was gay."

Indeed, Reardon and Rogers had first become friends at Rollins College, where they lived across the hall from each other. Reardon had started his college career as a business student, but he began to study music after his performance in campus musicals earned enthusiastic praise from students and faculty. A gifted baritone, Reardon graduated from Rollins in 1952, just a year after Rogers, and less than two years later he made his debut at the New York City Opera, where he sang regularly until 1972. He and Rogers remained friends throughout this time, and Rogers invited him to appear on *Mister Rogers' Neighborhood* shortly after the program went national.

Reardon accepted the invitation, and in his April 1968 debut he sang a selection from Mozart's *The Magic Flute* for King Friday in the Neighborhood of Make-Believe. It was the first of many appearances that Reardon—whose homosexuality was known on and off the set—made before he died twenty years later at the age of fifty-eight. Three years before his untimely death—the newspapers reported that he died of pneumonia—Reardon publicly described Rogers as "my best friend."[6] Clemmons characterizes the relationship between Reardon and Rogers as "extremely close."

During his tenure on *Mister Rogers' Neighborhood*, Reardon became a "big brother, big sister" to Clemmons, teaching him especially about discrimination against gays in the wider world and about places where he might be most comfortable living out his homosexuality. Rogers offered Clemmons similar counsel in the days, months, and years following their painful conversation. Though Clemmons was still feeling stung, he eventually experienced a sense of "healing" as Rogers listened to his innermost thoughts and feelings about his sexuality. "He was wonderful in not judging me," Clemmons says. "I never felt he pulled away or rejected me or turned his back. He stood there right with that issue . . . and we walked through it together."

After Clemmons divorced, Rogers shifted his tactics, urging him to find a stable, long-term partner with whom he could share his life. "He thought that was a worthy, positive, human thing to do," Clemmons recalls.

The shift in counsel was significant. By this point—it was the early 1970s—the Stonewall riots had occurred, and gays and lesbians were coming out in record numbers and publicly demanding basic rights—especially the right not to be discriminated against—in everything from employment to mental health to marriage. Rogers himself embraced this cultural shift in the sense that he stopped asking Clemmons to stay in the closet and discontinued his threat to fire him if he were to come out.

Nevertheless, Rogers's own shift went only so far. As his evolving counsel suggested, Rogers was not prepared to encourage Clemmons to enjoy the "free love" wing of the budding gay and lesbian rights movement. Rogers's progressivism had its limits. Because he found monogamous love to be the best expression of romantic relationships, Rogers focused instead on helping Clemmons see the value of having a stable, long-term partner. Still, he did not push the idea too hard, and he certainly did not go so far as to introduce Clemmons to any other gay men. "He was not meddlesome," Clemmons says. "He never interfered. . . . The kind of parenting he did was empowering."

Clemmons found Rogers's counsel especially helpful as the two talked about their parents. When he told Rogers about the "tremendous judgment" he felt from his mother back in Youngstown, Rogers refused to condemn her. He was "very nonjudgmental" and instead helped Clemmons try to understand that "she was who she was because of her experiences." On a more positive note, the Freudian Rogers also encouraged Clemmons to reconnect with his biological father, who was still living in Tuscaloosa, Alabama. "You have some unfinished business with your dad," he said. "Maybe you should go visit him."

Rogers made the suggestion several times, and Clemmons eventually decided to pick up the phone. To his delight, he got "a very positive, warm reception" from his father, and the two agreed he should visit the extended family in Tuscaloosa. The visit went remarkably well; he experienced both his father and stepmother as "very, very loving." During the amicable visit, he made sure to pull his father aside for a potentially explosive conversation. "There's something I want to tell you," Clemmons explained. "I'm gay. And I want to know whether that's okay with you, and I want to know if it's not okay. I want to know how you feel." Clemmons did not know what to expect, and he deeply feared that his father, like his biological mother, might turn judgmental and cast him away. But his father did not disappoint. "Son," he said, "if you find someone to love you in this life, consider yourself lucky. I don't care who he is." That positive reaction left Clemmons with "a feeling that I never had in my whole life—that this is where I belong. I belong to this man. I'm gay, and my daddy loves me. It was the most empowering and ennobling . . . conversation I've had with anybody."

He Understood

Empowered by fatherly love, Clemmons wanted to come out more publicly, not just to friends and family, and so in the early to mid-1970s he started talking with Rogers about "what it would be like to have a gay character on the show." Specifically, Clemmons wanted to come out publicly by appearing as a gay character on *Mister Rogers' Neighborhood*. The proposed character would allow him to blend his personal and professional lives in new and innovative ways, and Clemmons pitched his idea several times through the years.

But Rogers would have none of it. As Clemmons recalls their conversations, Rogers maintained that an openly gay character would be too radical for the more socially conservative areas that *Mister Rogers' Neighborhood* reached. A gay character, that is, would alienate significant portions of his viewing audience.

Once again, Clemmons was disappointed with his boss and friend. But once again, he did not allow his disappointment to interfere with their personal friendship and their ongoing conversations about gender and sexuality. "He understood," Clemmons says. "He had insights." When Clemmons shared that he felt feminine, for example, Rogers encouraged him to find a way to express his femininity, even suggesting that Clemmons might like wearing dresses and heels. And when he told Rogers that he loved children and felt maternal, Rogers assured him he would no doubt find a way to express his maternal feelings too. That feeling of confidence "was the impetus for me having my 'cosmic children,'" Clemmons says today, referring to the Middlebury College students he took under his wing during his tenure there as a musician-in-residence.

Rogers continued to exercise his limits too. While assuring Clemmons it was okay to be gay, he steadfastly refused to depict any hint of gay sexuality onscreen. This limit became dramatically clear when Clemmons began wearing an earring in the 1970s. "It was my way of silently rebelling and telling people quietly that I was gay. In those days, if you had an earring in your left ear, it meant you were gay. So I wore an earring in my left ear."

But Rogers also resisted that public expression. "Fred was not okay with it. He said I should take it out whenever I was filmed." Clemmons obliged, but the absent earring did not suffice for Rogers's purposes. "I was aware [the camera operators] often filmed me on the right side because my left side was pierced." Clemmons felt it was a concerted effort to avoid broadcasting images of the piercing.

"Whatever you do in your private life is your business," Rogers told him when explaining that the program would steer far away from expressions of Clemmons's gay sexuality. But there was a double standard at play, and Clemmons knew it. After all, Rogers wore his wedding ring on the program, as did David Newell (Mr. McFeely), Joe Negri, and Don Brockett (Chef Brockett), among others. Rogers had no qualms about filming those obvious signs of heterosexual relationships, but he would not show any hint of Clemmons's earring. That was too controversial, too potentially alienating to viewers who were still light years away from today's widespread acceptance of same-sex relationships. Concerned about losing these viewers, Rogers continued to act on his conviction that gay sexuality, unlike straight sexuality, should remain behind the camera lens.

The double standard irritated Clemmons, but he abided by Rogers's dictate. He also continued to grow bolder in publicly expressing his sexual identity behind the camera lens. In the years to follow, he even grew daring enough to invite gay friends and lovers to come by the studio at different times. "Everybody in the studio knew that I was gay," he says, and everyone knew his friends were gay too. He and his friends would hold hands and show physical affection for each other without trying to hide it from anyone, whoever they were. He was not out on *Mister Rogers' Neighborhood*, but he was as out as he could be in other settings.

Rogers grew less concerned too, moving far beyond his earlier warning that Clemmons should not be seen at gay bars. In fact, when Clemmons brought his gay friends to the studio, Rogers was "not uncomfortable" in their presence and "always treated them in a warm, honorable, loving way," Clemmons says. Perhaps more significantly, Clemmons offered the same back to his friend. Although Rogers had sought to shove him back into the closet several times, claiming it was all for the sake of the program, Clemmons remained a loyal friend and devoted co-worker for twenty-five years, appearing on *Mister Rogers' Neighborhood* for the last time during Love Week in 1993.

His second-to-last scene includes a wading pool, echoing back to the wade-in of 1968. Donning his police officer suit one last time—he's just "filling in" at the local precinct—Clemmons joins Rogers in the front yard as he is soaking his tired feet in a wading pool and thinking of different ways people say "I love you." Rogers invites Clemmons to soak his feet too, and the gentle police officer accepts the offer, stating that he likes to say "I love you" through his singing. After Clemmons sings "Many Ways to Say I Love You," Rogers smiles, tells Clemmons he's proud of him, and then uses a towel to help dry Clemmons's feet.[7]

Clemmons knew his Bible well enough to realize that the towel scene reenacted a Bible story in which Jesus expresses his love for his disciples by washing their feet and drying them with a towel. Clemmons would never be guilty of confusing Rogers with Jesus; perhaps better than most, he knew Rogers was human, imperfect, and sometimes in need of his own washing. But through it all he also believed that Rogers had sought to serve him well through the years—that he truly loved him as a friend, a colleague, and even as the gay man he would always be, on and off the set.

More Light at Sixth Church

Two years after Clemmons left *Mister Rogers' Neighborhood*, Fred Rogers attended a private dinner for the Rev. William Sloane Coffin Jr., former minister of the Riverside Church in New York City, at the Pittsburgh home of the Rev. John McCall, minister of Sixth Presbyterian Church, where the Rogers family had attended since the early 1970s. Known for his prophetic preaching and social activism, Coffin shot to national prominence when, as chaplain at Yale University, he became a leading voice in the peace movement opposing the Vietnam War. He later became a prominent voice against the nuclear arms race, his fame already assured by Garry Trudeau's use of him as inspiration for an ongoing character (Rev. Sloan) in the politically liberal comic strip *Doonesbury*.

Coffin's sermons and essays often had a national audience, and in 1993 he published *A Passion for the Possible*, a small and provocative book that offered a liberal faith perspective on such issues as abortion, sexism, racism, poverty, the environment, nuclear disarmament, and homophobia. On the topic of the Bible and homosexuality, Coffin wrote:

> In abolishing slavery and in ordaining women we've gone beyond biblical literalism. It's time we did the same with gays and lesbians. The problem is not how to reconcile homosexuality with scriptural passages that condemn it, but rather how to reconcile the rejection and punishment of homosexuals with the love of Christ. It can't be done. So instead of harping on what's "natural," let's talk of what's "normal," what operates according to the norm. For Christians the norm is Christ's love. If people can show the tenderness and constancy in caring that honors Christ's love, what matters their sexual orientation? Shouldn't a relationship be judged by its inner worth rather than by its outer appearance?[8]

Coffin's main point—it's what inside that counts—dovetailed nicely with the main point on *Mister Rogers' Neighborhood*: It's *you* I like, what's *inside* you. Indeed, McCall had invited Rogers to the private dinner knowing that he was sympathetic to Coffin's stance toward homosexuality.

At the time, Sixth Church was in the process of studying homosexuality and discerning whether publicly to identify itself as a congregation that welcomed gays and lesbians and supported their ordination within the Presbyterian Church (U.S.A.). A liberal like Coffin, McCall was clearly in favor of moving in this direction. This came as no surprise. Since arriving at Sixth Church in 1970, McCall had built a citywide reputation as an outspoken crusader for peace and social justice. His hard-hitting sermons opposed wars, backed labor unions, and called for fighting poverty in the blighted city. Not long after arriving at Sixth, he and others even developed a plan to tear down the church building and construct a high-rise tower that would include church space on the lower levels and low-income housing on the upper levels. Needless to say, the idea was controversial inside and outside of Sixth Church; local residents fearing a decline in their property values were especially vocal at public hearings. Rogers attended those meetings in support of the plan, but no one on the pro side wielded enough political power to make the plan succeed.

McCall was equally prophetic in addressing homosexuality, and he enlisted his friend William Sloane Coffin in the cause. On the night of the dinner with Rogers, Coffin stood in front of a packed Sixth Church and delivered a talk titled "Homophobia: In the Bible, in the Military, and in the Churches." Like his book, which was for sale at the event, the lecture encouraged Christians to let love cast out fear—to make friends of homosexuals, just as Jesus made friends with those his world had abandoned.

Fred Rogers attended the lecture, but he did not need to be convinced of Coffin's arguments. According to McCall, Rogers was already "very supportive" of the gay-friendly ministry that had been taking shape at Sixth since the late 1970s, when McCall had first led the congregation in studying an official Presbyterian report affirming homosexuals and the ordination of those within same-sex relationships.[9] After the General Assembly (the governing body of the Presbyterian Church (U.S.A.)) adopted the report without approving the recommendation to ordain sexually active gays and lesbians, McCall continued to fight for full inclusion of lesbian and gay people within his church, his city, and the wider denomination. For example, he joined and later chaired the Committee for Ministry with Homosexual Persons, a new committee in the Pittsburgh Presbytery. He appeared before the city council, testifying on the need to include sexual orientation in the city's antidiscrimination statute—a widely publicized testimony that resulted in more gays and lesbians attending worship at Sixth. And he consistently called upon Sixth to open its doors wide to gays and lesbians.

That's exactly what Sixth Church did in 1997, when it became the first of four congregations in the Pittsburgh Presbytery to join a movement called More Light Presbyterians, a coalition of congregations committed to ordaining qualified gay members to all church offices. The church board voted 17 to 1 in favor of joining More Light, and although Rogers could not cast a vote (Presbyterian ministers cannot be official members of local churches), there was no question that he supported the move. "Fred was supportive and stuck with us," McCall remembers. "He wasn't wishy-washy." He was firmly committed to Sixth's inclusive ministry and offered McCall personal support and encouragement as he crafted a gay-friendly ministry.

But Rogers offered his support quietly; he was not a loud crusader for LGBT rights either in or beyond Sixth Church. According to McCall, Rogers stated that "he had to be careful not to be identified publicly with these causes because of the potential effect on the program." Rogers was concerned that if he became widely identified as a crusader for gay rights, the program would suffer in its ability to reach as many children as possible. "He wasn't trying to protect his company," McCall says. "He was just concerned about reaching the children." So although Rogers had attended public hearings to support Sixth Church's proposal to build a high-rise building with low-income housing, he did not publicly demonstrate his support for gay and lesbian rights as they took shape at Sixth—or, for that matter, anywhere else.[10]

A few families left in protest over the decision to become a More Light congregation, but Sixth made up for the numerical losses by attracting more members of the LGBT community and families of all kinds. Among the long-time members was an openly gay radiologist who had joined Sixth almost a decade before the congregation voted to become More Light. He and his partner sat near Fred and Joanne on Sunday mornings, and the four became fast friends—more tangible evidence that Rogers, as Clemmons put it, was "not uncomfortable" in the presence of gays and "treated them in a warm, honorable, loving way." The radiologist so appreciated the friendship that he acted as Rogers's medical advocate in the difficult period leading to his death.

Fred Phelps and Rebekah Phelps Davis were thus partly right; Rogers never used his pulpit to denounce homosexuality, and he attended and supported a progressive church known for offering love and support to the LGBT community. But the Phelpses were wrong to suggest that Rogers was one of the "foremost proponents" of teachings that were explicitly gay-friendly.

Although his teaching of radical acceptance—"I like you just the way you are"—no doubt gave heart to many gays and lesbians, Rogers never made public comments about homosexuality or gay rights. The support he offered to gay friends and to the gay-friendly ministry at Sixth Church was typically quiet, exactly what one would expect from Fred Rogers. His quietist approach to homosexuality and gay rights meant that Rogers's Neighborhood was never entirely inclusive and that the peace of the Neighborhood was not as deep and wide as it might have been.

Rogers modeled healthy food choices for his young viewers. A long-time vegetarian, he often stated that he could never eat anything that had a mother.

Chapter 11

"I Love Tofu Burgers and Beets"

Animals and Mothers

Some pacifists don't think twice about killing game for food. In rural Pennsylvania, thousands of religious pacifists—Amish, Mennonites, and Brethren—head to the hills every November in search of a big buck or plump doe to fill their freezers. With a clear distinction between people and animals, their version of pacifism permits them to shoot and kill deer. But Fred Rogers did not embrace this type of pacifism. Not only did the Pennsylvania resident refrain from hunting; he also decided, not long after his program went national, to stop eating meat, fish, and fowl. The decision was part of his wider treatment of animals as valuable and lovable. Far from anthropocentric, Rogers's pacifist approach to life extended to the animal kingdom.

Spreading God's Love and Peace

In the early 1970s, the tiny vegetarian movement in the United States experienced a significant boost, thanks in part to the 1971 best seller *Diet for a Small Planet*. The book's twenty-seven-year-old author, Frances Moore Lappé, set forth a major critique of meat production, argued that a plant-based diet could help alleviate world hunger, and offered numerous recipes for easy-to-make vegetarian dishes. Lappé's book found a receptive audience among the Woodstock generation, with its embrace of all things natural, as well as with mainstream social progressives concerned about the population crisis.

As the vegetarian movement was taking off, Fred Rogers signed up. "I stopped eating meat, fish and fowl about ten years ago," he told *Vegetarian Times* for its November 1983 issue.[1] Rogers was the featured vegetarian of the month, and his smiling face graced the issue's cover. The profile's author was his good friend Paul Obis, the magazine's founder, who had converted to vegetarianism in 1970 while eating a hamburger at a Burger King in Chicago.

After an unsuccessful attempt to sell an article on vegetarianism ("Being a Vegetarian Means Never Having to Say You're Sorry—to a Cow"), he had put together a four-page newsletter titled *Vegetarian Times*.

The profile of Fred Rogers and his vegetarian lifestyle begins with a statement of faith. "I want to be a vehicle for God, to spread his message of love and peace," Rogers says.[2]

This simple faith statement suggests that treating animals nonviolently and adopting a vegetarian lifestyle were ultimately religious practices for Rogers—reflections and enactments of God's love for all creation. To be a vehicle for God, in his view, meant refraining from a diet that required the slaughtering of God's beloved creatures in the animal kingdom. Because he did not adopt vegetarianism until the early 1970s, Rogers did not always draw this connection between his dietary practices and his understanding of God. But no doubt before the publication of this profile, Rogers had grown to see his vegetarian practices as grounded in his conviction that God infuses and loves all creation, including animals.

The connection Rogers drew between vegetarianism and faith was a progressive stance in the early 1980s, and it remains so today. Many Christians continue to believe God's sole and holy purpose is to save humanity, the crown jewel of creation, and that animals are godless and inferior creatures—little more than fuel for human flourishing. But there is a growing movement among Christians that resists this dominion theology and sees vegetarianism as a faithful response to a God who is loving and peaceful toward all creation, not just the human part.

Empathy for Animals

In addition to making his faith statement, Rogers told Obis he had several reasons for becoming a vegetarian. "As I grew older," he said, "I found I liked [eating meat, fish, and fowl] less and less." It was a matter of taste; he simply began to prefer eating fruits, nuts, vegetables, and whole grains. But there were other reasons at play too—moral reasons. "Part of it has to do with the animals—it's hard to eat something you've seen walking around," he stated.[3] He expounded on this point a bit more colorfully in other settings. "I don't want to eat anything that has a mother," he often said.[4] By the early 1970s Rogers had developed empathy for all types of animals—empathy so deep that he didn't want to hurt these little sons and daughters in any way. He especially didn't want to stick them in his mouth, chew them, and swallow them.

Fred Rogers expressed an ability to empathize with animals long before his television program went national. In the 1960s, he even took up the cause of dyed Easter chicks. Colored peeps (made of flesh and feathers, not marshmallow and sugar) were a popular Easter gift at that time, and five-and-dime stores across the nation displayed them in their store windows, usually in cramped boxes under bright lights. A few animal activists at the time considered the practice abusive, and Rogers joined their efforts by writing a song titled "Don't Pick on the Peeps." His empathy for peeps and animals is loud and clear throughout this little-known song:

If you'd paint a cow, she'd holler
If you'd dye a dog, he'd squeal
If you'd color a cat, he'd scream just like that. . . .
Well, how do you think chickens feel?

Don't pick on the peeps this year
Don't dye us pink and blue
Don't pick on the peeps, you hear?
Find other things to do.

Please don't dye the ducks this year
We hate us to be chartreuse
Please don't dye the ducks this year
Don't even dye the goose.

Our fine feathered friends all think that it's foul
That fowl must take this lickin'
It gives us a pain. We *have* to complain:
We chicken . . . are chicken.

Don't pick on the peeps this year
Give chickens a chance to grow
If you've got to paint and smear
Just join an artist's studio (BUT WHATEVER YOU DO)
Don't pick on the peeps this year.[5]

Rogers did not halt the practice of coloring chicks—it's still legal in some states—but his message that chickens possess a dignity and integrity apart from human desires, and that we should stop treating them as playthings to color and paint, was certainly a progressive plea in the 1960s, when animals were often viewed not as ends in themselves but merely as means for human enjoyment. In the years to follow, Rogers implanted this ethic of care and deep empathy for animals in the national run of *Mister Rogers'*

Neighborhood. Early on, he did this not so much by touting vegetarianism but by focusing on the value of pets.

Pets Are Special

In the very first week of the show's national run, Mister Rogers sets up a wooden playpen, like the ones often used by human babies, for a "special visitor."[6] The guest turns out to be Lydia Stout, a St. Bernard puppy whom Mister Rogers adores. He pets her lovingly and even engages her in a pretend dialogue. Lydia, according to Mister Rogers, says she really doesn't care to be fenced in by a playpen, but he assures her that the playpen, equipped with a warm blanket, is for her own protection. Treating her as if she were a child, he also plays hide and seek with her and talks sweet baby talk to her. It's pretty clear by the end of the episode that Mister Rogers sees Lydia as special and lovable, not unlike the way he sees people.

Throughout the entire run of his program, Rogers staged a colorful and ongoing parade of dogs and cats, ducks and fish, skunks and pigs, lizards and iguanas, penguins and whales, bears and monkeys, and many others. Given his smiles and hugs and kisses, Mister Rogers seemed to love them all, as did Mr. and Mrs. McFeely, who were constantly opening their home to all sorts of needy animals; their home was the Neighborhood's rescue shelter. Mr. McFeely also played the role of Mister Rogers's personal animal instructor.

When Mister Rogers got his own pets in 1969—quiet goldfish, of course, so fitting for his personality—McFeely initially set up the aquarium and instructed Rogers on the proper ways to care for it. In the following episodes, and for years to follow, we see Rogers acting as a responsible and engaged pet owner. He feeds his fish faithfully—telling us along the way that if he ever forgets to feed them during the program he'll come back to do so later—and even talks and sings to them. Adult viewers might have occasionally found themselves thinking, "Uhhh—they're just fish," but to Mister Rogers they're beloved pets worthy of conversation and song.

His most poignant moment as a loving pet owner occurs when one of his goldfish dies. In this moving episode, which was broadcast during the program's second year, Mister Rogers invites us to look at the fish in his aquarium. "Oh, what's that right down there?" he asks. "Do you see a dead fish?" As he looks directly at us, he explains that a dead fish "would be one that isn't swimming or breathing or anything at all." Sure enough, the close-up camera shot shows what appears to be a lifeless fish lying at the bottom of the aquarium.

But Mister Rogers takes extra special care in this surprising moment. "Someone told me one time if you put a very sick fish in some water with salt, it might revive it—bring it back," he says. So he uses a small net to scoop the fish out of the aquarium and place it in a smaller container filled with water. He then adds salt to the water, but the fish is clearly dead. "I guess the salt isn't going to help it," he says. "I guess we'd better bury it."

Mister Rogers uses his fish net again and puts the dead fish on a paper towel. After silently wrapping it in a small square, he grabs a spade and heads to the backyard, where he digs a hole and buries his beloved pet. It's a quiet, peaceful scene, punctuated only by a memory from his childhood:

When I was very young I had a dog that I loved very much. Her name was Mitzi. And she got to be old, and she died. And I was very sad when she died because she and I were good pals. And when she died I cried. And my grandmother heard me crying, I remember, and she came and she just put her arm around me because she knew I was very sad. She knew how much I loved that dog. My dad said we'd have to bury Mitzi, and I didn't want to. I didn't want to bury her because I thought I'd just pretend that she was still alive. But my dad said her body was dead and we'd have to bury her. So we did.

Back in the house, Mister Rogers shows us a picture of Mitzi and adds, "Even now I can still remember Mitzi's prickly fur and her curly tail. . . . I really missed her when she died."[7] While it's clear he did not have the same type of emotions when he discovered his goldfish had died—the two were not as close as he and Mitzi had been—what's most obvious, especially as we watch him wrap and bury his fish, is that he cares deeply for his pets, in life and death. Nothing, not even death, can prevent Mister Rogers from caring for and loving his pet fish.

Rogers's devotion to pets continued for years to follow, even receiving a weeklong focus in 1982.[8] Unsurprisingly, the special series is all about the positive message of enjoying and caring for pets as valuable in and of themselves. Together with Mr. McFeely and others, Mister Rogers helps us see and accept pets as special family members, to be loved and cared for, just as we love and care for human family members. The series is full of images of children and adults doting on their pets; there is lots of grooming, hugging, feeding, bathing, walking, running, and playing with all sorts of pets.

"Caring for animals helps them to know you love them, too," he tells us just before singing "I'm Taking Care of You" to a stuffed pet dog.[9] It's Rogers's way of inviting us to see animals as valuable, as deserving of our love, and as desirous of our care.

Children and Eating Meat

Importantly, though, Rogers extended his ethics to animals that weren't exactly pets. In *Mister Rogers' Neighborhood,* all types of animals deserve, and receive, respect and care. Rogers was especially interested in showing his appreciation and care for cows—the unwitting contributors to all those fast-food hamburgers devoured by millions of children in the United States.

One of the most telling and amusing segments about cows shows Mister Rogers visiting Turner Dairy Farms in Pittsburgh during a 1984 special series on food. To get to the dairy barn, where the farm workers are milking cows, Rogers has to walk past a group of loudly mooing cows. But rather than simply hurrying past them, as many of us nonfarmers might do, perhaps with a bit of fear in our step, Mister Rogers smiles at them and says hello very gently, as if he were talking to little children playing in a neighborhood park. The cows, of course, keep on mooing, and this prompts Mister Rogers to do the same. Back in his television house, he says, "Weren't those cows *beautiful?*"[10]

Rogers's choice of a dairy farm rather than, say, one that butchers cows for hamburgers, reflected his longtime sensitivity about both animals and the negative effects of animal-eating on children. He first addressed this issue in a 1972 episode of *Mister Rogers' Neighborhood.* During a visit to Chef Brockett's bakery, Rogers suggests that some of us might find it difficult and troubling to eat the chef's new creation—a cake shaped like an adorable little lamb. We might, after all, imagine or believe that we're actually eating the little lamb. While Chef Brockett assures him it's just cake, Mister Rogers's uneasiness is palpable.[11]

It remained palpable for the rest of his career. In his 1983 interview with Paul Obis of *Vegetarian Times,* Rogers stated that when children "discover the connection between meat and animals, many children get very concerned about it." Their worries were another reason he adopted vegetarianism, he said.

Concern for children also led him to avoid showing images of people eating animals on his program. A 1982 episode that teaches children about dining at restaurants includes footage from a full-service restaurant, but without showing even one image of meat, fowl, or fish, and the 1984 special series on food successfully avoids any mention of eating animals. In the Neighborhood, animals are for enjoying and nurturing—not for eating and digesting.

Rogers did not, however, hesitate to show images of people, including himself, eating dairy products and eggs. He was not a vegan, but rather a conventional vegetarian who certainly consumed his fair share of eggs and dairy. When he places his lunch order in the 1982 restaurant episode, for example, he asks for a cheese, lettuce, and tomato sandwich on whole wheat. "I like whole wheat bread," he says. In another episode he eats baked goods with eggs among the ingredients.[12]

As a conventional vegetarian, Rogers was aware of a concern often raised by ethical vegans—that the processes used to extract eggs and milk cause undue suffering in animals. He briefly addresses this issue in a 1996 episode during which Mr. McFeely delivers not only a cup of delicious yogurt but also a video titled *How People in a Factory Make Yogurt*.

In his narration of the video, Mr. McFeely informs us that "when people make yogurt they start by milking cows." As the video shows a worker attaching a milking machine to a cow's udder, Mister Rogers says, "That doesn't hurt, does it?" It certainly looks as if it might be uncomfortable for the cow, now crammed into a narrow stall, but Mr. McFeely assures us otherwise. "Oh, no," he replies. "In fact, it makes the cow feel good!"[13] Neither Rogers nor McFeely speaks to the other ways cows might experience undue suffering during the course of their lives as milk producers for people, but as far as milking is concerned, they seem convinced the cow experiences no suffering at all.

As a conventional vegetarian, Rogers also openly touted his love of foods preferred by vegetarians. In the first episode of the 1984 series on food, for instance, we learn that Mister Rogers loves applesauce; we then watch him tour an applesauce factory. In the second episode he tells us he likes granola with raisins as he fills bags of this treat to share with his friends. This particular type of granola consists of honey, rolled oats, dried milk, coconut, wheat germ, sunflower seeds, and peanuts—"all sorts of good things," he says with a smile. In this same episode, Mr. McFeely even delivers an order of tofu to Mister Rogers, and together they view a film about people making tofu. "Tofu is a very good food," Rogers says. "It helps a lot of people to grow."[14]

In the third episode, he visits Chef Brockett's bakery, where the chef teaches him how to make a special peanut butter treat rolled in graham cracker crumbs. Brockett says the nutritious treat is "wonderful with vegetables and fruit," and as Mister Rogers is leaving, he spots, surprisingly, collard greens and kale in the chef's kitchen.[15] Mister Rogers seems more attracted to peanut butter, though, and when he returns home he puts peanut butter, raisins, and graham cracker crumbs on a banana.

In the fourth episode, he visits a vegetable soup factory and seems to like the vegetables almost as much as he did the peanut butter. Mister Rogers is a pasta fan too, and in the last episode of the week, he and Johnny Costa visit Johnny's son as he makes pasta from scratch, just as his beloved grandmother once did.

Soy products grab the spotlight a year later, in 1985, while Mister Rogers is visiting Chef Brockett again. Although long known for his cakes and cookies, the adaptable chef has now taken up the cause of foods preferred by vegetarians. He has just developed a "special new line of health foods—very healthy foods called soy foods," he says. Brockett then shows Mister Rogers his new items: soybeans, vegetarian burgers in cans, soy drinks, soy pancake and waffle mix, and tofu. "That's something I know," Mister Rogers says when he hears about the tofu. "I eat a lot of tofu—in all different ways!"[16]

He did indeed. Fred Rogers's diet, as he explained to Paul Obis, regularly featured tofu and other health foods. For breakfast he usually had milk and cereal or fresh fruit and toast. A true yogurt fan ("I love yogurt!" he announced in the 1996 episode), he often ate yogurt and crackers, or cottage cheese with peaches, for lunch.[17] And his dinner typically consisted of tofu and vegetables. "I love tofu burgers and beets," he told Obis. As for drinks, he avoided coffee, alcoholic beverages, and soda in favor of water with lemon juice.

Health Benefits

Rogers understood well that the foods he recommended on his program ran counter to taste buds formed in a culture ravenous for junk food. In the special series on food, Mister Rogers draws a sharp contrast between junk food and healthful food. Sitting at his kitchen table, he introduces us to a wonderful bowl of fruit before taking three items out of a brown recyclable bag: a bag of chips, a can of soda, and a candy bar marked "SUGARTIME." He seems disgusted, and as he puts the junk food on the table, he says, "There are some foods that are better than others. They taste better, and they help your body grow better."

"There are some people," he adds, "who cannot eat sugary things or salty things or deep fried things at all." He does not explain the reason for this, but he does deliver this news in a very somber tone. "And of course," he adds, "it's important that nobody eats or drinks too much of them."[18] Mister Rogers looks stern when he tells us this—just before cheerily revealing that cherries are one of his favorite foods.

Fred Rogers addressed childhood obesity long before most people had heard of it. Obese people, adults or children, simply do not appear in the Neighborhood; they're one of the few missing cross-sections of the population. It's not clear whether Rogers deliberately avoided having obese people on his program, but it's crystal clear that the characters of the Neighborhood tended to appear physically fit. Even Chef Brockett, a neighbor who struggled with his weight, dropped pounds in later programs, around the time he began to speak about nutritious food in his bakery. Mister Rogers observes the changes in Chef Brockett's body and tells his friend he looks good.

Rogers fought obesity on his program partly by showing children various ways to exercise their bodies—from walking and stretching to dancing ballet and playing sports. To say that he did not appear to be especially good at ball sports may be an understatement, but in an early 1982 episode he certainly proved he was a decent swimmer. "In fact," he says when introducing the swim segment, "a long time ago, many years ago, I promised myself that I would try to swim a certain length of time each day. And I've done that almost every day for more than ten years." He then shows a captivating video of himself sporting a Speedo at one of his local swimming pools. Mister Rogers appears to be a very trim and fit middle-aged man as he heads from the locker room into the pool; his muscles are toned, and his stomach is flat. Back at his television house, he says this about his daily swimming: "I know it's good for me, and I promised myself I'd do it every day."[19] He's modeling for us, of course, quietly encouraging us to take up a daily discipline of exercise.

Rogers also fought obesity, as we've seen, by urging children to eat meatless foods. As he put this in the *Vegetarian Times* article, "There are so many wonderful things to eat besides candy bars and sugary cereals. It would be nice for kids to explore the varieties of unusual fruits, nuts, and vegetables." Rogers himself enjoyed the personal results of his commitment to vegetarianism and cited them as yet another reason for deciding to become a vegetarian. "I also enjoy the health benefits," he told Paul Obis. "I weigh about the same now as I did when I was in college."

As an adult, Rogers was never a big eater, and for the last thirty years of his life he maintained a weight of 143. "I guess I just don't need a lot of food," he stated. Coupled with his moderate portions, his exercise and vegetarian diet helped him maintain his ideal weight. (The number 143, incidentally, was his favorite because it meant "I love you." As he explained to his friend Tom Junod, "It takes one letter to say 'I' and four letters to say 'love' and three letters to say 'you.' One hundred and forty-three.")[20]

Shamu

Rogers became a vegetarian because he (1) wanted to spread God's love and peace; (2) grew to prefer fruits, nuts, vegetables, and whole grains; (3) developed an empathy for all animals and saw them as valuable and lovable; (4)

disliked the effects of animal-eating on children; and (5) enjoyed the health benefits of a vegetarian diet. But can we also count him among the vegetarians who saw animals as possessing rights, as equal in value to humans?

In 1975, not long after Rogers became a vegetarian, philosopher Peter Singer published an influential book drawing attention to abuses animals suffered in factory farms and research laboratories. Now considered a classic, *Animal Liberation* argued that animals are equal in value to humans, and it urged us to stop harming and killing animals for human purposes. Fred Rogers was never quite as explicit as Singer or the militant activists who followed him. Although Rogers treated the animals in his care as valuable, lovable, and deserving of respect and care, he never claimed they were equal to humans. Nor did he ever say aloud that they possessed rights, even though he treated them as though they had a right to life. What is no doubt more troubling to animal activists is that Rogers did not always treat wild animals as though they had a right to liberty—freedom from human captivity.

Fred Rogers was a fan of circuses that used animals to entertain people, and he had a deep appreciation for marine mammal parks such as SeaWorld. In 1987, Rogers even broadcast a *Mister Rogers' Neighborhood* episode in which he visits with two killer whales in captivity at SeaWorld—Shamu and Namu. During the visit, Mister Rogers enjoys hearing Shamu's trainer claim that the killer whale "loves it here [at SeaWorld]. He likes the attention that we give him and all the playtimes that we have and the times we spend together just getting to know each other." After Rogers watches Shamu and Namu do tricks designed to delight human audiences—they wave their tails, spin, dance, and jump out of the water—he marvels at the "amazing things that people and animals can do with love."[21]

Animal activists did not see the captivity of Shamu and Namu, let alone their blatant use for human entertainment, as an act of love. But it wasn't just adults sensitive to the plight of captive whales who were displeased with this episode; so too were many children, especially those who watched reruns of the episode in 1993 and later. Part of the reason for their dissent was that *Free Willy*, a wildly popular movie among children in 1993, had inspired them to believe that killer whales like Willy should be free to swim the wide oceans where they belong. So after seeing Mister Rogers visit Shamu and Namu, more than a handful of young *Free Willy* fans wrote their favorite television neighbor letters of protest, informing him in no uncertain terms that it was not loving at all to keep killer whales in captivity. To this day, though, the Shamu episode is available for purchase.

Beyond the Neighborhood

Yes, Rogers tended to anthropomorphize animals, and he never joined the militant side of the vegetarian movement; he did not picket factory farms or join the Animal Liberation Front. Similar to his work for peace, his advocacy of vegetarianism and care for animals tended to be quiet, behind the camera, in speeches here and there, or on written pages. His commitment to vegetarianism, along with his opposition to animal cruelty, also took an activist form outside the Neighborhood.

Two years after Obis interviewed him for *Vegetarian Times*, he became a co-owner of the magazine, providing financial backing as Obis repurchased the periodical from a company he had sold it to years earlier. For Rogers, it was a form of activism through publishing; he didn't march, but he made sure people had access to pro-vegetarian writings. It also turned out to be a smart business move. When Obis and Rogers sold their vastly improved magazine in 1990, their profit totaled in the millions.

In the same year he bought into *Vegetarian Times*, Rogers also signed his name to a statement that Beauty without Cruelty USA, a pro-animal activist group, ran as an advertisement in newspapers across the country. Part of a campaign to undermine fur sales and pelt prices in the United States, the statement read, "Furs look best on their original owners. I am aware of the great suffering unavoidable in the production of fur coats. I would encourage compassionate people to find beauty without the cruelty involved in real furs."[22]

Both in and beyond the Neighborhood, then, Fred Rogers tried to show, however imperfectly at times, that peace on earth was not merely a matter of ending wars and properly managing one's mad feelings; it was also about treating animals nonviolently—refusing to eat them or abuse them for our own imagined or real needs, and caring for them as valuable creatures that deserve a full life. Even though he was no Peter Singer, Rogers stood in his own way against mainstream society's consumption of animals, its farm factories and slaughterhouses, and its meat-fueled obesity.

Rogers tapped into the expertise of oceanographer Sylvia Earle to emphasize the importance of caring for the natural world. In this particular series, he says, "If you were a fish, you wouldn't want someone dumping garbage into your home."

Chapter 12

"Take Care of This Wonderful World"

Peace on Earth

*O*n Earth Day in 1971, Keep America Beautiful joined efforts with the Ad Council in launching the famous "crying Indian" commercial. The spot featured actor Iron Eyes Cody dressed in traditional Native American leather and paddling his canoe in a river full of litter. With ominous drumming in the background, Cody floats past factories spewing thick pollution into the dark skies. After he disembarks from his canoe and surveys the surrounding land, a woman in a passing car throws a bag full of trash out the window. The bag breaks to pieces as it lands at Cody's feet, and a gravelly voiced narrator tells us: "Some people have a deep, abiding respect for the natural beauty that was once this country. And some people don't." As the camera zooms in on a tear falling from Cody's right eye, the narrator delivers a simple message: "People start pollution. People can stop it."[1]

Advertising Age named the memorable commercial, which ran from 1971 to 1983, as one of the top 100 campaigns of the twentieth century. Fred Rogers never received such public recognition for his program's pro-environment campaigns, nor did his ecological commitments ever attract such national attention. But three years before the Cody commercial aired, Rogers ran a special series devoted to protecting the environment; he did the same seven years after the commercial was pulled. The pioneering environmental programs show the importance he ascribed to both individual and governmental responsibility for taking care of the earth. When placed in conversation with other episodes, they also reveal that Rogers's faith fueled his progressive stance toward the environment. For Rogers, peace on earth requires caring for the environment as a gift from God.

Litterbugs in the Neighborhood

In 1968, two full years before the first Earth Day, Rogers used three segments of the Neighborhood of Make-Believe to promote individual and governmental responsibility for keeping the world clean. It was not an entirely new message: Keep America Beautiful, a consortium of government and private groups, had been delivering anti-littering messages since 1953, and a year earlier the Pennsylvania Resources Council, an environmental organization that helped to jumpstart Keep America Beautiful, had run a "Don't Be a Litterbug" campaign in Rogers's home state. Although not brand-new, Rogers's programs were part of an emerging movement prompted by the growing problem of litter that followed the construction of the interstate highway system.

The simple and short Make-Believe storyline begins with King Friday's alarm at the "40 million litterbugs in this country."[2] The king "has litter on his mind," as Handyman Negri puts it, and is fiercely determined to make a change. "There are a million pieces of litter descending on this country every day of every year," he says, "and we're going to have them stopped!" To support the effort, Friday instructs Negri to conduct a survey of Neighborhood residents, with the most important question being: "Were you ever or are you now a litterbug?"

Negri carries out his task with typical care, and his findings leave him hopeful. "My final report after checking with everyone in the Neighborhood is that at some time or another they have been litterbugs but that they try not to be litterbugs anymore," he says. Pleased with the report, Friday calls for a continuation of the "cleanup campaign," even suggesting a song for it:

> Clean up the streets.
> Clean up the land.
> Keep all the litter
> Right in your hand
> Until you find a litter basket.

Inspired by factory owner Cornflake S. Pecially, who has donated a litter basket to support the campaign, Friday then charges Lady Aberlin with placing wastebaskets throughout Make-Believe. And because he's not content with merely a voluntary effort, he also instructs Lady Aberlin to enforce a new rule requiring people to stop littering. If anyone is found guilty of littering, he or she must wear a coned hat, not unlike a dunce cap, with the word *litterbug* written on it. In Make-Believe, rules made by the king lead the way in solving the litter crisis; individual goodwill does not suffice.

Shortly after receiving her royal orders, Lady Aberlin catches Lady Elaine Fairchilde littering indiscriminately; she's acting out her anger at Chef Brockett for not giving her a cookie in a timely manner. With the litterbug hat perched atop her head, Fairchilde gripes about Friday's decision to enlist citizens in the anti-littering campaign. "Why doesn't *he* get out there and clean it up then?" she asks. "Well," Lady Aberlin replies, "it's better if each person cleans up his own." Lady Elaine becomes convinced of this too, but only after Lady Aberlin and Chuck Aber agree to help her pick up the trash.

King Friday is doubly pleased about his pro-environment campaign when he learns that the Committee for World Clean-Up has given him a citation of meritorious service for his commitment to litter education, uncovering the causes of litter, and setting an example for royalty and citizens. Major Smith, a representative of this important committee, delivers the citation and a trophy—a royal broom. "He who sweeps clean is a clean sweep," Smith says.

Interestingly, back in his television house, Mister Rogers encourages his viewers to back their anti-littering efforts by reusing products normally thrown away. He does this ever so subtly in a short segment in which he marvels over presents that children have made out of such items as shoeboxes, paper tubes, egg cartons, jelly jars, and other paper and glass products. The unspoken lesson is that reusing old glass and paper products, in addition to throwing litter in trash baskets, can help keep the Neighborhood clean.

A Dump Crisis

On the issue of recycling, Rogers both reflected the frugal past of U.S. history, when the Depression and World War II had strongly encouraged people to recycle, and pointed to the coming future. While U.S. citizens in the late 1960s were less concerned than before about recycling, the early 1970s saw the arrival of the nation's first recycling plant as well as laws requiring recycling. Rogers fully supported the emerging recycling movement, and in 1990, when many cities were still not requiring their residents to recycle, he devoted an entire week of programs to the theme of recycling and caring for the environment.

The ecologically minded series begins with Mister Rogers walking through the door with a greeting card in hand. "I'm interested to know what people do with greeting cards," he says.[3] "I'm sorry to say that a lot of people just throw them away. But some people make scrapbooks of them. They collect them and save them. Other people turn them into other greeting cards so they can use them again." This is what Mister Rogers himself does, and he carefully shows us how to recycle a greeting card and its envelope.

Mr. McFeely arrives and expresses his approval when he learns that Mister Rogers likes to save things. The speedy deliverer says that he likes to save everything he can, that he's recently become concerned about the huge size of the Neighborhood dump, and that his community service this week will focus on doing something about the problem. Just before leaving, he also gives Mister Rogers some important advice: "Before you throw anything out, just think. Just think. All righty? And don't buy anything you don't really need."

There's a dump crisis in the Neighborhood of Make-Believe too. The dump cannot hold any more trash, and the smell of overflowing garbage has become so bad that Make-Believe residents have to wear "nose muffs" supplied by King Friday. The concerned king fully realizes the muffs won't solve the ecological crisis, so he instructs Lady Aberlin to find a new dump for all the stinky garbage. "Simply find a new dump," he says. But Lady Aberlin soon discovers the job isn't that simple. Two nearby dumps, one at Westwood and the other at Southwood, are also full and overflowing.

There's only one location left—Northwood, home to lots of goats, who, of course, are longtime experts in getting rid of trash. In learning of the dump crisis, Old Goat and New Goat travel to the three dumps to assess the situation, and while they're napping shortly after arriving, Lady Elaine comes up with two other ideas. "Number one is, throw it all in the ocean. The ocean's plenty big for everything." But Lady Aberlin throws cold water on the idea by saying that was what they had (wrongly) thought about the existing dump—that it would be plenty big for all the garbage. Chuck Aber adds another reason for dismissing the idea. Dressed in a wet suit, he reports that while he did indeed check the oceans as a possible option, "they're too beautiful to dump things into."

So Lady Elaine shares her second idea—appear on *The Universe Today,* a local call-in television show, to share news about the crisis and see whether any viewers might help out. When Lady Elaine and King Friday do exactly this, Sue Goat of Northwood calls in to the program to explain that she and her team from Northwood will "divide and conquer" the overflowing dumps. "A team of highly experienced goats will come and divide all the garbage so that it can be recycled," she explains. To top things off, Hilda Dingleboarder, an employee of Corney's factory, appears on the show to demonstrate her new invention. "It takes one kind of garbage at a time and turns it into something useful," she says.

So the goats will divide the overflowing and stinky garbage, and the new invention will make useful items out of it. With the crisis under management, the respective parties express a sigh of relief, and Patrice, the host of the program, concludes on a happy note: "Until next time, peace from Patrice." In Make-Believe, peace demands caring for the world.

Back in his television house, Mister Rogers shares a similar message throughout the week. He uses a paper bag he found outside for a new "bag ball game"; he later uses toilet paper tubes to make pretend trees and learns how to make birdfeeders out of milk cartons. He and Mr. McFeely also visit a recycling center that crushes cans and glass jars brought in by everyday citizens concerned about the environment. "If I take [cans, bottles, and jars] to the recycling place, then they won't have to go fill up some dump somewhere," he explains. After he returns from the center, he adds to his lesson. "There are lots of ways everyone can help," he says. "Just not waste things, for one. Just not use any more than we really need of anything." For Rogers, wasteful living, materialism, and overconsumption are some of the biggest dangers to the environment.

The World Is Fancy

Mister Rogers also encourages his viewers to "be friendly" toward the environment, to develop an attitude that sees the world and everything it holds as special and worthy of our attention and care. He and oceanographer Sylvia Earle communicate this point in a conversation right after they've gone snorkeling in the ocean. Sitting at the back of the boat, Mister Rogers asks, "What can we do to take care of places like this—these seas of ours?"

Earle's answer fits well with Rogers's values and morals. "One of the most important things is to do just what we were doing—to get out and know the place," she says. "It's hard to care about something if you don't understand it, if you haven't seen it, so being in the seas is an important first step in the right direction. Get to know the fish. Get to see the corals."

When we begin to understand that "the ocean is vital to the good health of the planet," she adds, we will see that "it's just part of good common sense to take care of this ocean that, in its own way, has taken care of us." It's also important that we share our understandings with others and encourage behavior that respects the ocean—to "mind our manners . . . and watch what we do." Nodding his approval, Rogers adds his own angle. "And be friendly!" he says. "And be friendly!" Earle replies.

Back in his television house, Mister Rogers tells us that people like Sylvia Earle "are my heroes because they care about our world." Later, as he turns to the subject of caring for the ocean, he begins to explain the morality underlying such care, even invoking the Golden Rule. "If you were a fish, you wouldn't want somebody dumping garbage into your home," he says. "Nobody would want that."

That simple moral lesson takes on a deeper meaning, however, when he explains that the world and its inhabitants are special, just as people are. "I was just thinking," he says. "Every fish is fancy in one way or another. Just like every person is fancy in one way or another. . . . There is something fancy about every creature in the world, and there's something fine about each one of us, too. Each person, each fish, each animal, each bird, each living creature."

Friday's Comet

Rogers's environmentalism, like his vegetarianism, counters the common notion that there's a hierarchy of value with people at the top, advanced mammals one level down, and bugs and worms many, many levels down. Although he held that God identifies most with people, Rogers also believed that there's special value in *all* living beings, in the wider world, and even in worlds beyond.[4]

His egalitarian approach to environmentalism came into full view just after Halley's Comet, arguably the most well-known comet in our universe, visited Earth in March 1986. The news media granted an amazing amount of attention to the comet, which is visible from Earth approximately every seventy-five years, and Rogers decided to join the throngs of enthusiastic stargazers.

In May 1986, *Mister Rogers' Neighborhood* included a series of Make-Believe segments addressing the spectacle of a rarely seen comet. At the beginning of the week, King Friday announces that this comet is *his* comet, Friday's Comet, and that it will soon be appearing in the skies. He calls for a celebration to mark the occasion and gives detailed instructions for carrying out the event properly. When the comet finally appears at the end of the week, it flies just above the cheering neighbors and drops an important message for King Friday:

> I belong to you . . .
> AND to everyone
> else in the world.
> No one can own
> the stars, the moon,
> the planets, or a comet.
> No one owns you, King Friday.

No one owns your son, Prince Tuesday.
And no one owns us.
We heavenly bodies are for everyone to celebrate.
Thanks for the royal welcome.
I'll be back next time.

Although surprised, King Friday accepts the sobering lesson and halts his efforts to claim the comet as his very own. "Well, that is the lesson—nobody owns anybody, even a heavenly body," he says.[5] In Make-Believe, heavenly bodies, just like people and puppets, have their own special value that all should honor and celebrate.

This episode also points to a deeper understanding of heavenly bodies—one that lines up with Rogers's spiritual beliefs. After King Friday learns that he does not own the comet, the neighbors of Make-Believe gather for another celebration, this one a surprise birthday party for Henrietta. As they celebrate her birthday, Lady Elaine gives Henrietta an *Ojo De Dios* (Eye of God), a decorative weaving with roots in Native American culture and later popularized by Christians as a sign of divine presence, wisdom, and care. The gift is especially significant during this episode because some heavenly bodies, such as Helix Nebula, are known as "eyes of God."

This connection between Friday's Comet and God subtly suggests a spiritual dimension to Rogers's lesson about seeing heavenly bodies as having special value for all to enjoy—and, more generally, about his belief that all living things are "fancy" in and of themselves and worthy of our care and devotion. In fact, underlying his respect for the environment is his spiritual conviction that the world is a creation of God—that *God* made the stars and the moon, the rain and the rainbows, the mountains and the molehills. As Rogers's lyrics in "Creation" put it, "God made the world, made the people. God made it all."[6]

For Rogers, God made the world as an act of love, and so the world is for us to revere and celebrate as the expression of divine love. The world is for us to love as God loves—full of care and devotion.

Tree, Tree, Tree

Fred Rogers was not a militant environmentalist. He did not hug trees or set fire to backhoes demolishing woods to make way for new real estate. Nor did he lobby Congress to pass pro-environment legislation or pressure businesses and industries to cut back on their pollution. But he did offer us helpful hints about littering and recycling before most of the world paid attention to these matters.

For the sake of the environment, he also implored us to stop buying what we don't need, to counter the consumerism in which we are so steeped, and to slow down and take time to learn about the wider world of nature. But perhaps most important, he showed us how to express a sense of wonder at the world and to be reverential toward it—to see and love it as the special creation of God. "Take care of this wonderful world that we have," he said.[7] Fred Rogers did not urge us to hug trees but, as one of his most beloved songs shows, he certainly invited us to love them:

> Tree, tree, tree,
> Tree, tree, tree,
> Tree, tree, tree,
> Tree, tree, tree.
>
> We love you,
> Yes, we do.
> Yes, we do,
> We love you.
>
> Tree, tree, tree,
> Tree, tree, tree,
> Tree. tree, tree,
> Tree, tree, tree.[8]

As he sings this quiet song, we have no doubt that, for Mister Rogers, loving trees, fish, animals, and nature is a powerful act that can help transform our world into a neighborhood of peace and love for all.

Conclusion

The Compassion of Fred Rogers

*I*n January 2000, childhood friends Casey McNerthney, a student at Western Washington University, and Morgan Marshall, a Stanford student, were planning a summer trip when Mister Rogers popped up in the conversation. Rogers was front-and-center in McNerthney's mind at the time because he was hosting "Mister Rogers Fridays," a weekly breakfast during which he and his college friends watched reruns of *Mister Rogers' Neighborhood*. The breakfast gave McNerthney a way to relax right after his early morning shift at the college radio station, and best of all, time to revisit a wise old friend from his childhood years.

"You think we could meet Mister Rogers?" McNerthney wondered when chatting on the phone with his friend Marshall. They weren't sure, but after they decided to give it the old college try, McNerthney contacted David Newell (Mr. McFeely), who oversaw public relations for Family Communications and sometimes acted as gatekeeper to the program and its cast and characters. Newell, himself a gentle man, was so impressed with the earnestness of the college students that he suggested they come by at the end of June. "They're very charming kids, and they're not weird," he said at the time. "They're not coming in wearing cardigans or anything like that."[1]

Nevertheless, the young men's choice to visit Rogers was highly unusual. Nicole Brodeur, a Seattle reporter covering the trip, observed as much when she wrote that many guys planning an annual summer trek "would list the usual suspects: Lollapalooza. Daytona Beach. Yosemite. Anywhere with bikinis, beer or risk."[2] Settling on Rogers instead seemed downright anti-macho. But that didn't stop McNerthney and Marshall, and near the end of June the two packed up Marshall's van in Seattle and began a four-day trek to Pittsburgh, sleeping in 7-Eleven parking lots along the way.

Once they arrived at Family Communications, Rogers's secretary escorted them to his office. "Walking into his office was one of the coolest things,"

Marshall recalled. "He was just sitting there and said 'Oh, hello!' There was no fanfare. Just him."

Rogers told them he was honored they had come to visit, and for about an hour the three shared stories and memories. McNerthney was especially impressed with the way Rogers gently touched his arm after he had begun to stutter. Unlike the typical adult who tried to coax him out of his stutter, Rogers just touched his arm and waited. "It was unlike anyone else," McNerthney said. "He had a sense of what to do. That had a lot of meaning for me."[3]

The visitors had a lot of meaning for Rogers too. He later placed a framed photograph of the young men in his office, retrieving it for a national reporter who had asked him why he had devoted his life to children. "Well, the children become adults," Rogers explained, holding the photograph. "That's the most important time with which we can nourish the future."[4]

The future Rogers had nurtured, and witnessed, in his two visitors gave him evidence for feeling positive about days and years to come. "These kids give you such hope," he told the reporter. "Maybe they realize that you don't have to be macho to be acceptable, and that everybody longs to be loved and feel that he or she is capable of loving. I would hope that is one of the major influences of the Neighborhood."[5]

Rogers's hope was far from unfounded. Indeed, researchers of *Mister Rogers' Neighborhood* have suggested that the program's "prosocial impacts may be lifelong" in some viewers.[6] Prosocial behaviors, unlike those obsessed with beer and bikinis, include seeing others as worthy of empathy and compassion and acting in ways to help others and enhance relationships—the type of actions that contribute to personal, interpersonal, and social peace. In his two adult visitors, then, Rogers witnessed the lasting effects of his lifelong work to create peacemakers.

Rogers spoke a bit more about his legacy during another interview in 2000. "I'd like to be remembered for being a compassionate human being who happened to be fortunate enough to be born at a time when there was a fabulous thing called television that could allow me to use all the talents that I had been given," he said.[7] That seems fair enough—especially the part about compassion.

Thich Nhat Hanh likes to point out that the word *compassion* means "to suffer with" and that acting with compassion is our primary vocation. "Our responsibility as humans is to transform our suffering in order to transform the suffering of those around us," he states.[8]

We've seen that Fred Rogers embraced this vocation, transforming his suffering—that painful childhood experience of peers who did not accept him as he was ("Hey, Fat Freddy!")—into a constructive project that encouraged others who were suffering to create their own transformative experiences. There is no doubt that *Mister Rogers' Neighborhood* was Rogers's unique way of acting compassionately toward himself, others, and even the world.

But it's not enough to say that Rogers was a compassionate human being, especially if we restrict his compassion to the realm of sweet children and fuzzy feelings. However accurate they may be, those few words don't do justice to the Fred Rogers depicted here. They're not descriptive enough, and they're far too abstract for this ordinary, extraordinary man.

If we are to grasp the full significance of Rogers's legacy, we have to place his compassion in its historical context. Because context matters, it's far more helpful to say that Fred Rogers acted with compassion toward victims of the Vietnam War; people whose lives suffered under the absurd and astronomical costs of the nuclear arms race; children and soldier-parents whose familial bonds were shattered during the Persian Gulf War; and boys and girls who were scared that planes would attack them too during the War on Terror. As a compassionate human being, Fred Rogers countered the attitudes, policies, and practices of a political society poised to kill.

Rogers's compassion was not some vague feeling of kindness and sweetness suspended above time and place. He acted with compassion toward victims of racial discrimination during the modern civil rights movement, toward poor parents whom President Nixon characterized as lazy, and toward children whose bellies growled in the middle of the day as their parents rushed home with boxes of cheap cereal. Rogers also expressed compassion for boys and girls who, long before the sexual and gender revolution came to full expression, craved experiences far beyond those typically associated with their particular genders; for gays and lesbians longing to feel loved and lovable in the pre- and post-Stonewall eras; and for a natural world wrecked by industrial and postindustrial America. As a compassionate human being, Fred Rogers opposed the attitudes, policies, and practices of anyone who built walls between rich and poor, whites and people of color, men and women, gays and straights, people and the natural world—barriers that made individual and social peace impossible.

By placing Rogers in context, then, we can finally see that his compassion was not a vague feeling of warmth and fuzziness, but that it had concrete implications for politics and economics, and perhaps most fascinating of all, that it was edgy and radical—subversive of our wider society and culture. Fred Rogers was thus not merely a compassionate human being. He was a compassionate prophet—not so much the type who rails, rants, and rages against the powers that be, but the type who quietly builds an alternative *polis*, where the violence and injustice of the wider society and culture are subverted.

Placing his compassion in context also helps us avoid the common danger of deifying the beloved host of *Mister Rogers' Neighborhood*. Fred Rogers was compassionate toward those who were oppressed in various ways, but even today some of those individuals feel he could have done more than he did. François Clemmons believes that Rogers could have supported racial justice even more by depicting him and Betty Aberlin as an interracial couple in the program's operas, and that he could have offered more support for gay rights by having a gay character appear on *Mister Rogers' Neighborhood*. Aberlin believes that Rogers could have used his public platform to condemn the Persian Gulf War in no uncertain terms, just as other celebrities had done. And these are just a few examples; the files of viewer mail include other criticisms suggesting that Rogers did not do enough to advance peace and justice—that he was imperfect and inconsistent in his efforts to build the peaceable reign of God in the Neighborhood.

Rogers would most likely be among the first to remind us that he was not "all things to all people" (1 Cor. 9:22). He was just himself, with all his strengths and weaknesses, all his advantages and limitations, and he was that way for reasons unique to his own personal history, many of which we will never know. But perhaps we would do well, when pinpointing his shortcomings, to recall that in his own prayer life Rogers often sought divine guidance and wisdom— and especially forgiveness for those times he fell short of unconditional love.

This, of course, points us to another important dimension of his compassion. Fred Rogers was not just a compassionate human being; he was a practicing Christian who firmly believed that human compassion has its ultimate source in a God whose love for all of creation never ends. For Rogers, we can and should be compassionate because God is compassionate toward us— always and everywhere. Again, context matters here, and when we place Rogers's spiritual beliefs in their historical perspective—a time when Billy Graham's judgmental God was wildly popular—we can clearly see just how prophetic Rogers's compassion was.

But it's not enough even to say that he was a Christian prophet. Perhaps most of all, Fred Rogers was a Christian peacemaker. The compassion he expressed toward victims of violence and injustice was not for its own sake; it was ultimately for the sake of the peaceable reign of God. Rogers opposed all U.S. wars in his lifetime, as well as various barriers to individual and social peace, because he believed that the Prince of Peace beckons us to establish the peaceful reign of God here on earth—in our hearts, communities, and societies.

As a Christian peacemaker, Rogers took his cues from the parables of Jesus. His compassion did not come to expression in marches, rallies, and public protests, but in the quiet of a studio, behind the staring eye of a camera, and on a set he built for sharing stories about the peaceable reign of God—a place where individuals seek to resolve conflicts peacefully and love one another and the world as fully as possible. Rogers sought to bring the Prince of Peace into our lives by telling us captivating and compelling tales about a neighborhood of peace—peace within and between all of God's creation. This is the rich legacy of Fred Rogers; out of compassion, he built a neighborhood of peace and love just around the corner from the violent and unjust center of U.S. politics and economics.

Yes, Fred Rogers was a compassionate human being, and at times an imperfect one. But let's be sure to fill that out when we recall his legacy. As a compassionate human being, he was also a Christian prophet and peacemaker who sought to accept us as we are, with all our violence and injustice, while at the same time inviting us to visit a neighborhood marked by unconditional love for one another and the world—the peaceable reign of God—so that we can go back home and build similar neighborhoods in our own communities. Contrary to popular wisdom, Rogers wasn't content merely to accept us as we are; he wanted us to become prophets and peacemakers committed to making our neighborhoods bastions of compassion.

Can we really build neighborhoods of compassion? By taking Fred Rogers seriously, rather than dismissing him as a lightweight or deifying him in the clouds, perhaps we can at last see that his own steadfast commitment to peace in a time marked by relentless wars and terror gives us reason to hope against hope that the Neighborhood of Make-Believe—where King Friday orders his troops to put their weapons away—can indeed become our very own.

Notes

INTRODUCTION: JUST THE WAY HE WAS

1. Ellen Goodman, "Awareness Clicks In as the Persian Gulf Crisis Comes to Home," syndicated column published in the *Chicago Tribune,* January 20, 1991, accessible at articles .chicagotribune.com.

2. Fred Rogers to Ellen Goodman, February 19, 1991, EU14, folder "Goodman, Ellen," the Fred Rogers Archive (FRA) at the Fred Rogers Center, St. Vincent College, Latrobe, Pennsylvania.

3. youtube.com/watch?v=OFzXaFbxDcM, accessed May 29, 2014.

4. youtube.com/watch?v=yXEuEUQIP3Q, accessed May 29, 2014.

5. youtube.com/watch?v=LZbXM3Kzd7o, accessed May 29, 2014.

6. Claudia Rowe, "Some Things Never Change, and Thank Heavens Mister Rogers Is One of Them," *Biography Magazine* (March 2000): 104.

7. Quoted in Glenn Collins, "TV's Mr. Rogers—A Busy Surrogate Dad," *New York Times,* June 19, 1983. A few years earlier, Rogers had written the following to a friend: "There are those who make fun of my 'gentleness' and 'quiet' but I want so much to be honest. The medium of television itself seems to encourage the opposite. As I've told you, I need your prayers." See Fred Rogers to Sister Patricia Holly, November 20, 1979, CW10, folder "Lynch, Elaine, Daily file—November 1979," FRA.

8. Doreen Carvajal, "Still around the Neighborhood: 'Mister Rogers' Ends Production, but Mr. Rogers Keeps Busy," *New York Times,* April 10, 2001.

9. Mary Elizabeth Williams, "Where Have You Gone, Mister Rogers?" salon.com, March 13, 2012, accessible at salon.com. Williams describes Rogers as "one of the most radical figures of contemporary history," though she does not tend in any detail to his war politics.

10. Following the 1997 school shooting in Paducah, Kentucky, Rogers commented on the shooter—who had told his friends he was going to do something "really big" at school—by saying, "Oh, wouldn't the world be a different place if he had said, 'I'm going to do something really *little* tomorrow.'" Rogers then crafted a week of programs on the theme of "little and big," inviting his viewers to see the extraordinary potential of something, even an idea, that starts out very little. For an account of this, see Tom Junod, "Can You Say . . . Hero?" *Esquire,* November 1998, accessible at esquire.com.

11. Fred Rogers, letter to Pauline Hubner, November 5, 1979, FRA.

12. For more on Rogers as a storyteller, see George Gerbner, "Fred Rogers and the Significance of Story," in *Mister Rogers' Neighborhood: Children, Television, and Fred Rogers,*

ed. Mark Collins and Margaret Mary Kimmel (Pittsburgh: University of Pittsburgh Press, 1996), 3–13.

13. Fred Rogers, *Life's Journeys according to Mister Rogers* (New York: Hyperion, 2005), 47.

14. For more on the effects of Rogers's transitions, see Roderick Townley, "The Meaning of Transitions in *Mister Rogers' Neighborhood*," in *Mister Rogers' Neighborhood*, ed. Collins and Kimmel, 67–76.

15. "Mr. Rogers Sues to Stop T-shirts Picturing a Gun," *New York Times,* December 26, 1998.

16. Hedda Sharapan, "It's Contagious!" no date, accessible at fredrogers.org.

CHAPTER 1: "ISN'T PEACE WONDERFUL?"

1. Quoted in Mark Atwood Lawrence, *The Vietnam War: A Concise International History* (New York: Oxford University Press, 2008), 125.

2. For this chapter's quotations from this series of antiwar programs, see *Misterogers' Neighborhood*, episodes 1–5, originally broadcast February 19–23, 1968. ("Mister Rogers" was spelled "Misterogers" at this point in the program's history.)

3. Doug Harvey, "Zen and the Art of Make-Believe: A Date with Mister Rogers," accessible at dougharvey.la, states that "Mister Rogers' aim is clearly to arm his viewers with a full and intimate knowledge of the status quo, and the powers with which to—oh, so peacefully—overthrow it." This point will become even clearer in following chapters.

CHAPTER 2: "WAR ISN'T NICE"

1. John Corry, "TV: 13-Part History of Vietnam War on PBS," *New York Times,* October 4, 1983.

2. John B. Oakes, "Reagan's Path to War," *New York Times,* August 3, 1983.

3. Ronald Reagan, address to the National Association of Evangelicals, March 8, 1983, accessible at reaganfoundation.org.

4. For this chapter's quotations from this series of antiwar programs, see *Mister Rogers' Neighborhood,* episodes 1521–1525, originally broadcast November 7–11, 1983.

5. For more on this, see Davy Rothbart, "A Friend in the Neighborhood," *New York Times,* February 28, 2003. Rothbart asked Rogers why people sometimes seemed afraid to talk to each other. Here is his description of what followed: "Mr. Rogers sat quietly for 15 full seconds. 'Perhaps we think we won't find another human being inside that person. Perhaps we think that there are some people in this world who I can't ever communicate with, and so I'll just give up before I try. And how sad it is to think that we would give up on any other creature who's just like us.' His eyes seemed to be watering."

6. "War Enters World of Mister Rogers," Associated Press, published in *Calgary Herald,* November 8, 1983, accessible at neighborhoodarchive.com.

CHAPTER 3: "I LIKE YOU"

1. David K. Shipler, "The Summit; Reagan and Gorbachev Sign Missile Treaty and Vow to Work for Greater Reductions," *New York Times,* December 9, 1987.

2. Felicity Barringer, "Mister Rogers Goes to Russia," *New York Times,* September 21, 1987.

3. Quotations from his visit to the Soviet program can be found in *Mister Rogers' Neighborhood,* episode 1587, originally broadcast March 8, 1988.

4. "Mr. Rogers Tries Out His 'Puppet Détente,'" Associated Press, published in *The Free Lance-Star,* November 20, 1987.

5. Barbara Vancheri, "Mr. Rogers' Puppet Détente," *Pittsburgh Post-Gazette,* November 24, 1987.

6. Quotations from Vedeneyeva's visit to the program can be found in *Mister Rogers' Neighborhood,* episode 1589, originally broadcast March 10, 1988.

CHAPTER 4: "JUST THE WAY YOU ARE"

1. Rogers had presented the biblical theme of beating swords into plowshares in a much subtler form a year earlier, in a remarkably creative opera about a violent character named Wicked Knife and Fork (*Mister Rogers' Neighborhood,* episode 1505, originally broadcast July 2, 1982). Here's the storyline: Wicked has taken captive the sweet and innocent Purple Twirling Kitty in a bold effort to secure a piece of famous land known as Spoon Mountain. After they learn about this hostage situation, Prince Extraordinary and Park Ranger Betty Green, armed with spoons, set out to free Kitty. Halfway up the mountain they encounter Commodore, in full military attire, who offers them a resting place, where they learn more horrifying details about the situation: Kitty is now crying and in chains on top of the mountain.

When Prince Extraordinary and Betty Green arrive at the peak, a physical struggle ensues between them and Wicked Knife and Fork. Wicked wins the battle, but just when he is tying up his three hostages, Commodore arrives and secures the release of all three. Although he is clearly a military officer, Commodore uses no physical weapons in his successful rescue. All he does is untie the captives and sing about love: "There's a wonder in this mountain that is hidden from our eyes. . . . And that wonder's name is love."

Love melts the heart of Wicked, too, and he begins to cry. "All I ever wanted was a spoon," he says. But when he was younger no one ever gave him one; all they gave him was a bunch of knives and forks. "I was scared to death of all those knives and forks," he confesses. And so with fear deep in his heart, he simply lashed out in anger, becoming a "shrew" who "tried to undo everything that was true."

Prince Extraordinary is so moved by this shocking revelation, as well as his own mission of giving comfort to "the weak and heavy-laden," that he comes up with a plan to help Wicked. "Let's take your knives to the castle, where there's a spoon-making machine," he says. "We'll melt your forks at the castle." Back at the spoon-making castle, the characters celebrate their new lives—full of love, free of fear. Once again, love has cast out fear on *Mister Rogers' Neighborhood.*

2. Marian Christy, "How Mister Rogers Keeps Ticking," *Boston Globe,* February 17, 1985.

3. Fred Rogers, letter to Tom Junod, October 25, 1998, EU16, folder "Junod, Tom," FRA.

4. Fred Rogers, "God Doesn't POW Anybody," part of "Faith through the Eyes of a Child," a series of meditations for May 1–7, 1983, EU88, folder "These Days," FRA.

5. Rogers, letter to Tom Junod, October 25, 1998.

6. Fred Rogers, letter to Tom Junod, August 15, 1998, EU16, folder "Junod, Tom," FRA.

7. Alan Borsuk, "Everyone's Neighbor," *Milwaukee Journal Sentinel,* May 20, 2001.

8. Fred Rogers, "Invisible Essentials," sermon preached at Memphis Theological Seminary, Memphis, Tennessee, May 10, 1997, EU74, folder "1997," FRA.

9. Fred Rogers, "Sometimes Good and Sometimes Bad," EU88, folder "These Days," FRA.

10. Fred Rogers, commencement speech at Middlebury College, May 2001, Series VII, Final Projects 2001–2003, Subseries G, Speeches, FRA.

11. Fred Rogers, letter to William Trudeau, September 23, 1975, EU42, folder "Fred Rogers, daily, October 1997," FRA. Rogers was registering his complaint not against Trudeau, pastor of Turnagain United Methodist Church in Anchorage, Alaska, but against another pastor in the city.

12. Rogers, "Invisible Essentials."

13. Fred Rogers, "The Boundaries of Freedom," sermon preached at Sixth Presbyterian Church, Pittsburgh, August 27, 1972, EU3, folder "Sixth Presbyterian Church," FRA.

14. Fred Rogers, speech at Grove City, PA, June 13, 1979, CW10, folder "Lynch, Elaine: Daily file—June 1979," FRA.

15. Borsuk, "Everyone's Neighbor."

16. Fred Rogers, letter to Janet Harris, January 28, 1978, CW10, folder "Rogers, Fred, Daily—January 1979," FRA.

17. Wendy Murray Zoba, "Won't You Be My Neighbor?" *Christianity Today* (March 6, 2000): 46.

18. Fred Rogers, *Life's Journeys according to Mister Rogers: Things to Remember along the Way* (New York: Hyperion, 2005), 58.

19. Ibid.

20. See, for example, Wendy Murray Zoba, "Won't You Be My Neighbor?" 40.

21. Rogers, *Life's Journeys according to Mister Rogers*, 58.

22. Rogers, "Invisible Essentials."

23. Rogers, speech at Grove City.

24. Ibid.

25. Ibid.

26. Rogers, "Invisible Essentials."

27. Fred Rogers with Kathryn Brinckerhoff, "I Like You Just the Way You Are," *Guideposts* (September 1980): 4.

28. Fred Rogers, "Neighbor: Nourishing Our Life Together," *Living Pulpit* (July-September 2002): 3. See also Fred Rogers, *The World according to Mister Rogers: Important Things to Remember* (New York: Hyperion, 2003), 149.

29. Fred Rogers, untitled notes, n.d., EU19, folder "Canada," FRA.

30. Brian Knowlton, "'I Sinned,' He Says in Apology That Includes Lewinsky," *New York Times,* September 12, 1998.

31. Fred Rogers, letter to Tom Junod, September 14, 1998, EU16, folder "Junod, Tom," FRA.

32. "Direct Access: J. Philip Wogaman," December 16, 1998, accessible at washington post.com.

33. Rogers, letter to Tom Junod, September 14, 1998.

34. Fred Rogers, letter to Tom Junod, July 26–29, 1998, EU16, folder "Junod, Tom," FRA.

35. Fred Rogers, commencement speech at Middlebury College, May 2001.

36. Fred Rogers, "Intercession," March 6, 1977, EU3, folder "Sixth Church," FRA.

37. Rogers, speech at Grove City.

38. William Guy aptly summarizes Rogers on this point: "Far from serving solely as some kind of glorified Dr. Feelgood, bathing viewers in a vague glow of affirmation, Mister Rogers should be understood as proclaiming an ethic of challenge and responsibility. It is an ethic, however, that understands that care of others is not likely to be tendered by those who have been battered into submission or who doubt their own worth" ("The Theology of *Mister*

Rogers' Neighborhood," in *Mister Rogers' Neighborhood,* ed. Mark Collins and Margaret Mary Kimmel [Pittsburgh: University of Pittsburgh Press, 1996], 101).

39. Rogers, commencement speech at Middlebury College.

40. Ibid.

41. Ibid.

42. Rogers, "Invisible Essentials."

43. Ibid.

44. Ibid.

45. Ibid.

46. Fred Rogers, "Out of the Wilderness," sermon for the installation of the Reverend Kenneth L. Barley, January 15, 1989, EU4, folder "Installation of Kenneth Barley," FRA.

47. Rogers, "Neighbor: Nourishing Our Life Together," 5.

48. Rogers drew this quotation from Henri J. M. Nouwen, *Sabbatical Journey: The Diary of His Final Year* (New York: Crossroad, 2000), 179–80.

49. Rogers, "Out of the Wilderness."

50. Fred Rogers, "More Than We Know," speech at Saint Vincent College, Latrobe, PA, April 25, 1995, EU74, folder "1995," FRA.

51. Rogers, *Life's Journeys according to Mister Rogers,* 58.

52. Fred Rogers, speech at Washington and Jefferson College, 1984, EU84, folder "Washington & Jefferson College," FRA.

53. Fred Rogers, speech to Presbyterian Peace Fellowship, June 1994, EU83, folder "Peaceseeker Award," FRA.

54. Rogers, email to Tom Junod, October 25, 1998.

55. Leo Tolstoy, "Letter to Ernest Howard Crosby," in *Approaches to Peace: A Reader in Peace Studies,* ed. David P. Barash (New York: Oxford University Press, 2000), 178.

56. Rogers, email to Tom Junod, October 25, 1998.

57. Fred Rogers, letter to Martin Marty, February 13, 1992, EU33, folder "Marty, Martin," FRA.

58. Fred Rogers, speech at the Fourth Annual National Dropout Prevention Conference, March 29, 1992, MRNA. On a similar note, Rogers held that "the best way to understand about God and peace is to know about peace in our everyday lives" (Rogers, *World according to Mister Rogers,* 178.)

59. Frederick Buechner, *The Magnificent Defeat* (San Francisco: Harper & Row, 1985), 105.

60. Rogers, letter to Tom Junod, November 15, 1998, EU16, folder "Junod, Tom," FRA.

CHAPTER 5: "IT'S OKAY TO BE ANGRY"

1. Amy Hollingsworth, *The Simple Faith of Mister Rogers* (Nashville: Thomas Nelson, 2005), 99.

2. Gary Covert, "Breaking through the Violence Within—and the Violence Without," *Other Side* (April 1979): 21.

3. "Clinton Asks Men to Pledge Never to Strike Any Woman," *New York Times,* October 15, 1995.

4. Fred Rogers, "Invisible Essentials," sermon preached at Memphis Theological Seminary, Memphis, Tennessee, May 10, 1997, EU74, folder "1997," FRA.

5. For this chapter's quotations from the series on mad feelings, see *Mister Rogers' Neighborhood,* episodes 1691–1695, originally broadcast October 16–20, 1995.

6. Fred Rogers, *You Are Special: Words of Wisdom for All Ages from a Beloved Neighbor* (1994; repr., New York: Penguin, 1995), 168.

7. Ibid., 105.

8. Fred Rogers, *Dear Mister Rogers, Does It Ever Rain in Your Neighborhood?* (New York: Penguin, 1996), 19.

9. Ibid., 101.

10. Rogers, *You Are Special,* 26.

11. Ibid., 23.

12. Fred Rogers and Barry Head, *Mister Rogers Talks with Parents* (New York: Berkley Books, 1983), 60.

13. Rogers, *You Are Special,* 169.

14. Fred Rogers, *The Mister Rogers Parenting Book* (Philadelphia: Running Press, 2002), 108.

15. Rogers, *You Are Special,* 23.

16. Fred Rogers, *Life's Journeys according to Mister Rogers: Things to Remember along the Way* (New York: Hyperion, 2005), 25.

17. Rogers, *You Are Special,* 123.

18. Fred Rogers, speech to NATPE, New Orleans, January 15, 1997, EU30, folder "NATPE," FRA.

19. Fred Rogers, speech to PTA, Las Vegas, June 12, 1994, speech box 1, FRA.

20. Fred Rogers, "What Do You Bring to TV?" May 26, 1978, EU42, folder "Rogers daily, June 1978," FRA.

21. Fred Rogers, letter to James Komaniecki, February 1990, EU44, FRA.

22. Fred Rogers, speech to NAEYC Conference, Toronto, November 18, 1998, speech box 2, FRA.

23. See Fred Rogers, "Television and the Family," speech, April 26, 1975, box 1, folder 2.1.3, Fred Rogers Collection, Mister Rogers' Neighborhood Archive [MRNA], University of Pittsburgh.

24. Fred Rogers, acceptance speech at Television Hall of Fame, February 1999, EU123, folder "Fred Rogers Center," FRA.

25. Rogers and Head, *Mister Rogers Talks with Parents,* 60–61.

26. Fred Rogers, remarks for *The Protestant Hour,* February 25, 1976, EU42, folder "Basil Cox correspondence, January 1977," FRA. See also Fred Rogers, *Fred Rogers Writes and Sings about Many Ways to Say I Love You* (Valley Forge, PA: Judson Press, 1977), 7.

27. Fred Rogers, July 22, 2000, interviewed by Karen Herman for Archive of American Television, accessible at emmytvlegends.org.

28. Fred Rogers, *Mister Rogers' Special: Kennedy Assassination,* recorded June 7, 1968, transcript available at CW7, folder "Kennedy Special," FRA.

29. *Mister Rogers' Neighborhood,* episode 1468, originally broadcast February 6, 1980.

30. *Mister Rogers' Neighborhood,* episode 1469, originally broadcast February 7, 1980.

31. Rogers and Head, *Mister Rogers Talks with Parents,* 171.

32. See *Approaches to Peace: A Reader in Peace Studies,* ed. David P. Barash (New York: Oxford University Press, 2000), 9.

33. Sigmund Freud, "Why War?" in Barash, ed., *Approaches to Peace,* 9–13.

34. Rogers, "What Do You Bring to TV?"

35. Rogers, "Invisible Essentials."

36. Rogers, *You Are Special,* 168.

37. See Fred Rogers, "What Would You Do with the Mad That You Feel?" *Healthy Kids* (October-November 1997): 42–44.

38. "Margaret McFarland; Child Psychologist," obituary, *Los Angeles Times,* September 14, 1988.

39. Quoted in Patrick A. McGuire, "Welcome to the Neighborhood," *Baltimore Sun,* May 14, 1993.

40. Quoted in ibid.

41. Rogers, *Life's Journeys,* 15.

42. Rogers, *You Are Special,* 148.

43. Ibid., 154–55.

44. Rogers and Head, *Mister Rogers Talks with Parents,* 62–63.

45. For this chapter's quotations from the special, see *Violence in the News: Helping Children Understand,* originally broadcast May 20, 1981, FRA. For a transcript of the program, see "Violence in the News: Helping Children Understand," EU78, folder "Let's Talk about It—brochures," FRA.

46. Rogers and Head, *Mister Rogers Talks with Parents,* 154.

47. Ibid., 153.

48. Quoted in Jeff Garis, "The Passing of a Quiet Abolitionist in Pennsylvania," accessible at prisontalk.com.

49. Rogers, *You Are Special,* 105.

50. Rogers, *Mister Rogers Parenting Book,* 108.

CHAPTER 6: "A GROSS FORM OF ABUSE"

1. This is not to say that Rogers's program did not result in positive social behavior in child viewers. For evidence of the effects of *Mister Rogers' Neighborhood* on children's sociability, see Shirley G. Moore, "The Effects of Television on the Prosocial Behavior of Young Children," *Research in Review* (July 1977): 60–64. This excellent article includes analyses of various scholarly articles that explore the effects of *Mister Rogers' Neighborhood* on children. There is also a scholarly work on lifelong prosocial effects of the program. See Stephen D. Perry and Amanda L. Roesch, "He's in a New Neighborhood Now: Religious Fantasy Themes about *Mister Rogers' Neighborhood,*" *Journal of Media and Religion* 3, no. 4 (2004): 199–218. The authors explore religious themes in tributes to Rogers posted shortly after his death, and they offer the following conclusion: "The frequency with which the values and ideals of the program surface in the lives of those who watched the program is unclear, but there is some indication from the responses analyzed here that prosocial impacts may be lifelong" (217).

2. Fred Rogers, speech for migrant workers, April 27, 1987, EU74, folder "1987," FRA.

3. Fred Rogers, letter to Senator H. J. Heinz III, January 31, 1991, EU64, folder "FR daily, Jan. 1991," FRA.

4. Fred Rogers, speech for Association of Family and Conciliation Courts, May 15, 1991, EU64, folder "Rogers daily, March-July 1991," FRA.

5. Ibid.

6. Fred Rogers, letter to Larry Kutner, January 24, 1991, EU17, folder "Kutner, Lawrence, Ph.D.," FRA.

7. Ibid.

8. Sam Newbury, memo to general managers and program managers, January 15, 1991, EU64, folder "EL daily, Jan. 1991," FRA.

9. Transcripts of the spots are included in Sam Newbury, memo to Fred, Margy, Bob, Adrienne, David C., Kathy B., February 11, 1991, EU64, folder "EL daily, Jan. 1991," FRA.

10. Fred Rogers and Barry Head, *Mister Rogers Talks with Parents* (New York: Berkley Books, 1983), 118.

11. Ibid., 119.

12. Fred Rogers, *The Mister Rogers Parenting Book* (Philadelphia: Running Press, 2002), 24.

13. Rogers and Head, *Mister Rogers Talks with Parents,* 119.

14. Ibid., 119–20.

15. Fred Rogers, reflection for mass for Senator H. John Heinz III, April 1, 1992, EU15, folder "Heinz, John and Teresa," FRA. Rogers mentioned Heinz's efforts in several 1992 speeches. See Fred Rogers, Indiana University commencement speech, May 16, 1992, box 1, folder 2.1.4, MRNA; and Fred Rogers, "The Gift of Yourself," baccalaureate speech at Boston University, May 17, 1992, box 1, folder 2.1.4, MRNA.

16. *Mister Rogers' Neighborhood,* episode 1558, originally broadcast February 5, 1986.

17. *Mister Rogers' Neighborhood,* episode 1559, originally broadcast February 6, 1986.

18. Betty Aberlin, letter to Fred Rogers, February 2, 1991, copy in private papers of Betty Aberlin.

19. Betty Aberlin, letter to Peter Jennings, January 27, 1991, copy in private papers of Betty Aberlin.

20. Betty Aberlin, letter to Shirley Green, February 4, 1991, copy in private papers of Betty Aberlin.

21. For this chapter's quotations from this series, see *Mister Rogers' Neighborhood,* episodes 1631–1635, originally broadcast February 25–March 1, 1991.

22. Fred Rogers, letter to Scott Simon, March 14, 1992, EU107, folder "Papers with FR's notes on them," FRA.

23. Fred Rogers, letter to Tom Junod, September 5, 1998, EU16, folder "Junod, Tom," FRA.

24. See civilianpublicservice.org for a history of these camps.

25. Rogers, letter to Tom Junod.

26. Rogers and Head, *Mister Rogers Talks with Parents,* 183.

27. Rogers, letter to Scott Simon.

28. Fred Rogers, "Introduction to Dalai Lama," November 11, 1998, Greensburg, Pennsylvania, speech box 2, FRA.

29. Fred Rogers, "Adults PSA," EU95, folder "9/11 spots—scripts," FRA.

30. "Text of President's Speech," July 9, 2002, accessible at edition.cnn.com/2002/ALL POLITICS/07/09/bush.transcript/index.html.

31. Fred Rogers, "Dartmouth College," June 9, 2002, EU123, folder "Speeches," FRA.

32. Fred Rogers, *The World according to Mister Rogers: Important Things to Remember* (New York: Hyperion, 2003), 177.

CHAPTER 7: "A BLACK BROTHER"

1. Paula Lawrence Wehmiller describes Rogers as a "keeper of the dream" that Martin Luther King Jr. shared on August 28, 1963 ("Mister Rogers: Keeper of the Dream," in *Mister Rogers' Neighborhood: Children, Television, and Fred Rogers,* ed. Mark Collins and Margaret Mary Kimmel [Pittsburgh: University of Pittsburgh Press, 1996], 123).

2. Fred Rogers, speech to the American Academy of Pediatrics, July 19, 1989, New York City, EU74, folder "1989," FRA.

3. *The Arsenio Hall Show,* episode 69, originally broadcast January 6, 1993.

4. George Allen, letter to Fred Rogers, September 4, 1999, EU37, folder "Allen, George," FRA.

5. Fred Rogers, *Report for 1950–51,* Rollins College Archives, digital item accessible at archives.rollins.edu.

6. *Mister Rogers' Neighborhood,* episode 4, originally broadcast February 22, 1968.

7. Unless otherwise noted, this chapter's quotations of François Clemmons come from the author's interview of Clemmons, September 6, 2013, Middlebury, Vermont.

8. "Personal Histories: François Clemmons," interview by Joey Plaster, August 23, 2000, for Oberlin College LGBT Community History Project, accessible at oberlinlgbt.org.

9. *Mister Rogers' Neighborhood,* episode 119, originally broadcast August 1, 1968.

10. *Mister Rogers' Neighborhood,* episode 1065, originally broadcast May 9, 1969.

11. "Interview by Mike Wallace," June 25, 1958, *The Papers of Martin Luther King Jr.,* vol. 4, *Symbol of the Movement, January 1957–December 1958,* ed. Clayborne Carson, Susan Carson, Adrienne Clay, Virginia Shadron, and Kieran Taylor (Berkeley: University of California Press, 2000), 436.

12. "Excerpts from Supreme Court Ruling on Virginia Ban on Miscegenation," *New York Times,* June 13, 1967.

13. *Mister Rogers' Neighborhood,* episode 1402, originally broadcast March 4, 1975.

14. Tony Chiroldes, email to Michael Long, November 12, 2013, in author's possession.

15. *Mister Rogers' Neighborhood,* episode 1543, originally broadcast February 6, 1985.

16. *Mister Rogers' Neighborhood,* episode 1389, originally broadcast May 16, 1974.

17. *Mister Rogers' Neighborhood,* episode 1478, originally broadcast February 18, 1981.

18. *Mister Rogers' Neighborhood,* episode 1543.

19. *Mister Rogers' Neighborhood,* episode 1581, originally broadcast November 23, 1987.

20. "Klan Barred from Playing Phone Tapes," Associated Press, *Los Angeles Times,* October 11, 1990.

21. *Mister Rogers' Neighborhood,* episode 1663, originally broadcast February 24, 1993.

CHAPTER 8: "FOOD FOR THE WORLD"

1. Unless otherwise noted, this chapter's quotations of François Clemmons come from the author's interview of Clemmons, September 6, 2013, Middlebury, Vermont.

2. Fred Rogers, keynote speech for migrant educators, April 27, 1987, EU74, folder "1987," FRA.

3. Fred Rogers, "Invisible Essentials," speech delivered at Memphis Theological Seminary, Memphis, Tennessee, EU74, folder "1997," FRA.

4. Doris Kearns, "Do the Poor Want to Work?" *New York Times,* September 17, 1972.

5. Ibid.

6. For this chapter's quotations from the series on Mr. Appel's poverty, see *Mister Rogers' Neighborhood,* episodes 1216–1218, originally broadcast March 20–22, 1972.

7. "Report Says U.S. Hunger Is Widespread and Rising," Associated Press, *New York Times,* February 7, 1984.

8. For this chapter's quotations from the series on food and hunger, see *Mister Rogers' Neighborhood,* episodes 1536–1540, originally broadcast November 19–23, 1984.

9. Arthur Simon, *The Rising of Bread for the World: An Outcry of Citizens against Hunger* (New York: Paulist Press, 2009), 75.

10. Ibid., 93.

11. Jonathan V. Last, "Mr. Rogers among the Savages," *Weekly Standard,* June 6, 2011, accessible at weeklystandard.com.

12. Rogers, keynote speech for migrant educators.

13. Ibid.

14. *Mister Rogers' Neighborhood,* episode 1710, originally broadcast August 30, 1996.

15. Fred Rogers, *The Giving Box: Create a Tradition of Giving with Your Children* (Philadelphia: Running Press, 2000), 11–12.

16. Ibid., 13.

17. Ibid., 14.

18. Ibid., 13.

19. Ibid., 14.

20. Ibid., 80.

21. Ibid.

22. Fred Rogers, letter to Bo Lozoff, September 29, 1997, EU33, folder "Lozoff," FRA.

23. Comment by Joe Pytka, November 2, 2009, accessible at deadline.com.

24. *Mister Rogers' Neighborhood,* episode 1529, originally broadcast April 7, 1984.

25. *Mister Rogers' Neighborhood,* episode 1569, originally broadcast November 27, 1986.

26. Fred Rogers, July 22, 2000, interviewed by Karen Herman for Archive of American Television, accessible at emmytvlegends.org.

27. "Mr. Rogers Evicts Burger King's TV Ad," Associated Press, *Pittsburgh Post-Gazette,* May 9, 1984.

28. Rogers, interview with Karen Herman.

29. Fred Rogers, speech to NATPE, January 15, 1997, Las Vegas, EU30, folder "NATPE," FRA.

30. Rogers, interview with Karen Herman.

31. Fred Rogers, letter to Roger Richardson, May 25, 1998, EU36, folder "Richardson, Roger," FRA.

CHAPTER 9: "I'M TIRED OF BEING A LADY"

1. For this chapter's quotations from this episode, see *Mister Rogers' Neighborhood,* episode 16, originally broadcast March 11, 1968.

2. For this chapter's quotations from this episode, see *Mister Rogers' Neighborhood,* episode 50, originally broadcast April 26, 1968.

3. Quoted in Lucy Freeman, "The Feminine Mystique," *New York Times,* April 7, 1963. Freeman, incidentally, found it "superficial" of Friedan to fault "culture" for women's restricted identity.

4. For this chapter's quotations from this episode, see *Mister Rogers' Neighborhood,* episode 1068, originally broadcast February 4, 1970.

5. Susan Linn states that "in Lady Elaine we recognize a characteristically amoral, limit-pushing, and curiosity-driven aspect of early childhood" ("With an Open Hand: Puppetry on *Mister Rogers' Neighborhood,*" in *Mister Rogers' Neighborhood: Children, Television, and Fred Rogers,* ed. Mark Collins and Margaret Mary Kimmel [Pittsburgh: University of Pittsburgh Press, 1996], 95).

6. *Mister Rogers' Neighborhood,* episode 1139, originally broadcast February 25, 1971.

7. *Mister Rogers' Neighborhood,* episode 1664, originally broadcast February 25, 1993.

8. For this chapter's quotations from this episode, see *Mister Rogers' Neighborhood,* episode 1764, originally broadcast August 30, 2001.

9. Elizabeth Flock, "Princess Diana and Kate Middleton: A Tale of Two Princesses," posted April 28, 2011, at washingtonpost.com.

10. *Mister Rogers' Neighborhood,* episode 1015, originally broadcast February 28, 1969.

11. *Mister Rogers' Neighborhood,* episode 1009, originally broadcast February 20, 1969.

12. *Mister Rogers' Neighborhood,* episode 1707, originally broadcast August 26, 1996.

13. Fred Rogers, speech at Yale University, December 2, 1988, speech box 1, FRA.

14. *Mister Rogers' Neighborhood,* episode 1183, originally broadcast April 28, 1971.

15. *Mister Rogers' Neighborhood,* episode 1615, originally broadcast November 24, 1989.

16. For this chapter's quotations from this episode, see *Mister Rogers' Neighborhood,* episode 26, originally broadcast March 25, 1968.

17. Steven Mintz, "From Patriarchy to Androgyny and Other Myths," in *American Families Past and Present: Social Perspectives on Transformations* (New Brunswick, NJ: Rutgers University Press, 2006), 23.

18. Ibid., 24.

19. Rogers, speech at Yale University.

20. *Mister Rogers' Neighborhood,* episode 1623, originally broadcast August 1, 1990.

21. *Mister Rogers' Neighborhood,* episode 1573, originally broadcast March 11, 1987.

22. *Mister Rogers' Neighborhood,* episode 1622, originally broadcast July 31, 1990.

23. *Mister Rogers' Neighborhood,* episode 1621, originally broadcast July 30, 1990.

24. *Mister Rogers' Neighborhood,* episode 1625, originally broadcast August 3, 1990.

25. Fred Rogers and Barry Head, *Mister Rogers Talks with Parents* (New York: Berkley Books, 1983), 14.

26. Ibid., 11.

27. Ibid., 32.

28. Ibid., 34.

29. Ibid., 32.

30. Ibid.

31. Ibid.

32. For this chapter's quotations from the series on working parents, see *Mister Rogers' Neighborhood,* episodes 1611–1615, originally broadcast November 20–24, 1989.

33. *Mister Rogers' Neighborhood,* episode 1519, originally broadcast April 28, 1983.

34. Fred Rogers, note to Hedda Sharapan, no date, EU44, FRA.

CHAPTER 10: "HE UNDERSTOOD"

1. A. J. Daulerio, "Mr. Rogers Is Going to Hell, the FDNY Is Evil but He Loves Them Anyway: The Gospel according to Pastor Fred Phelps," interview posted April 2, 2003, at blacktable.com.

2. Quoted in Ralph R. Reiland, "God, Buggery, and Mister Rogers," posted May 15, 2003, at capitalismmagazine.com.

3. Unless otherwise noted, this chapter's quotations of François Clemmons come from the author's interview of Clemmons, September 6, 2013, Middlebury, Vermont.

4. François S. Clemmons, *A Song in My Soul: An Autobiographical Folktale,* unpublished book manuscript held in the private papers of François Clemmons.

5. Ibid.

6. "John James Reardon," *Palm Beach Post,* April 5, 1985.

7. *Mister Rogers' Neighborhood,* episode 1663, originally broadcast February 24, 1993.

8. William Sloane Coffin, *A Passion for the Possible* (Louisville, KY: Westminster John Knox Press, 1993), 65.

9. This chapter's quotations of McCall are from the author's interview with the Rev. John McCall, January 27, 2014.

10. Rogers did not hesitate to enter the public square on issues with which he felt comfortable. For example, in 1968 he served as chairman of the Forum on Mass Media and Child Development at the White House Conference on Youth, and a year later he appeared before the Senate in a lobbying effort to safeguard funding for PBS (see his moving testimony before Senator John Pastore at youtube.com). For more on this, see Robert A. Levin and Laurie Moses Hines, "Educational Television, Fred Rogers, and the History of Education," *History of Education Quarterly* 43, no. 2 (2003): 262–75. This excellent article also looks at Rogers in light of the troubling issue of the commercialization of children's television.

CHAPTER 11: "I LOVE TOFU BURGERS AND BEETS"

1. Paul Obis, "Fred Rogers: America's Favorite Neighbor," *Vegetarian Times* (November 1983): 26.

2. Ibid., 23.

3. Ibid., 26. All following quotations from this article are found on p. 26.

4. "The Legacy of Fred Rogers," accessible at fredrogerscenter.org.

5. Fred Rogers, "Don't Pick on the Peeps," undated, EU54, folder "Coral," FRA.

6. *Mister Rogers' Neighborhood,* episode 4, originally broadcast February 22, 1968.

7. *Mister Rogers' Neighborhood,* episode 1101, originally broadcast March 23, 1970.

8. *Mister Rogers' Neighborhood,* episodes 1496–1500, originally broadcast May 31–June 4, 1982.

9. *Mister Rogers' Neighborhood,* episode 1499, originally broadcast June 3, 1982.

10. *Mister Rogers' Neighborhood,* episode 1527, originally broadcast April 5, 1984.

11. *Mister Rogers' Neighborhood,* episode 1232, originally broadcast April 11, 1972.

12. *Mister Rogers' Neighborhood,* episode 1508, originally broadcast November 17, 1982.

13. *Mister Rogers' Neighborhood,* episode 1710, originally broadcast August 30, 1996.

14. *Mister Rogers' Neighborhood,* episode 1537, originally broadcast November 20, 1984.

15. *Mister Rogers' Neighborhood,* episode 1538, originally broadcast November 21, 1984.

16. *Mister Rogers' Neighborhood,* episode 1551, originally broadcast November 25, 1985.

17. *Mister Rogers' Neighborhood,* episode 1710, originally broadcast August 30, 1996.

18. *Mister Rogers' Neighborhood,* episode 1538.

19. *Mister Rogers' Neighborhood*, episode 1493, originally broadcast March 3, 1982.

20. Tom Junod, "Can You Say . . . 'Hero'?" *Esquire,* November 1998, accessible at esquire.com.

21. *Mister Rogers' Neighborhood,* episode 1572, originally broadcast March 10, 1987.

22. "Beauty without Cruelty," May 1990, EU4, FRA.

CHAPTER 12: "TAKE CARE OF THIS WONDERFUL WORLD"

1. Commercial produced by Keep America Beautiful and the Ad Council, 1971, accessible at youtube.com. See also Jane L. Levere, "After the 'Crying Indian,' Keep America Beautiful Starts a New Campaign," *New York Times,* July 16, 2013.

2. For this chapter's quotations from this series, see *Mister Rogers' Neighborhood,* episodes 72–74, originally broadcast May 28–30, 1968.

3. For this chapter's quotations from this series, see *Mister Rogers' Neighborhood*, episodes 1616–1620, originally broadcast April 16–20, 1990.

4. Fred Rogers, "Over Time," speech at Moravian College, May 30, 1992, MRNA.

5. *Mister Rogers' Neighborhood*, episode 1564, originally broadcast May 8, 1986.

6. Fred Rogers, "Creation," lyrics, EU54, folder "Coral," FRA.

7. *Mister Rogers' Neighborhood*, episode 1620, originally broadcast April 20, 1990.

8. Fred Rogers, "Tree, Tree, Tree," lyrics, EU85, folder "Songs (Words)," FRA.

CONCLUSION: THE COMPASSION OF FRED ROGERS

1. Nicole Brodeur, "A Most Beautiful Day in the Neighborhood for Students on Quest to Meet Mister Rogers," *Seattle Times,* August 6, 2000.

2. Ibid.

3. Ibid.

4. Doreen Carvajal, "'Mister Rogers' Ends Production, but Mr. Rogers Keeps Busy," *The New York Times,* April 10, 2001.

5. Ibid.

6. See Stephen D. Perry and Amanda L. Roesch, "He's in a New Neighborhood Now: Religious Fantasy Themes about *Mister Rogers' Neighborhood," Journal of Media and Religion* 3, no. 4 (2004): 199–218. The authors explore religious themes in tributes to Rogers posted shortly after his death, and they offer the following conclusion: "The frequency with which the values and ideals of the program surface in the lives of those who watched the program is unclear, but there is some indication from the responses analyzed here that prosocial impacts may be lifelong" (217).

7. Fred Rogers, July 22, 2000, interviewed by Karen Herman for Archive of American Television, accessible at emmytvlegends.org.

8. Thich Nhat Hanh, *Creating True Peace: Ending Violence in Yourself, Your Family, Your Community, and the World* (New York: Free Press, 2003), 25.

Index

Aber, Chuck, 93, 171, 172
Aberlin, Betty, 69–70, 112–13, 180
Abzug, Bella, 119
"the accuser," 29–30, 31, 43
advocate, Jesus as, 29–32
African American mayor, 92–93
Allen, George, 81–82, 83
ambulance corps, 75
American Civil Liberties Union, 141
Amish, 157
anger, "It's okay to be angry . . . ," 45–61
Animal Liberation (Singer), 166
animals. *See* vegetarianism
Another Mother for Peace, 120
Arlington National Cemetery, 3
arms race, in "Conflict Week," 11–15
Arsenal Family and Children's Center, 56, 57, 109–10
Arsenio Hall Show, The, 82
assassinations, 51, 52, 59, 85
Ayres, Lew, 75

Baldwin, James, 144
Band Aid, 105
Barnett, Marilyn, 91–92
beauty myth, 127–28
Beauty Myth, The (Wolf), 128
Beauty without Cruelty USA, 167
Bishop, Maurice, 10
Bixby, Bill, 52
Black Power movement, 84
Bread for the World, 106, 107–8
breakdancing, 94
Brethren, 75, 157
Brewer, Brad, 131
Brezhnev, Leonid, 23, 37

Brockett, Don, 151
Brodeur, Nicole, 177
Brown, H. Rap, 88
Brown, J. Larry, 105, 109
"Budyesh Ty Moi Sosyed?" 22
Buechner, Frederick, 34, 43
Burger King incident, 116
Bush, Barbara, 70
Bush, George H. W., 63, 69, 70, 73
Bush, George W., 77

Calvin, John, 30, 33
Cantini, Virgil, 121, 122
channeling, 45, 53–54, 61, 68
charity, 99–104, 112–14
Charles, Prince of Wales, 129
child abuse, Persian Gulf War and, 63–73, 179
children
    safeguarding, Gorbachev's view, 21
    Soviet children compared to U.S. children, 23–24
    vegetarianism and, 162–64
    See also poverty
Chiroldes, Tony, 93–94
Christian peacemaker, 180–81
Cisneros, Jose, 92
Citizens Commission on Hunger, 105
civil disobedience, 7, 18
Clemmons, François, 85–92, 96–97, 99–100, 143, 144–52, 154, 180
Clergy and Laity Concerned about Vietnam, 3
Clinton, Bill, 35–36, 45–46
Cody, Iron Eyes, 169
Coffin, William Sloane, Jr., 152–53
Cold War, 21, 23, 24, 37
coloring chicks, 159

197

comets, 174–75
compassion, of Rogers, 177–81
"Conflict Week" episodes (Nov. 7–11, 1983),
    9–19, 69–70
consumerism, 99, 115, 116, 117, 176
"Creation" (song), 140–41
Cronkite, Walter, 3
cruise missiles, 10, 37
crying corney, 130–32

Dalai Lama, 76
David, Keith, 92
Davis, Doris, 92
Davis, Mary Lou, 85
Davis, Rebekah Phelps, 143, 154
Day After, The (television series), 10
death instinct, 53
death penalty, 61
derivative nature, of political power, 6–7
détente, puppet, 21, 22–25
Detroit riots, 84
devil, 29
Diana, Princess of Wales, 129
Diet for a Small Planet (Lappé), 157
diversion, 53
diversity and race, 81–97
divine spark, 33–38, 42
    accept all people as they are, 34
    all are under providence and care of God, 37
    constancy of love for others, 36–37
    forgiveness of others, 35–36
    help others to grow, 34–35
    as "holy thing," 38
    identify with and understand those who hurt
        us, 35
    love God as God loves, 33
    love ourselves, 37–38
Donnelly, Thomas J., 106
do no harm principle, 50–51
"Don't Pick on the Peeps" (song), 159
Doonesbury, 152
"Do They Know It's Christmas?" 105
dump crisis, 171–73

Earle, Sylvia, 173
Earth Day, 169, 170
economic simplicity, of Rogers, 114–17
Edwards, Maurice, 59, 60
Einstein, Albert, 53
environment, 169–76
    Friday's Comet, 174–75

Iron Eyes Cody commercial, 169
    litterbugs, 170–71
    recycling, 171–73
    "Take care of this wonderful world that we
        have," 176
    trees, 175–76
    world is special, 173–74
equality issues, 129–30
Erlanger, Jeff, 95
Ethiopia, 105
evil empire speech, 10–11, 21
"the evil one," 29
"extraordinary, ordinary people," 33–38

Family Communications, 66, 96, 115, 177
"Fat Freddy," 34, 46, 178
fathers. See gender roles
Feminine Mystique, The (Friedan), 124
Ferrigno, Lou, 52
First Presbyterian Church of Latrobe, 27
Food for the World, 106, 110, 140
forgiveness, 31–32, 35–36
Foundry United Methodist Church, 36
Frampton, Mama Bell, 35
free will, 38
Free Willy (film), 166
Freud, Sigmund, 45, 53–54
Freudian perspective, of Rogers, 45, 53–54,
    63, 149
Friday's Comet, 174–75
Friedan, Betty, 119, 124, 125
Friends (religious society), 33, 75

Gandhi, Mohandas, 6–7
Geldof, Bob, 105
gender roles, 119–41
    beauty myth, 127–28
    crying corney, 130–32
    early gender bending, 119–20
    equality issues, 129–30
    fathers and music, 135–37
    fathers as nurturers, 132–35
    God with feminine and masculine qualities,
        140–41
    men with yarn, women with hammers, 120–22
    rough-and-tumble girls, boys taking care,
        122–27
    sensitivity in men, 130–32
    working mothers, 137–40
giving box, 110–12
Giving Box, The (Rogers), 110

God, of Rogers, 28–33
  as faithful and nonviolent, 27–29
  forgiveness of, 31–32
  God and neighbor are somehow One, 39–40
  God continues to try to find us, 29
  God forgives everyone, 30–32
  God of Hebrew Bible, 28
  God progresses, 28
  God within us, 32–33
  as Great Appreciator, 29–30
  maleness and femaleness of, 140–41
  peace of God emanating from our hearts,
    41–43
  as unconditional love, 27, 34, 77, 180, 181
"God's foolishness is wiser than human wis-
    dom . . ." (1 Cor. 1:25), 39
Golden Rule, 174
Goldman, Ronald, 45
"good feeling of self-control," 50–53
goodness, in all people, 15, 30
Good Night, Little Ones (Spokoinoi Nochi),
  21–23
Goodwin, Leonard, 102
Gorbachev, Mikhail, 21, 24
Graham, Billy, 31, 180
Great Appreciator, 29–30
Great Commandment to love (Mark 12:29-31),
  33
Grenada invasion, 10, 16, 19, 63
"gross form of abuse," 65
Groveland rape case, 83

Halley's Comet, 174
Hanks, Tom, 74
Harlem Spiritual Ensemble, 97
Harvard Physician Task Force on Hunger, 109
Hatcher, Richard, 92
heaven, 31–32, 68, 101
Hebrew Bible, 8, 27, 28
Heinz, John, 65, 66, 68
hell, 28, 147
hello (zdravstvuitye), 22
Helms, Jesse, 21
hernia repair incident, 64
heroes are helpers, not killers, 73–75
Hoffman, Abbie, 3, 7
Hollingsworth, Amy, 45
Hollingsworth, Joey, 91
Holocaust, 28, 42
holy ground, 38–39
Holy Spirit, 25, 29, 31, 38–39

Holy Trinity, 30
"Homophobia: In the Bible, in the Military,
    and in the Churches," 153
homosexuality, 143–55
hucksters, 115, 116
Hughes, Langston, 144
Human Kindness Foundation, 113
hunger, 104–12
Hussein, Saddam, 63, 73

"I am the way, the truth, and the life," 32
"I Like to Take Care of You" (song), 136
"I like you just the way you are," 34, 89, 95,
    155
Incredible Hulk, The, 52
inner violence, 45, 53
intercontinental ballistic missiles, MX, 41
Interfaith and Race Relations Committee,
    82–83, 100
interracial life, 89–92
Iron Eyes Cody, 169
Isaiah 2:4 (Hebrew Bible), 8, 27
Israelites' use of violence, Hebrew Bible, 28
"It's okay to be angry . . . ," 45–61
"It's You I Like" (song), 77, 95, 153

Jennings, Peter, 70
Jesus of Nazareth
  as advocate, 29–32
  "I am the way, the truth, and the life," 32
  second person in Holy Trinity, 30
John, Gospel of, 32, 57
John Paul II (pope), 59
Johnson, Lyndon, 3, 7, 84, 85, 120
Junod, Tom, 28–29, 36, 41, 74–75, 165
justice, 78

Kennedy, John F., 51
Kennedy, Robert F., 51, 120
Kernick, Cynthia, 96
Kerry, John, 9, 10
killer whales, Shamu and Namu, 166
King, Martin Luther, Jr.
  assassination of, 51, 85
  Clemmons and, 89
  economic ethics of, 116
  on interracial marriage, 90
  male personalities in peace movement, 120
  Rogers compared to, 7, 81, 88
  vigil at Arlington National Cemetery, 3
kingdom of heaven, 68, 101

Koppel, Ted, 21
Ku Klux Klan incident, 96
Kutner, Larry, 65–66

Lappé, Frances Moore, 157
L'Arche Daybreak community, 113
Last, Jonathan, 108
legacy, of Rogers, 178–81
Lennon, John, 59
Lenox, Annie, 105
levitating the Pentagon, 3, 7
Lewinsky, Monica, 35–36
litterbugs, 170–71
Little Prince, The, 14
"little quiet moments," 39
Littman, Lynne, 10
Living Hungry in America (Brown, J. L.), 109
lost coin parable, 29
lost sheep parable, 29
love
    constancy of love for others, 36–37
    diversity and, 95–96
    love ourselves, 37–38
    love your enemy, 43
    unconditional, 27, 34, 77, 180, 181
loving punishments, 60–61
Loving v. Virginia, 90
Lozoff, Bo, 113
Luke, Gospel of, 29, 100, 108
Luther, Martin, 30–31
Lydia Stout (St. Bernard puppy), 160

Ma, Yo-Yo, 136–37
mad feelings, 45–61
Malcolm X, 84
"Many Ways to Say I Love You" (song), 151
March on Washington for Jobs and Freedom, 75
Mark, Gospel of, 33
Marsalis family, 136–37
Marshall, Morgan, 177–78
Marshall, Thurgood, 82
Marty, Martin, 42
materialism, 116, 117, 173
matryoshka dolls, 22
Matthew, Gospel of, 68
McCall, John, 152, 153–54
McCarthy, Eugene, 120
McCartney, Paul, 105
McFarland, Margaret, 55
McFeely, Fred Brooks, 34, 100

McGovern, George, 120
McNerthney, Casey, 177–78
meat eating. See vegetarianism
Medal of Freedom, 77
Mennonites, 75, 157
men with yarn, women with hammers, 120–22
"A Mighty Fortress Is Our God" (song), 30–31
mite box, 112
Monica Lewinsky scandal, 35–36
More Light Presbyterians, 154
mothers, working, 137–40
Mother Teresa, 117
Murray, Pauli, 119
MX intercontinental ballistic missiles, 41
My Lai massacre, 73–74

NAACP, 82, 83, 88
Namu, 166
National Association of Evangelicals (NAE), 10–11
Nation of Islam, 84
Negri, Joe, 138, 139, 151
Newell, David, 21, 61, 151, 177
Niebuhr, Reinhold, 30
Nightline, 21
Nixon, Richard, 101–2, 179
Noah and flood, 28
nonviolence
    Gandhi, 6–7
    God's, 27–29
    inner violence, 45, 53
    Israelites' use of violence, Hebrew Bible, 28
    "It's okay to be angry . . . ," 45–61
    punishing the violent, 58–61
    of Rogers, 19, 42–43
    television violence, 48–50
    Tolstoy, 42
    violence against women (Clinton speech), 45–46
    See also pacifism; vegetarianism
Nouwen, Henri, 33, 34, 40, 113
nuclear weapons, 9, 10–11, 16, 21, 37, 41
nurturing males. See gender roles

Oakes, John B., 10
obesity, 164–65, 167
Obis, Paul, 157–58, 162, 164, 165, 167
O. J. Simpson trial, 45–46
"One little word shall fell him," 31
Organization of Eastern Caribbean States, 10
Orr, William, 29–31, 100–101

pacifism
   killing animals and, 157
   of Rogers, 9, 27, 42–43
   of Tolstoy, 42
   See also vegetarianism
parables, 29, 180–81
Parham, Glover, 144–45
Passion for the Possible, A (Coffin), 152–53
patriarchal culture, 120, 124, 129
PBS, Vietnam documentary, 9–10
"Peace and Quiet" (song), 19
peace as possibility, 16–19
peace balloons, 4, 5, 6, 7, 17
"the Peacemaker," 41
peacemaking, 6–7
   making peacemakers, 61
   Rogers as Christian peacemaker, 180–81
peace theology, 27–43
   "extraordinary, ordinary people," 33–38
   God and neighbor are somehow One, 39–40
   God of Rogers, 28–33
   holy ground, 38–39
   peace of God emanating from our hearts,
       41–43
Pentagon, 3, 7, 64, 65, 66
Persian Gulf War, child abuse and, 63–73, 179
pets as special, 160–61
Phelps, Fred, 143, 154
physical challenges, 94–96
political power, as derivative, 6–7
Poor People's Campaign, 99
poverty, 99–117
   charity, 99–104, 112–14
   hunger, 104–12
power punishments, 60
predestination, 33
Presbyterian minister, Rogers as, 27–28, 33
prince of darkness, 31
Prison Ashram Project, Lozoff's, 113
prosocial behaviors, 178
public service announcements, subversive, 66–68
punishing the violent, 58–61
puppet détente, 21, 22–25
Pytka, Joe, 114

Quaker, Rogers as, 33

race and diversity, 81–97
radical acceptance, 30–32, 54, 155
rape case, Groveland, 83
Ray, James Earl, 85

Reagan, Ronald
   assassination attempt, 59
   evil empire speech, 10–11, 21
   Gorbachev and, 21, 24
   Grenada invasion, 10, 16, 19, 63
   militaristic foreign policy, 9, 16
   MX intercontinental ballistic missiles, 41
   nuclear weapons proliferation, 10–11
   U.S. forces in Central America, 10
   "war isn't nice" message compared to, 16
recycling, 171–73
Ride, Sally, 127
riots, 84–87, 146, 148
Robert Hungerford Normal and Industrial
       School, 83
Rogers, Fred
   as absolutist on war issue, 16
   charity and, 112–14
   as Christian peacemaker, 180–81
   Clemmons and, 85–92, 96–97, 99–100, 143,
       144–52, 154, 180
   compassion of, 177–81
   economic simplicity of, 114–17
   environment and, 169–76
   "Fat Freddy," 34, 46, 178
   Freudian perspective of, 45, 53–54, 63, 149
   Gandhi compared to, 6–7
   God of, 28–33
   in *Good Night, Little Ones* episode, 22–23
   Hoffman compared to, 3, 7
   homosexuality and, 143–55
   "I like you just the way you are," 34, 89,
       95, 155
   Junod's relations to, 28–29, 36, 41, 74–75,
       165
   Kerry compared to, 9, 10
   King, Martin Luther, Jr., compared to, 7,
       81, 88
   legacy of, 178–81
   nonviolence of, 19, 42–43
   nurturing, family roots, 133–35
   Obis and, 157–58, 162, 164, 165, 167
   pacifism of, 9, 27
   peace theology of, 27–43
   photos of, 26, 44, 80, 118, 156, 168
   as Presbyterian minister, 27–28, 33
   puppet détente, 21, 22–25
   as Quaker, 33
   on sin, 30, 36
   in Soviet Union, 21–23
   as Tolstoyan, 42

Rogers, Fred (*continued*)
   Vedeneyeva and, 22, 23–24, 25
   vegetarianism of, 157–67
   wealth of, 100, 112–14
   See also songs
Rogers, Jamie (older son), 64, 133, 134
Rogers, Jim (father), 36–37, 100, 134, 137
Rogers, Joanne (wife), 30, 64, 74, 85, 112, 114, 154
Rogers, Johnny (younger son), 64
Rollins College, 77, 82, 83, 100, 148
Romney, George, 84
Roth, Audrey, 126
rough-and-tumble girls, boys taking care, 122–27
Rustin, Bayard, 75

SALT II nuclear disarmament talks, 37
Satan, 29
Saunders, Mrs., 84, 85, 125
Saving Private Ryan (film), 74
Seattle Special Olympics story, 37
selective nuclear proliferation, 10
self-control, "good feeling of self-control," 50–53
sensitivity in men, 130–32
Sesame Street, 90–91
Shamu, 166
Simon, Arthur, 106
Simon, Paul, 106
Simon, Scott, 73–74, 76
Simpson, Nicole Brown, 45–46
Simpson, O. J., 45–46
sin, 30, 36, 144
Singer, Peter, 166, 167
Sixth Presbyterian Church, 152–55
songs
   "Creation" 140–41
   "Don't Pick on the Peeps," 159
   "I Like to Take Care of You," 136
   "It's You I Like," 77, 95, 153
   "Many Ways to Say I Love You," 151
   "A Mighty Fortress Is Our God," 30–31
   "Peace and Quiet," 19
   to Tatyana Vedeneyeva, 24
   "Tree, Tree, Tree," 176
   "The Truth Will Make Me Free," 57–58
   "What Do You Do?" 50–52
   "Won't You Be My Neighbor?" 23, 66
   "You Are Special," 87
Southern Christian Leadership Conference, 88

Soviet Union, Rogers in, 21–23
Special Olympics story, 37
Spock, Benjamin, 56, 120
Spokoinoi Nochi. See Good Night, Little Ones
St. Bernard puppy (Lydia Stout), 160
Stewart, Maggie, 46, 55, 92–93, 96
Stewart, Mrs., 34, 46
Sting, 105
Stokes, Carl B., 92
Stomp, 55
Stone, Lucy, 130
Stonewall riots, 146, 148
Student Nonviolent Coordinating Committee, 88
sublimation, 45, 53–54
subversive public service announcements, 66–68
Swann, Lynn, 135–36
Swenson, Mr., 132–33
"Swing Low, Sweet Chariot" (song), 97

"Take care of this wonderful world that we have," 176
talk, don't shoot, 70–73
Task Force on Food Assistance, 105
television, violence on, 48–50
Television Hall of Fame speech, 49
Testament (film), 10
Tet Offensive, 3
"That which is essential is invisible to the eye," 14
"They shall beat their swords into plow-shares . . ." (Isa. 2:4), 8, 27
Thich Nhat Hanh, 178
Third Presbyterian Church, 85, 86
Thompson, Chrissy, 94–95
Thompson, Hugh, 73–74
Thompson, J. Walter, 116
tofu, 163–64
Tolstoy, Leo, 42
Tom and Jerry, 22
trees, 175–76
"Tree, Tree, Tree" (song), 176
Trinity, 30
Trudeau, Gary, 152
"The Truth Will Make Me Free" (song), 57–58
Turner Dairy Farms, 162
tzedekah box, 112

U2, 105
unconditional love, 27, 34, 77, 180, 181

Vaughan, Jermaine, 94
Vedeneyeva, Dmitri, 23–24
Vedeneyeva, Tatyana, 22, 23–24, 25
vegans, 162, 163
vegetarianism, 157–67
    Animal Liberation (Singer), 166
    Beauty without Cruelty USA, 167
    children and eating meat, 162–64
    empathy for animals, 158–60
    health benefits, 164–65
    obesity and, 164–65, 167
    pets as special, 160–61
    reasons for, 165–66
    Shamu and Namu, 166
    spreading God's love and peace, 157–58
    tofu, 163–64
Vegetarian Times, 157–58, 162, 165, 167
Vietnam War, 3–10
violence. *See* nonviolence

wade-ins, 87–89, 96–97, 151
Walters, Barbara, 127
war and peace programs (1968), 4–7

"war isn't nice" message, 9–19
War on Terror, 76–78, 179
Washington, Booker T., 83
wealth, of Rogers, 100, 112–14
Weber, Sam, 135–36
Western Theological Seminary, 29
Westmoreland, William, 3
"What Do You Do?" (song), 50–52
Williams, Robin, 82
Wogaman, J. Philip, 36
Wolf, Naomi, 128
Women for Peace, 120
Women's International League for Peace and
    Freedom, 120
Women Strike for Peace, 120
"Won't You Be My Neighbor?" (song), 23, 66
Woodward, Kenneth, 83
working mothers, 137–40

Yoshi Ito, 92
"You Are Special" (song), 87

zdravstvuitye (hello), 22

Made in the USA
San Bernardino, CA
22 May 2015